Directive
Family
Therapy

Directive Family Therapy

Alfred Lange, Ph.D.
and
Onno van der Hart, Ph.D.

Translated by Marion Alhadeff
and John Quysner

BRUNNER/MAZEL, Publishers • NEW YORK

Library of Congress Cataloging in Publication Data

Lange, Alfred, 1941-
  Directive family therapy.

  Translation of: Gedragsverandering in gezinnen.
  Bibliography: p.
  Includes indexes.
  1. Family psychotherapy. 1. Hart, Onno van der,
1941-   . II. Title. [DNLM: 1. Family therapy.
WM 430.5.F2 L269g]
RC488.5.L3513   1983   616.89'156   83-3907
ISBN 0-87630-335-1

Copyright © 1983 by Alfred Lange and Onno van der Hart

Published by
BRUNNER/MAZEL, INC.
19 Union Square West
New York, N.Y. 10003

MANUFACTURED IN THE UNITED STATES OF AMERICA

FOREWORD

These days it is embarrassing to call oneself an "eclectic" therapist, since the term commonly implies one is a "fence sitter" unable to choose between the different and self-contained schools of psychotherapy. However, this book represents a step in psychotherapy's evolution toward a phase of deliberate and systematic eclecticism, a time when to be eclectic will not be synonymous with feeling ashamed. We are ably helped toward this goal by the sophisticated Dutch therapists, Lange and van der Hart.

At first, psychotherapy developed discrete theoretical models through which practitioners identified themselves with certain colleagues and distinguished themselves from others by adhering to the doctrines and practices of a well-defined orientation. This early developmental phase was the "separation-individuation stage" of psychotherapy.

This separation-individuation phase has its benefits and liabilities. The main benefit is a wild proliferation of new ideas. Unfortunately, wild proliferations result in an abundance of weeds as well as flowers, and this stage brought with it a regrettable conservatism and a reflexive, dependent grasping to perspectives espoused by Masters. And so it continues that therapists are judged by their orthodoxy, sectarianism is promoted in training institutions, and therapists define and limit themselves as "Ericksonians," "structural family therapists," etc.

This book will not change all that, but it's a start. Rather than a volume of new inventions, we have here a deliberate attempt to organize, unify and include seemingly discrepant orientations. Therapeutic interventions are not dogmatically ruled out—instead, interventions are drawn from systems theory, strategic approaches, analytic-interpretive models, social psychology, Gestalt family therapy, behavior therapy, etc.

Although there is a clear theoretiacal tone, the volume has a practical orientation and is directed toward clinical situations. Without neglecting individual pathology, emphasis is placed on assessment of the family structure and the concomitant communication patterns. The reader is presented with a clear overview of many techniques and strategies which can be used, step by step, in order to evoke change.

Moreover, this is a text about conducting effective psychotherapy, not just a book about becoming a "directive therapist" or a "family therapist." As such, it is a welcome addition to the literature and a progressive step toward a unified, nonsectarian approach to helping people.

I first traveled to Holland in 1980 to lecture at a meeting of the Netherlands Society of Clinical Hypnosis. I was immediately impressed with the quality of therapy in the Netherlands, which is among the most sophisticated in Europe.

The leaders of the Dutch school include Kees van der Velden, Richard Van Dyck, Kees Hoogduin, Leen Joele, Dick Oudshoorn, and the authors of this volume. This group published two volumes in Dutch entitled *Directive Therapy;* the approach described therein was formulated in the manner of the present-day strategic schools. The *Directive Therapy* volumes are extremely popular in Holland and have markedly influenced the development of psychotherapy there. The present volume advances the ideas of Lange and van der Hart, two of the more "family" oriented members of the Dutch group.

The Dutch group's amalgam of approaches is different from that commonly found in the United States, where directive/strategic therapists (especially those with a family orientation) are distinct from hypnotherapists. In the Netherlands, there is a definite movement to join these approaches, as demonstrated by the Dutch group's recent initiation of the *Journal of Directive Therapy and Hypnosis,* which emphasizes the commitment to draw from both sources.

I was impressed not only by the Dutch group's sophistication, but also by their productivity and spirit of cooperation. They met regularly to critique each other's clinical and theoretical work, and they published a private journal of working papers consisting of thousands of pages of manuscript. Only after a thorough critique were papers published in the *Directive Therapy* volumes and other psychotherapy journals. These Dutch therapists have much of relevance to say to American therapists and are now, through this volume, more accessible to them.

The authors of *Directive Family Therapy* are innovative and have much to say that is relative to American therapists. Onno van der Hart's recent volume, *Rituals in Psychotherapy*, has been translated into English (Irvington Publishers, 1983). Lange has published many articles in English social psychology and psychotherapy journals.

Directive Family Therapy is a book for both the novice and experienced psychotherapist. Because it is a textbook containing well-constructed models, novice practitioners will not have to reinvent strategic family therapy. Yet the complexity and subtlety of its analysis will please even experienced practitioners—the authors use reframing, rituals, and social psychological maneuvers in clever and unique ways. The experienced practitioner will also be interested in the training methods described, including the Dutch style of "intervision," as opposed to supervision.

The authors write nicely, with clear, concise and scholarly language, providing case reports for illustration. And Lange and van der Hart provide instruction in manageable bits—the same teaching style that they espouse.

This practical book is directed to clinical situations rather than theory. It emphasizes changing the structure of communication patterns in order to change behavior and provides a well-conceived approach to understanding and utilizing the communicational determinants of family behavior.

The strength of *Directive Family Therapy* is its systematic organization, providing a well-conceived outline of the discrete stages of family therapy in which the authors place the techniques and interventions described. While providing a model for instructing clients to be more skillful problem-solvers, it will also help therapists to be more skillful problem-solvers.

Most practitioners will find something new and useful here, and hopefully the Dutch therapists will soon be better known in the United States. As these innovative therapists become more familiar to us, we welcome them.

Jeffrey K. Zeig, Ph.D.
Director,
The Milton H. Erickson Foundation,
Phoenix, Arizona

CONTENTS

INTRODUCTION

During the past 30 years family therapy has evolved into a major treatment modality. Not only in the United States, where family therapy originated, but throughout the world, family therapy centers have been set up and many existing treatment centers have included family therapy in their programs. Each year has brought an increasing number of books and journals on the subject and training opportunities are now available everywhere.

Developments in other parts of the world often closely followed the progress made in the United States. Following the rapid growth of family therapy in the U.S., American leaders have given workshops and teaching seminars abroad and many therapists have gone to the United States to participate in family therapy training programs.

In the Netherlands, the input from America has consisted of various family therapy approaches, in particular structural family therapy, approaches based on the general systems theory and communication theory, Gestalt family therapy, and behavioral family therapy. In recent years, the innovative work of the Milan group has made its impact upon the Dutch family therapy scene.

In *Directive Family Therapy* an attempt is made to integrate principles from the above mentioned approaches, as well as ideas from social psychology—in particular from the attribution and self-perception theory—into one comprehensive treatment model. The focus of the book suggests not only the particularly strong influence of Jay Haley's earlier work but also the need to fit the treatment approach to

the family instead of the other way around. This is illustrated for example in the importance we attach to the use of judo principles in
therapy. We must also mention Nathan Epstein's problem-centered systems therapy of the family, in which one of the authors was trained in
the early seventies. The emphasis in this book on thorough family
assessment and contracting, for instance, reflects in particular Epstein's
influence.

Directive Family Therapy systematically describes all the stages of
family treatment and demonstrates the application of techniques in
concrete terms, with the use of examples. The book consists of three
parts. Part I focuses on basic concepts. In Chapter 1 attention is paid
to system and communication concepts and to the *life cycle of the
family.*
     In Chapter 2 the treatment model is described and schematically
explained. Six basic strategies which form the foundation of the treatment model are outlined. Treatment is described as a process in which
clients gradually learn the methods and techniques which will enable
them to detect and overcome problems themselves. To this end a number of communication rules which have their origins partly in Gestalt
therapy may be used. No therapy model is effective in, or applicable
to, all treatment situations. When the rational problem-solving model
cannot be applied, other strategies must be used. The principles of
restructuring and the *judo approach* described in 2.2.4 and 2.2.6 are
important here. After discussing the basic strategies, an elaboration on
the different stages in family therapy follows. The chapter closes with
a diagram and an accompanying explanation.

Part II concerns the practical aspects of the treatment, beginning with
Chapter 3, which indicates the way in which families, or parts of them,
can end up in family or couple therapy. We discuss, among other things,
the extent to which it is useful and desirable for the therapist to gather
information beforehand about the family he is to treat.
     In Chapter 4 a first session *(assessment)* with a family is extensively
described and analyzed. We indicate the points the therapist should
take into account during such a session, how the conversation can be
structured, and how even a first conversation can have therapeutic
value because it provides the therapist with the opportunity to demonstrate a number of principles. We also describe how the therapist
should assess the affective relationships in the family. Finally, the importance of making a treatment contract is emphasized.
     A large number of *techniques* involved in treatment are discussed in

Chapter 5, which shows how the therapist can help the family to relate directly to one another instead of talking about one another, while trying to solve their mutual problems. We describe how behavior exercises, modeling, topographical interventions, paradoxical assignments, etc., can be used. In the section on monitoring we systematically explain various forms of registration and the ways in which the information which emerges can be made known. Exact instructions for both are provided in the appendices. Techniques which can help the clients to apply in their daily lives what they have experienced during therapy sessions are dealt with again. There are sections on the treatment of sexual problems and on timing in family treatment. The end of the chapter is devoted to a consideration of the style and attitude of the therapist.

In Chapter 6 the ways in which *behavior contracts* can be negotiated are described in detail, using an example. Various applications of the *treatment contract* are also discussed.

Chapter 7 describes how individual problems connected with the past can be worked on in family therapy. Different forms of *therapeutic rituals* are also dealt with.

Chapter 8 is about divorce. It discusses the issues encountered by the therapist and his clients when there does not seem to be any point in the partners staying together. *Trial separation* and ways of implementing it are set out.

Part III departs from treatment itself and deals with education and training in family therapy. In Chapter 9 various types and forms of training are described. A detailed account is provided of the course given by the authors for the staff of a psychiatric clinic, and the aids and exercises we have developed in the last few years for training in family therapy are reviewed.

Directive Family Therapy is intended for practicing mental health clinicians, such as psychiatrists, psychologists, and social workers, and for family therapists, marriage therapists, marriage and family counselors, and pastoral counselors. The book is also designed as a textbook for the curricula of the above professions. In addition, it may be of use to general readers interested in improving their relationships. Anyone who has a permanent relationship may benefit from a number of the communication principles and techniques for bringing about change described in Parts I and II. With couples, this will yield the best results if these sections are read together.

Throughout the book the male pronoun is used when referring to therapists. We hope that readers will not mistake this for a male bias. It was simply a practical decision, as all the examples used are from our own practice and we happen to be male therapists.

ACKNOWLEDGMENTS

We are indebted to Frieda Aelen, Peter Poelstra, Gerda Methorst, Robert Aarsen, Kees van der Velden, Wil Zeegers, Joost Beek, and the late Professor T.T. ten Have, who have read the various parts of the manuscript critically and carefully. Their comments were invaluable. We also should like to thank Jeffrey K. Zeig who showed our manuscript to Brunner/Mazel. We are grateful to Marion Alhadeff and John Quysner for their dedication and skill in translating the main part of this English edition, while Angie Pleit-Kuiper and Arno Pleit took care of Chapter 2. Special thanks go to Japke Stol and Barbara Meulenberg for their help in the actual preparation of the manuscript.

We owe many thanks to Marcelle, Tanja, Tamar, Yasha, Shulamith and Eyal, our family members who inspired us while we were writing this book.

We wish to thank the following for permission to quote material in this book:

Haley, J. *Uncommon Therapy: the Psychiatric Techniques of Milton H. Erickson, M.D.*, New York, Norton & Co., 1973.
Gardner, R.A. *The Boys and Girls Book about Divorce*, New York, Jason Aronson, 1970.
American Orthopsychiatric Association to reproduce the table from Cleghorn, J.M., and Levin, S. Training family therapists by setting learning objectives. *American Journal of Orthopsychiatry*, 1973, 43(3), 439-446.

Directive Family Therapy

PART I

Background

CHAPTER 1

The Family

as a System

1.1 SYSTEMS APPROACH

When people consult therapists about their problems, they usually talk about individual complaints. They may think that there is something physically wrong with them because they suffer from headaches, stomachaches, or dizziness or they may be suffering from anxiety, suddenly burst into tears, fly into a rage, or feel that they simply cannot cope anymore. One traditional response by therapists was *to regard the individual as the unit of treatment.* There were many ways in which this could be done, for instance by dealing with the physical complaints, in the belief that once bodily health was restored, the psychological problems would also disappear. Alternatively, symptoms could be viewed as evidence of deeply-rooted psychological disturbances which had to be dealt with first before the superficial complaints, such as bouts of anxiety, would disappear—more or less as in psychoanalysis. An approach developed from the psychology of learning principles interprets psychological symptoms as conditioned responses that can be unlearned. Behavior therapy, which is based on this approach (cf. Bandura, 1969) has always regarded these principles as central.

In treatment geared to the individual, attention occasionally focuses on the "patient's" environment—as an aid to treatment—but the "patient" and his social environment (such as his family) are never explicitly viewed as the unit of treatment. In the 1950s in particular, a number of therapists whose work was based on treating the individual

5

began for the first time to concentrate on the social environment of people with problems (cf. Haley, 1970, 1971a). Experience had shown that an individual-based approach could be successful with some clients, but that it could also have unforeseen and unpleasant side effects. For example, once a woman was cured of frigidity, her husband became impotent. As one child stopped having temper tantrums, or behaving antisocially, a brother or sister started to exhibit the same tendencies—or the problems recurred after a certain interval. Therapists who were aware of this came to the conclusion that the individual could not fully account for these phenomena. Apparently what was happening between the patient and the rest of the family was undoing the good done by therapy. These therapists, therefore, invited whole families for interviews (cf. Ackerman et al., 1961), even though only one person had been presented as the patient. As a result, there was a gradual shift of emphasis away from the individual towards the husband and wife or the family as a whole. The interactions *among* people, rather than the individual's intrapsychic conflicts, came to be regarded as central.

According to this new approach, the way the members of the family relate to one another and the role the presenting problem plays in their relationships would need to be examined and changed. Therapists observed, for example, that families which presented the child as the patient were often concealing an unresolved conflict between the father and the mother. Attempts to bring the problem out into the open were often sabotaged by the "patient," who drew attention to himself and away from the parental relationship by behaving strangely or in an otherwise deviant fashion. In seeking explanations for this kind of behavior, some therapists came into contact with general systems theory, which was gaining ground at that time and which linked up with all the sciences by stressing their common characteristics. General systems theory is not in fact a theory in the conventional sense, relating to a particular scientific discipline in which hypotheses can be formulated and tested. It is far more abstract, and it would therefore be more accurate to refer to it as a metatheory or philosophical orientation.

General systems theory influenced family therapy in two ways. It provided a conceptual framework which some people felt could be used to describe or even explain family phenomena. The fact that it is so abstract, however, created great confusion as to what could or could not be included in a certain concept in specific instances. This led to innumerable semantic debates which did nothing to clarify the actual subject under discussion. Terms directly derived from the general systems theory, such as "homeostasis," "negative feedback," and "equifinality," are therefore not really relevant to present purposes (for more information about them see Watzlawick et al., 1967, and Hoffman, 1981). The terms "deviation-amplifying processes" and "deviation-counteracting processes" (Section 1.4.1) are useful, however, because they enable individual problems to be seen in their context. The conceptual framework of general systems theory is, therefore, not useful in all respects, but the theory itself forms the basis of the systems approach which is essential to family therapy. This means being aware of the cyclical processes which occur in natural groups: Changes in one part of a group are followed by changes in other parts of the group (cf. Zelditch, 1955).

The family can be regarded as a system in many respects: a system of communication, a power system, an affective system, etc. In this chapter we shall be dealing with a number of aspects of communication which are important in the analysis of patterns of family interaction. Jackson (1965) pointed out that, when one adopts this approach, theoretical assumptions about the individual are not necessary—only assumptions about the nature of communication as communication (cf. Wertheim, 1973). To a large extent, we take the same view. At the same time, however, we feel that the family therapist must also be aware of individual problems. In the course of treatment it will often be necessary to incorporate aspects of individual therapy, for example to teach someone to look after his own interests better (cf. Section 5.8.3), to draw up a better weekly schedule for himself, or to "let go" of a deceased parent (see Chapter 7). The therapist must also be capable of anticipating which members of the family will be capable of responding to which suggestions. On some occasions, a psychological test will be appropriate—for instance, with a child who has learning difficulties. At other times a medical or neurological examination will be necessary—when, for example, the client says he blacks out from time to time. It can also be vitally important to monitor interaction between the members of the family and outside systems such as a school or place of work, in addition to interaction within the family itself. A number of examples in this chapter will illustrate this. We underline Spiegel's conclusions (1969) that (a) if we are aware that changes in one system will also work through into other systems, and possibly meet with opposition there, then we should draw our conclusions from that; and (b) once therapy has begun, every system on which the therapy may have an influence should be identified as precisely as possible and the anticipated effects predicted.

After we have illustrated thinking in terms of systems, we go into this chapter to consider principles of communication. Another way of looking at the family within the systems approach is in terms of power relations. A communication-based approach can reveal a good deal, but in view of the fact that the balance of power frequently creates problems in families, we feel that it warrants separate treatment.

1.2 SYSTEMS APPROACH: A CASE
EXAMPLE

The following example shows how a problem for which a family is seeking help can be construed in terms of various systems. There is an individual complaint of a psychosomatic nature, which turns out to be closely connected with the way in which the family functions as a whole (cf. Minuchin, 1974, Chapter VII).

Rick Landman, age nine, is referred to a child guidance center by his family doctor because he is suffering from psychosomatic stomach pains. According to the doctor, this is in some way connected to the fact that Rick sometimes refuses to go to school. He says he is afraid of the other children in his class—if they come home to play with him, Rick shuts himself in his room.

The staff of the child guidance center build up the following picture of Rick on the basis of an interview with him: He seems to be the victim of an unsatisfactory relationship between his parents. He has guilt feelings about their quarrels because he thinks he is the cause of them. He deals with his guilt feelings by either escaping into a fantasy world or trying to improve his relationship with each of his parents separately, in an attempt to compensate for the lack of genuine relationships within the family. He is afraid of noise, which seems to indicate repressed anger and feelings of hostility. He is capable of establishing contact with people and of responding in an appropriate way, but his parents are turning him into an emotional cripple by condemning him for expressing his feelings. He seems to be an intelligent boy who can amuse himself with all kinds of interesting, even fascinating, hobbies. Rick's teacher has this to say about him: "He is a likable, quiet boy, but excessively shy and oversensitive. In class he tends to be rather solitary, although he does join in with group work and he has lots of good ideas. He has a tendency to daydream. Generally speaking, he is doing reasonably well at school but his spelling and dictation are absolutely awful."

Rick's mother is also asked for her explanation of her son's problems. She says he has no self-confidence and feels he only creates problems for other people. He wants to run away from home because he thinks that would be best for all concerned. When he comes home from school, he locks himself in his room and often refuses to come down for dinner. He can be aggressive and he screams and cries a lot. Small problems upset him quickly. He is afraid of school and very reluctant to go—sometimes he refuses outright. He is obsessed with fire and is always playing with matches. "He thinks that I smother him with affection and he hates me for it. I think that at school he's much too polite and afraid of authority."

This information confirms that Rick has a number of emotional problems stemming from influences in his environment and that he does need treatment. The staff of the child guidance center could, for example, decide that he needs play therapy or psychoanalysis in order to help him cope with the introjected family conflicts. Although this approach recognizes the influence of the environment on the patient, it concentrates on intrapsychic problems and treating them as such (cf. Montalvo and Haley, 1973). In fact, the staff of the child guidance center decide to have another interview with the whole family: Rick, his mother, Barbara, his father, Keith, and his younger sister, Marian, age seven.

During the first interview, the information provided by Barbara about Rick comes up for discussion. She says that Marian can also be a handful: "She is so busy trying to avoid problems, you can't make out what's really going on. If you ask her to do anything, she always says yes but then often doesn't do as you ask. Rick, of course, usually just says no in the first place." The conversation reveals that Barbara devotes a lot of time to bringing up the children. She also reads books on the subject, which she recommends to her husband, who shows a complete lack of interest. He knows the root of the problem: His wife is too lenient with Rick. If Rick complains of stomach pains, Barbara takes him seriously and lets him stay at home. In this way, he gains the upper hand. On the other hand, Keith says it would not be fair to blame his wife too much because his own way of dealing with Rick does not work either. If Rick refuses to go to school, and the father is still at home, he gets angry and shouts at him. Usually, he starts by asking Rick in a reasonable tone of voice to do something. If the boy fails to respond after having been asked six or seven times, Keith loses his temper with him. He abuses the child, hits him, or simply leaves the room. This has no effect either—Rick still does not go to school.

Barbara says she does not like her husband shouting at the children when they annoy him—something which happens quite frequently. Every evening after dinner, Keith wants to be left in peace to read the newspaper, but the two children always manage to make a tremendous amount of noise in the same room. Neither parent has an answer to this recurrent problem. If Keith loses his temper, Barbara becomes upset and shows it. He then feels that she is making a fool of him in front of the children, but he does not do anything about this because "parents should not criticize one another in front of the children." Barbara agrees with her husband that this is a problem. However, she cannot accept his shouting, which she considers to be unreasonable. He says that he cannot help the way he is.

Barbara and Keith clearly have different approaches to bringing up the children. Barbara's attitude can be described as reasonable "laissez faire"—she presents Rick with arguments as to why he should or should not do something. If he fails to respond, she drops the subject. Keith is more specific when asking Rick to do something, but he does not stress the point any further when Barbara becomes upset with his shouting. He is as ineffectual as she is because, in following his wife's example, he tries to be reasonable and get the children to do things by asking, but he will not even get up out of his chair to take Rick out of the room when this is necessary. He consciously stops himself because he feels that his wife would then criticize him in front of the children. This makes him feel castrated, in a manner of speaking. He only allows this to happen because he feels that parents have to be consistent in front of the children, but everyone else in the family can see that a united front does not exist and that this is producing tension. When the two of them are alone, they cannot solve this problem either, because if they quarrel, Barbara bursts into tears and Keith feels obliged to console her.

The two parents here have different approaches to bringing up their children and they are also incapable of supporting one another. Rick is clearly caught in the crossfire. His parents' disagreement on how to deal with him is so important to Rick that the only way he can cope with it is by trying to establish contact with one parent at a time. He regards himself as the reason for the conflict between his father and mother. This is a vicious circle which affects other family conflicts, such as Barbara's wanting to get a job and Keith's inadequate participation in household chores, and prevents their being discussed, let alone resolved.

1.3 LEVELS OF SYSTEMS

In Section 1.2, we describe a case in which a family therapist is confronted by a family, one of whose members is regarded as the "problem." The therapist finds out more about what is wrong with Rick and at the same time observes how the father and mother react to Rick independently and how he reacts to them. He also makes a special study of the relationship between the mother and the father and eventually develops a total picture of how the family functions. Finally, he also examines the relationship between the family and certain representatives of the outside world, such as the school and the family doctor.

The family therapist brings the problem into focus on a number of levels simultaneously, after which he decides to concentrate primarily on the relationship between the husband and wife. We should now like to describe in more detail the various levels (cf. Minuchin, 1974) on which a therapist can operate with the case of Rick and a number of other cases.

1.3.1 The individual family member as a unit

Rick suffers from headaches and stomach pains but he has been examined by his family doctor who says that, medically speaking, there is nothing wrong with him. The pain must, therefore, be caused by stress. This may be true, but there could also be a somatic problem which needs to be treated by a doctor. If a family therapist is to deal with interaction in a family, he must at least know what the somatic problems are, if indeed such problems exist. If Rick's mother had not first taken him to see a doctor, the therapist would have had to insist on an examination by a pediatrician at the child guidance center. The same applies to children who are referred to a center because of learning difficulties when, at the same time, the teacher suspects problems at home.

Leo, age six, is an extremely active little boy who is not doing very well at school. His parents think there is something wrong with him and seek the opinion of a neurologist, who comes to the conclusion that Leo is quite normal and of average intelligence. Leo's parents' attitude makes the neurologist suspect that the boy's "problem" could be caused by tension within the family. This is confirmed by the family therapist at the child guidance center. The whole family comes across as tense. The mother says there is a great deal of friction between herself and her husband connected with his rapid promotion at work and her feeling that she has been left behind. She feels inferior and "sees the same thing in Leo."

Family therapy would seem to be appropriate here. The parents continue to maintain, however, that there is something physically wrong with Leo, so the therapist decides to conduct more psychological tests to avoid having to keep asserting that he is perfectly normal. The results of the tests show that Leo has a visual motor handicap. Knowing this, his teacher will be able to give him extra help at school. The parents are satisfied and attention can now be focused on other problems within the family.

In the case described above, the therapist decided to test Leo at the insistence of the parents. The results show that even if they had not been so insistent, these tests would have been extremely useful in coming to grips with the family's problems. A family therapist must also consider other issues relating to individual members of the family, such as "How much (more) tension can this person take?" or "To what extent is he or she capable of changing?"

Experience confirms that diagnostic tests on individuals are best carried out as early in treatment as possible. If the family therapist comes to the conclusion that tests are necessary only after a number of sessions with the whole family, he runs the risk of increasing the family's resistance to further therapy. Their attention then focuses only on the "identified patient" and they deny that anything else is wrong.

1.3.2 Dyadic subsystems

The smallest social (sub)system consists of two people. Rick in the example above is the identified patient—he will not go to school. How does this fit in with interactions between Rick and his mother and Rick and his father?

Mother/Son

Early in the morning, Rick starts moaning and complaining vociferously that he has a headache or pains in his stomach and therefore cannot go to school. His mother tries to convince him that the pain will go away and that he should go to school because otherwise he will fall behind. Instead of getting better, Rick's complaints get worse and his mother manages to persuade him to go to school only on a limited number of occasions. When Rick stays at home, his mother spoils him because she understands that life is not easy for him ("I was the same myself as a child"). In other words, if Rick succeeds in staying at home, his mother rewards him for his behavior.

Father/son

If Rick is refusing to go to school before his father has left for work, then the pattern is quite different. Keith asks him about six times to go to school, each time without result, at which stage he loses his temper. He shouts at Rick, hits him, drags him to the car, and takes him to school. But this method is equally unsuccessful. Rick is usually back home half an hour later crying his eyes out to his mother who "loves him." The father sees this as sabotaging what he is trying to achieve and gives up. From time to time he says that Rick should be going to school, but if that does not help, he keeps quiet. As a result, he suffers from tension at work.

Father/mother

The subsystem of the parents does not appear to be functioning properly. If the father shouts at Rick, the mother distances herself from him. He then says nothing because "parents should not contradict one another in front of the children." When the parents are alone together, he says how much he dislikes the way she humiliates him in front of the children. A quarrel ensues, and fairly soon she is in tears. He then feels sorry for her and guilty for making her cry. The conflict stagnates and nothing is resolved.

Other differences of opinion between the spouses end up in precisely the same way. Barbara accuses Keith of not wanting her to go out to work and he replies by accusing her of neglecting her household duties. She starts crying and the ensuing argument again terminates without anything being resolved. As their differences of opinion about Rick assume more importance, they push other contentious topics into the background. A striking feature of this situation is the fact that the mother has to be included in any discussion of the father/son dyad. This section also shows just how much the children, particularly Rick, influence the husband/wife relationship. We shall be dealing with this in more detail in Section 1.7 under the heading "Perverse Triad."

1.3.3 The whole family as a system

In Section 1.3.2 we inevitably referred by implication to the family as a system. The mother criticizes the father in front of the children and he restrains himself from reacting. This enables Rick to do as he pleases. The parents behave differently when they are alone. We have here a family system in which the individual problem of one member of the family (a child of school age) is very closely associated with the way in which each of the parents deals with him and the differences in the way they treat him. Rick's symptomatic behavior creates tension within the family, which is accentuated by the way in which Rick's parents respond to this. Another way of looking at the situation would be to regard it as a problem of power relations between the parents (see Sections 1.5.4 and 1.7)—a struggle which takes place over Rick's head. Rick himself also provokes the conflict with his symptomatic behavior, but in so doing prevents attention from being focused completely on the struggle between his mother and father.

1.3.4 The family and its surroundings as a system

Rick also has problems at school. Because he is often absent, he falls behind. In his case, involving his teacher in the treatment does not really seem to be the answer. She likes Rick and understands that there are problems at home. The therapist does not think that the school itself is responsible for Rick's absenteeism or makes any significant contribution towards it, even though he does not mix very much with other children of his age. The family's problems are the most striking and serious, so the therapist concentrates entirely on the family.

Frank, age seven, who is referred for therapy by his teacher at the child guidance center, has problems of a different kind. He has not been at the school very long, but he is disobedient and his behavior is often described as "unacceptable." His teacher is convinced that the parents, whom he regards as difficult and unpleasant people, are at the root of his problems. Whenever he talks to them about Frank's problems, their reactions are hostile and they accuse the school of being responsible. They claim they do not have any problems with the child.

The family therapist at the child guidance center gets all the parties together: Frank's teacher, the head of the school, and the family (cf. Aponte, 1976). In the ensuing discussion he gets the impression that the family does not really have any serious problems. There are no difficulties as far as bringing up the children are concerned. The parents do seem somewhat authoritarian, but they manage to maintain a harmonious atmosphere at home. Frank's class is also characterized by a pleasant atmosphere and good discipline—with the exception of Frank himself, according to his teacher. The latter puts a strong emphasis on the children being responsible for their own actions and likes them to work independently.

The therapist concludes that there are discrepancies between home and school. Frank is used to an authoritarian upbringing at home and does not know how to respond to the more democratic approach of his new teacher. The latter gets caught up in a vicious circle of mutual recriminations and accusations with the parents, with both parties convinced that they are in the right. The argument is anything but constructive and, moreover, places Frank in the firing line. Just like Rick, Frank is caught up in a conflict between two parties. Frank, too, contributes to the problems by the way he himself behaves. The atmosphere between parents and school is so strained that each demands of the other a change of style.

A compromise seems completely out of the question for the time being. The therapist does not see any reason to start working with the family, which would mean implicitly siding with the school. The parents may be somewhat authoritarian, but that is their privilege—it does not create any problems for the children. On the other hand, it would be difficult for him to advise the teacher to deal with Frank in a different way, since this would not achieve anything. In view of the attitude of the parents and the school, his solution is to suggest that Frank should go to a different school where there is a more traditional approach in keeping with that of the parents. The only disadvantage is that it will probably be further away from home, but despite this all the parties agree that it would be the best idea.

During a follow-up session with the family a few months later the therapist asks them how things have worked out. They report that the new arrangement has been a success. To begin with, Frank experienced problems having to adjust to yet another new school, but he soon settled down and no longer has any discipline problems.

Many conflicts between members of families stem from situations outside the home, although this is not entirely the case with Rick and Frank. Adults often have comparable problems, such as tension at work, the threat of bankruptcy in business, quarrels with relatives over the terms of a will, or clashes with neighbors about noise. Some of these problems need to be tackled in terms of the relationship between the family and the outside world, as in the case of Frank. Often, however, the family therapist finds that the problem has its roots in the specific ways the members of the family deal with one another and the role that this plays in a relationship, for example that between husband and wife. If the therapist succeeds in bringing about changes at this level, it is important for him to establish whether they are making themselves felt in a wider context too.

Hans, age 40, has had problems at work for a number of years. The situation there is characterized by strained relations between colleagues, management suffering from stress, and frequent absences on sick leave. There comes a point when Hans can take it no longer and he, too, goes on sick leave. Clearly there are serious problems in the company, but the therapist to whom Hans is referred by his general practitioner thinks that it would be best to start by talking with the whole family—Hans, his wife and children—followed by a series of interviews with Hans and his wife Mary. The following picture emerges: Job satisfaction has always been very important to Hans, much more so than a big salary, although he is concerned with providing for his family properly. Mary would like him to be more ambitious, as she is afraid that colleagues will be promoted ahead of him. She can think of many ways in which they could spend the extra money promotion would involve. She is also concerned with status. Under pressure from her, Hans accepted a promotion when the man in the job was unable to carry on. Before long, Hans broke down as well.

The therapist concludes that Hans has difficulty standing up for himself, both at work and in relation to his wife. Therapy would teach him how to get to grips with the problem—something the therapist feels he is quite capable of doing. Mary, who says she wants her husband to be a "man," could in therapy be shown how her own behavior is contributing to the weak stand Hans takes. When he says he can no longer cope, she spoils him, which acts as a kind of reward. She does not reveal anything of her own problems, making it seem as if she is "strong" and he is "weak."

During the course of therapy, Hans and Mary come to regard one another as equals. He learns to stand up for himself and she finds out how to get support from Hans when she needs it. Hans then goes back to work. His problems there are discussed during therapy, but now in terms of what he wants to achieve for himself, how he can best set about fulfilling his goals and how he and Mary can discuss things fruitfully.

The above indicates how problems are sometimes connected with contacts in the outside world. The "ecological system approach" (Auerswald, 1968, 1972; Minuchin, 1970; Sager, 1972; Scheflen, 1971) takes this a stage further by devoting as much attention as possible to the family's natural surroundings. This involves analyzing how the family lives, the type of dwelling they have, the neighborhood, geographical mobility, the links members of the family have with friends, acquaintances, relations, neighbors, people at work, and with organizations, clubs, and societies. Information like this can show, for instance, that the family leads an isolated existence, that the parents have no one to turn to if they have problems in bringing up their children, and that they have only one another to satisfy their need for friendship, support, and affection. Scheflen and Ferber (1972) believe that this is an unhealthy state of affairs. In every respect families need contact with the outside world. In other words, a family must be sufficiently "open" in order to be able to function (of course, a family is never completely shut off from the rest of the world: cf. Chin, 1964). This applies to all families but is even more important for single-parent families. One of the jobs of a family therapist can be to teach members of the family to establish meaningful contacts with other people.

On the other hand, some families have too many outside contacts. If the father and mother and each of the children have their own separate interests and many social contacts outside the home, then there is a danger that the family will come to resemble a number of guests living by coincidence in the same hotel (cf. Section 4.3.1.7). Another type of situation which is normal and generally accepted in some cultures is where the family sees only relatives to the virtual exclusion of anybody else. It has open "borders" with the rest of the family clan, but is "closed" to the rest of the world.

1.3.5 Conclusion

Problems with which people require help from a therapist can take place within the framework of several different systems at the same time. The therapist must be capable of analyzing the situation on all of these levels and then deciding whether family therapy, marital therapy, or individual therapy is the appropriate treatment. Problems which can be expressed in other terms can often be dealt with effectively as family problems. Sometimes, however, the family therapist will have to work in terms of other systems.

This brings us to a terminological question. Family therapy is not simply therapy with families, but rather a form of therapy in which the identified patients are treated in conjunction with their relevant social context, which may consist of the immediate family but can also include friends and members of the wider family. For this reason, Minuchin (1974) prefers to talk about "therapy with natural groups" rather than family therapy. For present purposes, we shall be using the terms "family therapy" and "couple therapy."

1.4 DEVIANT BEHAVIOR AND THE FAMILY AS A SYSTEM

1.4.1 Deviation-amplifying and deviation-counteracting behavior

As we saw in Sections 1.2 and 1.3, the problems of the Landman family are closely connected with the way in which Rick and his parents react to one another and the way in which the parents behave towards one another when they have a difference of opinion. The parents concentrate more and more on Rick's behavior—which does indeed warrant attention—but in so doing they devote less and less time to their own differences, which, among other things, relate to how they feel Rick should be brought up. Rick and his parents are locked in a vicious circle which can be described as a "deviation-amplifying process" (cf. Hoffman, 1971, 1981). Tension grows within the family because the parents cannot solve their problems. The stress this creates for Rick comes out in his behavior in the form of increased anxiety, stomach pains, and shutting himself in his room more often. Barbara spends more time and energy on her son's problems. She reads books about child management and starts keeping a diary in which she records his behavior. Everything he does is seen as part of his problem, even the fact that he is too polite to his teacher and is afraid of authority. When Rick misses school because of a stomachache, his mother's excessive pampering is like a reward for his behavior. The same thing happens when she criticizes her husband's attempts to get Rick to go to school by force. This provides Rick with a respite and the chance to do as he pleases; at the same time, the atmosphere is such that his complaints get even worse. In other words, the way in which Rick's parents manage him and his response to them constitute a deviation-amplifying process. Rick's behavior deteriorates and he increasingly comes to be seen as the "deviant," the "patient," or the "problem" with which the rest of the family (in this case the parents) has to contend.

At the same time, a deviation-counteracting process is in operation with the family. It is the sum total of the interaction within the family which serves to minimize or deny the existence of differences or deviant behavior between particular members of the family. This is what is happening with Barbara and Keith. Their conflict about how to manage Rick receives less attention although it is always there in the background. Other sources of tension, such as whether Barbara should go out to work, are completely ignored.

During the first session, Keith is able to make certain observations about the problems between himself and his wife, which Barbara does not deny. This means that the deviation-counteracting process has not progressed so far that husband and wife refuse to admit that there is anything wrong with their relationship. In families where this has happened, the parents start believing that they have the perfect marriage and that the only problem is the difficult, disobedient, or disturbed child. If, in such cases, the therapist tries to draw the conflict between husband and wife out into the open, the "identified patient" may try to divert attention by strange or aggressive behavior. Jackson (in Haley and Hoffman, 1967) calls this the "rescue operation."

Deviation-amplifying and deviation-counteracting processes often occur at one and the same time. The same interaction and the same vicious circles then suggest that both processes are taking place simultaneously. In order to understand how this works, it is necessary to think in terms of levels of systems. That which amplifies Rick's deviant behavior in relation to the rest of the family (on the *family level*) counteracts the deviant behavior on the level of the subsystem of the parents and vice versa (cf. Hoffman, 1971, for a brilliant analysis of this). If the therapist is unaware of this, his intervention can have unforeseen consequences for the family.

The following example, described by Van der Hart and Defares (1973), illustrates the above. Mr. and Mrs. Madder have been referred for couple therapy because of the husband's alcoholism and the friction this creates within the marriage. The wife also drinks but that does not appear to create problems. In the course of therapy it becomes clear how the husband's drinking and his verbal abuse of his wife when he is drunk are part of a vicious circle. The husband's behavior evokes certain responses from his wife, which in turn make him drink even more. During the week, when he cannot afford to drink because of his work, she consistently and systematically belittles him and remonstrates with him because of his drinking. In this way she gives vent to the resentment she feels over the weekend when he is drunk and abuses her or even hits her. When this happens, she does not say anything at the time because she is afraid of him. His violence is a reaction to her criticism during the week and so on. This is a deviation-amplifying process between husband and wife which can also be interpreted as a punctuation problem (cf. Section 1.5.1.2).

Involving the three children (aged 11, 12, and 14) in the therapy reveals that they are afraid of their father. Over the years, he has apparently directed his anger against the eldest daughter as well as the mother. The children sympathize with the mother, who takes their side when she attacks her husband during the week about his attitude towards them. The deviation-amplifying process not only plays a role, therefore, between husband and wife, but also characterizes the husband's behavior in relation to the rest of the family (mother and children). Simultaneously, the same behavior of the members of the family constitutes a deviation-counteracting process—the differences between the mother and her children grow smaller as the differences with their father become greater. The danger of these processes within this family is crystal clear. The result of the deviation-amplifying process is that the mother is eventually admitted to hospital after being beaten by the father. The police are called in and the father is prosecuted. This provides everyone concerned with a certain amount of breathing space, but because nothing changes fundamentally, the old pattern soon repeats itself.

As with the Landman family, the therapist here is faced with a choice as to the system in which he should primarily intervene. With the Madders, the therapist has to keep a close watch on the whole family system. After both father and mother have stopped drinking (the first step), the distance between the father and the children grows smaller, creating problems for the mother. The gap between her and the children grows wider, as the unpleasant sides of her character become more apparent. She tries to remedy this situation, thereby instituting a deviation-counteracting process which is at the same time a deviation-amplifying process (between herself and the father on the one hand and herself and the children on the other). She does this by telling the children what she disapproves of in their father and letting them know how much she needs their sympathy. (This process is analyzed in detail in Section 1.7.4 in terms of power relations and coalitions.) The therapist must operate consciously on two levels here: The gap between the father and mother must not be allowed to become too great and a satisfactory relationship between the mother and children must not develop at the expense of the father.

With Barbara and Keith Landman, Rick's parents, it is not difficult for the therapist to decide on the first working points (cf. Kempler, 1974). Keith says of his own accord that the problems between him and Barbara are open to discussion and both of them make it quite clear that they want to see changes in their relationship. This enables the therapist to place the emphasis on breaking down the deviation-counteracting process taking place between the parents. He invites them for a number of interviews without the children. There is a risk that the original deviation-amplifying process between Rick and his parents will be reinforced. Numerous family therapy treatments break down because after the therapist has brought concealed differences and tensions between parents out into the open, he does not do anything constructive about them. This only results in the reinforcement of existing processes: The parents close ranks and devote increasing attention to the "deviant," who once again starts exhibiting symptomatic behavior. In such cases, the therapist will sometimes have to deal with the behavior of the identified patient first. In so doing, he may appear to be going along with the deviation-amplifying process in the existing system, which is so preoccupied with the "problem." For situations like this, the experienced therapist develops judo-like interventions which seem to be aimed specifically at the identified patient but have in fact been designed to restructure the existing system (cf. Minuchin, 1974; Sections 2.2.4, 2.2.6, and 5.1.2).

Deviation-amplifying and deviation-counteracting processes can be seen in all families. They are not harmful if they alternate with one another in a flexible manner. When, however, they are rigidly confined to certain prescribed channels, such as attempting to gloss over any kind of conflict between father and mother and attributing every kind of deviant behavior to one member of the family, the family clearly has problems.

1.4.2 The role of the scapegoat in the family

Vogel and Bell (1960) described what has been dealt with in Section 1.4.1 in terms of systems, in terms of functions of certain roles for the whole or rest of the family. Their analysis was extremely important—the concepts they used are still applied today—and therefore merits consideration here.

Vogel and Bell and later authors (Haley, 1964; Mishler and Waxler, 1968) compared families in which a child was the identified patient (problem families) with families where this was not the case. They discovered that in problem families there was conflict between the parents in which a child, the "patient," had become involved (in the Landman family it was Rick). In their control group of "non-problem" families, the conflict was either less pronounced or dealt with in such a way that the child did not become pathologically involved. A child in a position like Rick's is described by Vogel and Bell as the "scapegoat." Hoffman (1971) prefers to talk about the "deviant" because the term is less emotionally loaded. All the feelings of dissatisfaction and frustration are turned against the scapegoat. In an individual diagnostic session with Rick it became clear how this affects him on an intrapsychic level: He feels he is to blame for all the tension at home and for the fights between mother and father, which he hears when he is in bed. He thinks the best thing would be for him to leave home in order to make everyone else happy again. Without knowing it, Rick is describing the fate of the original scapegoat in the Bible and what in fact happens in many families: The scapegoat is removed or expelled. Numerous "identified patients" are admitted to clinics, hospitals, or institutions. Sometimes there is no other solution. However, family therapy has shown that it is sometimes possible to change the structure of the family and thereby make it unnecessary for the scapegoat or his or her successor to be admitted to an institution in this way.

Vogel and Bell have also observed that the whole family, including the scapegoat, often forms a united front to the outside world. People do not want to hang out their dirty linen in public—neither the problems between mother and father nor those of the scapegoat. But the family pays a high price for the scapegoat mechanism or maintaining the family myth as a way of solving problems (cf. Ferreira, 1967; Van der Pas, 1969).

The deviation-amplifying process between the scapegoat and the rest of the family imposes more and more stress on all concerned. The deviant behavior becomes progressively more serious and at a certain point the problems can no longer be concealed. Outsiders such as teachers and neighbors become involved because the situation creates problems for them, too. At the same time the behavior of the scapegoat becomes more and more disturbed. When the parents can no longer do anything with him/her, they have to ask for help.

1.4.3 Conclusion

In families where a child is presented as the patient, the child's symptoms often serve to mask conflicts between the parents or other members of the family, and as a result, the child becomes the scapegoat. The child's deviant behavior is emphasized more strongly all the time, and a deviation-amplifying process takes place between the "deviant" and the rest of the family rather than between the parents. Hoffman suggests that this is a safer alternative for the people involved, as it diverts attention from conflicts between the father and the mother —concentrating on that aspect could threaten the very foundations of the family. When conflicts between the parents are so serious that they can no longer be ignored, a deviation-amplifying process takes place, often with escalating quarrels as a component. At the same time, however, deviation-counteracting processes occur which serve to reduce the distance between the "non-deviant" parent and the children. This at least ensures the continued survival of "the family," even if the "deviant" parent disappears from the scene. The mother gathers the children around her to form the family when the father, the deviant party, leaves home.

In contrast to the above, family problems can often be effectively analyzed in different ways. Examples are outlined in Sections 1.5.1.2 (punctuation problems) and 1.7 (power problems). The advantage of thinking in terms of deviation-amplifying and deviation-counteracting processes is that the therapist can watch the main features of the system as it develops, thereby assessing the amount of progress the family is making in localizing the "deviant behavior."

In other words, in this way, the therapist is able to assess how rigid or flexible the family structure is in relation to the presenting problems. This enables him to predict how much effort and what sort of strategy will be needed to bring about change in the family. The rational, problem-solving model we present in Chapter 2 is geared towards families with at least some degree of flexibility, i.e., with a clear tendency towards transformation (Andolfi, 1979). For families with a very rigid structure, i.e., wth a strong tendency towards homeostasis, the "judo" approach (cf. Section 2.2.6) or paradoxical strategy is initially recommended (cf. Andolfi, 1979; Papp, 1977, 1980; Selvini Palazzoli et al., 1978; Van der Hart & Defares, 1978). If this approach leads to significant changes in the rigid structure of deviation-amplifying and deviation-counteracting processes, the therapist can then shift to a more congruent, problem-solving strategy.

1.5 THE FAMILY AS A COMMUNICATIONS
     SYSTEM

The above description of deviation-amplifying and deviation-counteracting processes in families is somewhat abstract. In an actual interview with a family, a therapist can pinpoint such processes only by
observing the way in which the members of the family interact. During
the session the therapist sees and hears how they communicate. He
notices how they keep getting stuck at certain points in their exchanges.
Keith and Barbara never get anywhere when they quarrel, because either
Barbara starts crying or Keith clams up. The therapist is trained to alter
the interaction pattern in such a way that the members of the family
can solve their problems themselves. A great deal has been written on
the communications approach, particularly by members of the Palo
Alto group, such as Jackson (1968), Haley (1963) and Watzlawick et al.
(1967), to which literature the reader is referred. Here we shall be
dealing with those aspects of communication which are important in
the light of the latter parts of this book or where we feel they need
elaborating or amending.

1.5.1 Basic rules and defining the terms of
       the relationship

Watzlawick et al. (1967) define an interactional system, such as a
family or a marriage, as a process in which two or more people are
engaged in defining the nature of their relationship. This process could
be further described as making proposals to one another, implicitly or
explicitly, about what the relationship should be like. Haley (1963)
puts it even more clearly. In his view people involved in a relationship
always face the same problem of establishing:

(a) "what messages, or what kinds of behavior are to take place
    in this relationship" and
(b) "who is to control what is to take place in the relationship and
    thereby control the definition of the relationship" (p. 9).

In short, the point is who has the most say and about what. Haley's
description accentuates the power aspect present in every relationship,
something that is always there when people have to deal with one

another. Frequently, this consists of confirming existing, implicit agreements as to who has the most say on certain matters, but people are not always aware of this. Many family conflicts which reach the family therapist have their origins in a failure to define the "basic rules." Often the clients have not identified the problem as such, and even when they have, the remedies sought are often inadequate.

The Landmans are to some extent aware that the ground rules have to be defined, but they are still unable to solve their problems by themselves. Keith's ideas about how the children should be brought up, and particularly about how to tackle Rick's refusal to go to school, are different from Barbara's. He thinks that the two of them should use the same approach. In other words, he is making a proposal concerning their relationship to the effect that both of them adopt the same kind of behavior, but he wants it to be the behavior he has envisaged. Barbara, on the other hand, wants them both to adopt her "reasonable" approach. This leads to Barbara "sabotaging" Keith when he is strict with Rick, which in turn causes Keith to withdraw more and more from the task of bringing up the children. Neither of them realizes that the essence of the problem is not merely a difference of opinion, but rather who should make the decision on this matter.

1.5.1.1 Content and relationship aspects

At a birthday party the conversation turns to food. Margaret says that she and her husband, John, had a delicious meal at a Chinese restaurant called the Shanghai. "No, Margaret," says John, "we went to the Tong-Lie last month, not the Shanghai and it was this month, not last month." It would appear that John and Margaret only wish to establish where and when they had the Chinese meal, as if they are merely concerned with the content aspect of their communications (cf. Watzlawick et al., 1967). At the same time, however, they are doing something more. They are dealing with the problem of how they wish to define their relationship. Watzlawick et al. (1967) call this the "relationship aspect" of communications. Bateson (1951) goes as far as calling it the "command aspect."

When John corrects Margaret he is implying that he has a better recall of events than she has ("Look how clever I am, and how stupid she is . . ."). Margaret, in turn, is incensed by John's correcting her and wants to put him in his place ("You don't know better and if you make a fool of me, I'll do the same to you").

As far as the relationship aspect is concerned, facial expression, stance, movement, and tone of voice all play an important role, in addition to what is actually said.

In many interactions the distinction between the content and the relationship aspect is blurred. Many people are in fact preoccupied with who will decide or who is the boss (ground rules), but the battle is waged in terms of content, without either party necessarily being aware of the true nature of the conflict. John and Margaret, for example, are aware of the conflict involved in the question of the Chinese meal, but fighting it out in terms of content does not usually produce a solution to the problem of ground rules. Many people never get past the confusion between the content and the relationship aspect, and do not achieve much more than scoring points against one another.

1.5.1.2 Punctuation problems

"Barbara, it's your fault that Rick won't go to school. When I try to be strict with him you make a fool of me in front of the children."

"But you treat him so badly that I have to intervene to stop you."

"That's the whole problem. You are much too lenient with him. That's why he does as he pleases, and why I have to be so strict."

The aspect of communication which emerges here is "punctuation" —introducing punctuation marks into a flow of communication. By doing this people indicate what they think is the starting point in a chain of causally connected behavior, about which there is disagreement. Often this is itself the cause of the disagreement. Keith feels obliged to react so vehemently to Rick because Barbara is too lenient with him. Barbara's starting point is a stage further back: Because Keith is so aggressive towards Rick she has to protect him, and so on. Neither realizes that they have landed up in a vicious circle in which each of them is reinforcing the other's behavior.

The original starting point is not important. What is essential in resolving this type of conflict is that neither person should concentrate exclusively on the other's shortcomings, but should try to gain insight into the effect of his or her own behavior on the other. Changes occur when one modifies one's own behavior.

Problems can also arise when all the parties involved agree on the starting point of an unsatisfactory sequence of interaction. If Keith were to say to Barbara "It's all my fault, I'm much too hard on Rick"—in other words if he stopped accusing her and adopted her approach, this might seem like the beginning of a solution to their conflict, but it will only be the semblance of a solution. Barbara will not learn to be aware of the effects of her own behavior and Keith will then become the scapegoat—which is clearly what has happened to the alcoholic father in the Madder family (Section 1.4). During the week, he complies with the mother's way of looking at things, and probably believes that he is the guilty party, that his drinking and drunken behavior are the cause of all their misery. Once he has had too much to drink over the weekend, however, his resentment towards his wife comes to the surface. Generally speaking, where there is unanimous agreement on the cause of the problem, all of the family members, including the "identified patient," concentrate on the latter's "illness," instead of looking for real solutions to their problems (cf. Section 2.2.1). Should the "patient" or "guilty party" protest, the rest of the family sees this as a confirmation of his problems.

1.5.2 Symmetrical, complementary, and parallel interaction

Bateson (1958) distinguishes between two types of interaction between two people or subgroups who have a long-term relationship. The first he describes as *symmetrical* interaction, meaning that the behavior of one party is followed by similar behavior from the other. For example, if one person makes an insulting remark, the other responds in kind. The characteristic feature of this type of behavior is sparring with one another, frequently resulting in an escalating power struggle, which comes to an end only when one of the two gives up (usually in order to regain strength for the next round).

Bateson describes the second type as *complementary* interaction, characterized by opposite responses which link up with and complement one another. One person lectures while the other listens; one person is cheerful and the other depressed; one person looks after the other who allows himself to be looked after (as with Sharon and Ray in Section 1.5.4). In complementary interaction the proportions become more extreme all the time. The "patient" becomes progressively more ill, and the "nurse" does more and more nursing.

The therapist endeavors to introduce more complexity into the clients' interaction. Couples who exhibit a predominantly symmetrical pattern of interaction learn to use a more complementary pattern with one another. In Section 6.2, we describe the drawing up of behavior contracts, in which mutual recriminations (a symmetrical pattern of interaction) are replaced by mutual requests and attempts to comply with those requests. The reverse approach is used on partners or family members with predominantly complementary behavior patterns. If a person is always ready to help another member of the family, it is often important that he or she learns to ask for help too. The aim is to be capable of alternating different types of behavior in an appropriate and productive manner (cf. Harper et al., 1977). Summarizing Lederer and Jackson (1968) on this subject, Harper et al. (1977) describe alternating symmetrical with complementary behavior as *parallel* interaction or "situationally appropriate exchanges that alternate between complementary and symmetrical behavior."

1.5.3 Inconsistent communication

Among the forerunners of family therapy in the United States, the Palo Alto group strongly emphasized the communicative phenomena which they called "double bind" (cf. Bateson et al., 1956). Since then much research has been done on this subject and a great deal of literature has been published. Lange (1973) has shown that, to a large extent, the various authors have their own interpretation of what they understand by the term "double bind" (cf. Berger, 1965; De Klerk, 1973; Olson, 1972; Ringuette & Kennedy, 1966; Sluzki and Ransom, 1976; Sojit, 1971; Van der Hart, 1973; Watzlawick et al., 1967).

Lange concludes that the concept should either be drastically redefined or dispensed with completely. We shall not be attempting a new definition here, but dispensing with the term does not, of course, mean that the effect of "double bind" phenomena in family relationships should be underestimated. The Palo Alto group did at least succeed in focusing attention on the negative effect of this sort of contradictory "message" on the functioning of the "receiver." A "message" from one member of a family to another can incorporate contradictory elements in various ways (cf. Lange, 1973; Van der Hart, 1973).

1.5.3.1 The paradoxical message

Demands members of a family sometimes make of one another, such as, "Peter, you should behave more spontaneously," or "John, you shouldn't be so obedient," are classic examples of paradoxical messages. Watzlawick et al. (1967), Haley (1973), and many other authors have pointed out that this sort of demand cannot be met because it is a contradiction in terms. The moment Peter attempts to act spontaneously, he is not being spontaneous, but responding obediently to someone else's request. When John tries to be disobedient, he is not really being disobedient—he is only trying to please his mother, who thinks that he is too well-behaved for a little boy of his age.

These kinds of demands are made more often than one might think. During a couple therapy session, Shirley accuses her husband, Jeff, of never getting angry when she criticizes him. Jeff says that he never gets angry because he always wonders if Shirley is not perhaps right. In any case, it takes a lot to get him angry. Whether Jeff defends himself sufficiently or accepts too much from Shirley and other people is debatable. Perhaps he should try to change in that respect. Be that as it may, the way in which Shirley orders him to get angry paralyzes him completely. For him to be angry in such a situation would be obedience rather than anger.

Another example: For a long time Andy had wanted his wife, Maria, to go to church with him. One Sunday Maria agreed. Andy asked her why—was it only to please him or did she really want to go? Maria told the truth—she was doing it for his sake. This led to an argument, because Andy thought it was pointless for her to do it only to please him; she had to want to go herself. This may seem slightly different from the previous example, but on examination the paradoxical elements in Andy's "message" are obvious. Maria has to do something to please him but at the same time is also commanded to enjoy it. Instead of being appreciated by her husband for doing something which is difficult for her and which she does not enjoy, she is punished. In a situation like this, it is difficult to do the right thing if one may not do anything to please the other person without enjoying it oneself.

Many more examples of paradoxical commands could be cited, but it will be clear that they are much more common than one would expect. Not every paradoxical command has negative results, however. If Maria had responded to Andy by saying "In that case I won't go," and Andy had accepted her decision, that would have been the end of it. The problem was that Andy was putting so much pressure on Maria to go.

In some cases the paradoxical commands do not have negative results because the people involved can discuss what they find difficult to accept. Watzlawick et al. (1967) correctly point out that the paradoxical command is particularly harmful in situations where there is a complementary relationship (for example parent/child) and the weaker party is on the receiving end. He or she will probably be aware that something is wrong, but will not be able to, or not dare to, put this feeling into words.

The therapist's outlook influences his perception, especially as far as paradoxical communication is concerned. This is illustrated by the following example. Mia, age 25, the "identified patient," suffered from serious depression and suicidal tendencies. Her husband, Ken, was the dominant partner in the relationship. During a therapy session, they reported having had a terrible quarrel one weekend. The therapist asked them to describe exactly what had happened. Mia explained that Ken came home and said, "Give me a kiss, darling." She did not respond and from that point things started to deteriorate. Mia could not explain why she had been unable to give Ken a kiss. The therapist, however, saw that Mia was very sensitive about being forced to do so many things by Ken. It was difficult for her to resist, because he always won the argument; he was more articulate and logical. When he said, "Give me a kiss, darling," she had interpreted it as an order to show affection, which she was unable to do on command.

Not every therapist would have thought of paradoxical communication here. Even when one is less wary of the paradoxical message than this therapist, there are many obvious cases with harmful consequences which do need to be made explicit.

1.5.3.2 Contradictions in various channels of communication

In many of the "double bind" studies referred to earlier, the authors have concentrated on the effect of the simultaneous "transmission" of contradictory "signals" through various channels—verbally (the words used), vocally (tone of voice), and nonverbally or visually. Olson (1972), Waxler and Mishler (1970), and Lange (1973) describe these in detail.

A simple example of a situation of this kind is when a mother, without changing her very harsh facial expression, says, "Of course we love you, John." The reverse is also possible—saying something extremely unkind with a friendly expression. Besides discrepancy between content and facial expression, there can also be a discrepancy between content and tone of voice.

Various authors, including Beakel and Mehrabian (1969) and Bugental et al. (1971, 1972), correctly make a connection between consequences of this sort of communication process and learning theory principles. Since Pavlov, many investigators have placed emphasis on the neurotic effects induced by contradictory stimuli (cf. Bandura, 1969; De Moor and Orlemans, 1972). Loeff (1966) reports interesting findings in this connection. He compared a random sample of "normal" girls with that of girls said to be schizophrenic. He had previously recorded a number of statements with an alternately "happy" or "unhappy" content but in a different tone of voice: One-third was spoken neutrally; one-third in a tone of voice which contradicted the content; and one-third in a tone appropriate to the content. Contrary to expectation, the "normal" girls did not perceive the incongruities any better than the "schizophrenic" girls, although the latter were more influenced by the contradictions. This corresponds with the view of Bateson et al. (1956) that "schizophrenic" children are more sensitive to statements with a double bind character. Loeff found, moreover, that where there was a contradiction, the "normal" group tended to pay more attention to the content than the tone of voice. This conflicts with the finding of Mehrabian and Wiener (1967) that it is in fact the tone of voice that makes the most impression.

1.5.3.3 Contradictions within one channel of communication

"I love you; or do I?" (Faber, 1972) is an example of a verbal message which is immediately undermined. In terms of learning psychology, simple theories can be advanced on the negative effects of communicating in this way. Mishler and Waxler (1968) give a survey of the opinions of a number of researchers who have studied the effects of this type of communication (obscurity, hidden meanings, disqualifications) in families. The results, however, are ambiguous. There is no conclusive evidence to suggest that in families with "schizophrenic" children, this sort of deviant communication pattern is predominant.

A special kind of inconsistency within one communication channel occurs when what is said by one person is constantly undermined by the response of another. The British film "Family Life" strikingly illustrates a number of examples of this. On one occasion the so-called schizophrenic girl is visited in an institution by her parents. Her father says, "You shouldn't be ashamed of being here, you know," to which she replies, "I'm not." The mother then says, "That's the trouble with you, you're never ashamed."

Learning psychology again places a great deal of emphasis on the harmful consequences of this type of inconsistency, particularly when parents contradict each other in front of their children (cf. Patterson,

1971). The family described in Section 1.2, in which Rick is the "identified patient," is an example of what happens when parents cannot agree on a common approach.

1.5.4 Symptomatic behavior

Ray, age 30, has a breakdown because he "can no longer handle his job." He goes on sick leave and is looked after at home by his wife, Sharon, age 29. They are both convinced that there is something physically wrong with him, as he suffers from headaches and often faints. Intensive tests and examinations reveal nothing, so the complaint must be "psychological." Ray, however, continues to be the "patient" and Sharon carries on looking after him. Their family doctor refers him to a psychotherapist, who wants to see husband and wife together. During the first interview the therapist asks them to specify the situations in which Ray's symptoms appear. Piecing together scraps of information from them both, it emerges that Ray gets a headache or faints when visitors turn up unannounced or stay too long. When this happens, Sharon has to entertain the guests on her own. Headaches also sometimes come on when Sharon suggests they go out together, which means that they cannot go and Sharon has to look after her husband. She puts him to bed, makes him tea, and gives him a tablet. Both of them agree completely about the nature of the relationship: Ray is "ill" and Sharon is the "nurse."

Ray's headaches and dizzy spells and his complaints about them are known as symptomatic behavior. They are physical complaints which are not somatic in origin (just as Rick suffers from headaches and stomach cramps when he has to go to school). Other forms of symptomatic behavior are phobias (from which Ray also suffers—he is afraid of public transport), compulsive thoughts and behavior, depression, and a whole series of conspicuous and inconspicuous types of behavior which have been dealt with in psychiatric literature (cf. Costello, 1970).

According to Haley (1963), before we can speak of a psychiatric symptom, it must have a severe effect on other people. Symptomatic behavior occurs frequently, but only seldom reaches the attention of a psychiatrist or therapist.

The greater the effect of the symptomatic behavior on others, the sooner help will be sought from a family doctor, psychiatrist, or psychotherapist. Barbara Landman contacted a child guidance center only when Rick started becoming excessively emotional while getting ready for school and she felt she could not do anything with him anymore.

Another aspect which Haley (1963) attributes to psychiatric symptoms is also characteristic of every kind of symptomatic behavior: The person concerned says that he is powerless to do anything about it. What is striking in Ray and Sharon's case is that Ray's complaints usually occur in situations where he is actually trying to make it clear that he does not want to do something. Instead of saying "no," which he finds difficult, he gets a headache. In this way he is able to exert his influence and get what he wants anyway. Sharon has to entertain visitors alone, or she cannot go to the movie she badly wants to see with Ray. The fact that she has to make the best of situations in which Ray is reluctant to participate is not in itself the problem. The real danger of situations like this is that the people involved cannot communicate as responsible adults in terms of "what-do-you-want-and-what-do-I-want." Sharon cannot really resent Ray's implicit "no" because he is after all "unable" to do anything about it. Haley regards symptomatic behavior like this as interpersonal maneuvers which are extremely powerful because the person is, in fact, saying, "I can't help behaving the way I do."

We must also consider the aspect of reward for symptomatic behavior. When Ray gets a headache or faints, Sharon spoils him with something he enjoys and expects of her. When Rick wins the battle and is allowed to stay home from school, his mother lets him play with his favorite toys and cares for him as though he were ill. Kanfer and Saslow (1965) call this "secondary gain" from symptomatic behavior (as opposed to primary gain, which is the elimination of fear). According to Liberman (1970), who has given this matter much attention, "intermittent reinforcement" (for example, nursing Ray on one occasion and not doing so or becoming angry on the next) ensures long-term continuation of this behavior. Generally speaking, however, Liberman's therapeutic strategy is aimed not so much at teaching the other members of the family to pay less attention to the "identified patient," as at changing the reasons for giving attention and the moment at which it is given. For example, Sharon has to avoid paying attention to Ray's symptoms and stop looking after him when he faints. On the other hand, she is to "reward" him more when he explicitly says what he wants or does not want.

Liberman's approach is still strongly based on altering the "social context" in order to enable the patient himself to change. Thus, he is basically engaged in individual therapy, although he is using the couple or the family as a whole. In family therapy, we must also consider the benefits of symptomatic behavior for the other members of the family or the husband or wife. Here the element of reciprocity plays a role. Ray's headaches give Sharon the opportunity of looking after him, which she enjoys doing. As a girl she often cared for members of her family when they were ill and this gave her great satisfaction. Ray's headaches were convenient for her for another reason too: She was afraid of arguments. If their differing needs and desires were to lead to conflicts, then this might suggest that they were unsuited to one another and therefore ought to separate. This was a frightening thought for her and thanks to Ray's symptoms she could keep it at bay.

1.6 THE LIFE CYCLE OF THE FAMILY AND SYMPTOMATIC BEHAVIOR

1.6.1 The life cycle of the family

A newly married couple has totally different problems from those of a couple married for 20 years. Parents of small children do not encounter the same difficulties as parents of adolescents. Recognition of the existence of these differences has led to the term "life cycle of the family" (Carter and McGoldrick, 1980; Haley, 1973; Minuchin, 1974) or the "developmental stages of the family" (Rubinstein, 1971; Solomon, 1973). These concepts tie in with older ideas in family sociology (cf. Duvall, 1962; Hill and Rodgers, 1964; Rodgers, 1973).

The life cycle of the family can be divided as follows:

1) The childless phase: from living together or marriage until the birth of the first child;
2) Expansion: from the birth of the first child until the birth of the last child;
3) Stabilization: the period of bringing up the children, until the first child leaves home;
4) The phase in which the children leave home;
5) "The empty nest": when the couple is alone together after the departure of all the children;
6) The phase in which one partner is left alone after the death of the other.

This division is fairly arbitrary. Endless variations are possible, dependent on such factors as a sudden change in the number of children or a change in the professional status of the breadwinner. Furthermore, there are numerous families which do not fit in with any scheme, for example, families with children at different stages of development, families with children from a previous marriage, and single-parent families.

Whatever its structure, every family has specific tasks to carry out which belong to a particular stage in the life cycle. Frequently, the problem of a family seeking help can be traced back to the failure to carry out these tasks properly. Between the various stages there are also transitional stages, such as children starting school or getting married. Each transitional stage requires a major adjustment on the part of the members of the family. Usually a period of stability follows until the next transition. Some transitions are easy for a family to make, while others present problems. For example, a young couple may be very happy with the arrival of children and manage to integrate them well into the family, but later may not succeed in "letting go." The children's leaving home is then postponed and is eventually accompanied by all kinds of problems.

An unsuccessful transition may result in instability in the next phase of family life, as the unstable nature of the transition is maintained. Well-intended interventions by the therapist to help the family adapt to new circumstances may be rejected because the new phase itself has not yet been accepted. Partly for this reason, it is important for the therapist to win the family's confidence (cf. Section 5.1) and to not try to achieve too much at once (the principle of "taking small steps," Section 2.2.5).

1.6.2 Psychiatric symptoms and the life cycle of the family

Haley (1973) places psychiatric symptoms within the framework of the life cycle of the family: "Symptoms appear when there is a dislocation or interruption in the unfolding life cycle of a family or other natural group. The symptom is a signal that a family has difficulty in getting past a stage in the life cycle" (pp. 24-25).

With the Landmans (where Rick was the "identified patient," cf. Sections 1.2 and 1.3) problems arose when the younger child started going to school all day. Rick developed symptoms because the family had not succeeded in adapting satisfactorily to the phase in which the children start school. When Rick, the first child, was born, Barbara, his mother, gave up her job as a nursery school teacher and devoted all her time to household chores and bringing up the children. Once the children were in school all day she did not have much to do. Her husband, who was not very "liberated," was opposed to her going back to work, because he felt that he was the breadwinner. Apparently she was satisfying her need for a meaningful existence by an intense preoccupation with Rick's problems; in other words, she needed Rick's problems and Rick obliged by producing them for her.

Another example is provided by the Jackson family, which we analyze in Section 1.7.4 in terms of a coalition. The family is made up of father, mother, and the "identified patient," Barry, age 20. Barry's symptoms (passivity and depression, among others) can be interpreted as a sign that the parents are finding it difficult to let their child go. This means that Barry is unable to lead his own life. The aim of family therapy here should be to help the family with the disengagement process between the parents and Barry, enabling Barry to go and live by himself and make friends of his own without breaking off the relationship with his parents.

> Although we don't know much about how a child disengages himself from his parents and leaves home, it looks as if he would lose if he went to either of two extremes. If he leaves his family and vows never to see them again, his life usually goes badly. If, in this culture, he stays with his parents and lets them run his life, that too goes badly. He must become separated from his family and yet remain involved with them (Haley, 1973, p. 44).

The parents should also be helped to lead their own lives together in the new phase. One solution, according to Haley, lies in preparing them to become grandparents. From that point of view communication between the generations is essential for them too.

> If young people cut themselves off from their parents they deprive their child of grandparents and also make it more difficult for their parents to get past stages in their own lives. Each generation is dependent upon every other generation in complex ways that we are beginning to understand as we watch the disruption of the families in these changing times (Haley, 1973, p. 45).

We may conclude that psychiatric symptoms are sometimes bound up with transition problems. Often a family goes through a transition, but is not capable of adequately carrying out the tasks appropriate to the new phase, resulting in complaints on the part of various members of that family.

According to Solomon (1973), families that have failed to perform certain tasks at some point in the past are usually characterized by chronically problematic family interactions. This is inevitably accentuated if the same is true of their families of origin. Families that have carried out their tasks well exhibit problems which relate specifically to a transition or phase.

1.7 THE FAMILY AS A POWER SYSTEM

Section 1.5 dealt with a number of communication principles. These are usually best illustrated by means of social systems which consist of two people. In practice, however, families usually consist of more than two people—a father, a mother, and one or more children, each of whom is a separate entity. They are all involved in defining the ground rules (Section 1.5.1), determining who has the most to say about what in the family. The children also play a role in the power struggle between the parents.

In the following section we shall discuss the form the power struggle can take when more than two parties are involved.

1.7.1 The "go-between"

According to Zuk (1966), there are primarily two parties in a struggle for power (for example, father and mother, or one parent and a child). Very often they draw in a third party, such as another member of the family or an outsider, who can fill a number of roles within the triad—the "go-between" being the most important, according to Zuk. The "go-between" mediates between the conflicting parties and is therefore often in a position to alter the nature of the conflict. For example, when a quarrel threatens to get out of hand, the "go-between" can tell one person that the other person did not really mean it seriously. In some families certain people always fight and others always mediate; for example, the father and son fight, and the mother is the mediator. There is never a conflict between the father and the mother or the mother and the son. Zuk tends to view this as an undesirable situation and will sometimes try to make the mother a party in a conflict rather than a "go-between." The mother's mediation is sometimes a maneuver to avoid an open conflict with her husband.

1.7.2 The "enjoying third"

Simmel (1950) makes a distinction between the role of the go-between and that of the "tertius gaudens" or "enjoying third" who takes advantage of the conflict between the other two. The opponents compete for his support and favor, for which he exacts a price. Both the quarreling parties want him on their side, once they have rejected one another. We see this in conflicts between parents when both parents want to use the child's support as a weapon against the other. The child does not really take sides, but enjoys the favor bestowed on him by both parents and in this way he becomes the most powerful member of the family. The power thus acquired is not used for the good of the family or for either one of the conflicting parties, but purely for the benefit of the "enjoying third."

1.7.3 The "oppressor"

Simmel also singles out the "oppressor" who stimulates the conflict between the two other parties and uses it for his own ends by consciously adopting a policy of divide-and-rule. The oppressor is always on the lookout for possible coalitions (two or more parties together) directed against him, which he tries to forestall. His position, therefore, is not the most advantageous. The go-between, on the other hand, usually has so much status in the family that he can afford to sanction the development of a coalition between the other two members of the triad.

Making a distinction between the conflicting parties and a third party who fills the role of go-between, "enjoying third," or oppressor can provide valuable information about the power struggle within a family. There is, however, a danger of becoming obsessed with roles if a family conflict is analyzed only in terms of roles. Concrete behavior patterns with which the people involved influence one another can easily be overlooked and the therapist begins to lose his grasp on the pattern of interaction.

1.7.4 Changing coalitions

The Jackson family consists of father and mother (both around 50) and their son, Barry, age 20, the "identified patient" who has lost his job and sits around at home, passive and depressed. In the family interview it becomes clear that Barry has many conflicts with his parents, who in turn have problems in their relationship. All three of them are involved in the struggle for power.

There are coalitions but they are not lasting, because conflicts keep arising between the members. The composition of the coalitions keeps changing. In the first family therapy session Barry implies a mother/father coalition when he accuses them of bringing him up badly. He has all kinds of psychiatric problems because they did not understand him. According to Barry, this not only happened in the past but is still going on. He illustrates it with examples of some of the points of dispute, such as the watching of television and the use of the record player. The parents defend themselves by saying, "We've always done our best. It's your fault; you're lazy." The rift between the parents themselves becomes apparent when Barry says that his father is equally bad-tempered. The mother reacts immediately with "My husband is the cause of Barry's problems, because he is always so grumpy. But he can't help it, he's always been like that." This remark reveals the existence of tension between the parents. The mother keeps the conflict under control by saying that her husband cannot help his ill-temper. The son takes his cue and launches into a tirade against his father, which the mother readily joins.

The same pattern recurs in subsequent sessions. The therapist finds it very difficult to do anything to change it. It seems as if the family can only survive in terms of the two constantly varying coalitions, which makes for a very weak family foundation. All three of them see change as a threat to their continued existence as a family. On one occasion the therapist tries to work on the father/son relationship and keeps the mother out of the conversation for a while. When it becomes obvious that father and son have resolved a conflict and seem to be getting somewhere, the mother reacts vehemently with "It's all wrong between those two. You will never manage to change it. You won't change my husband, believe me!" Barry immediately begins attacking his father again and the old mother/son coalition is restored. At that moment the mother is the oppressor, but this label is not in itself sufficient to explain what is happening in the family. A coalition between father and son means that the central figure in the family, the mother, is isolated. She is threatened and so, therefore, is the continued existence of the family.

The Madder family, which we discussed in terms of deviation-amplifying and deviation-counteracting processes in Section 1.4, can also be described in terms of power struggles and coalitions. For some time there has been a coalition of mother and children against the father, relating specifically to his drinking habits. Family therapy brings about a shift in the balance of power. The father stops drinking, and the children begin to like him more. At the same time they start seeing some of the more unpleasant sides of their mother. For example, she often loses her self-control and becomes abusive. The coalition between the mother and children weakens slightly and the bond between the father and children improves. This happens before the husband and wife have done anything to solve the problem of defining the basic rules between them. The children take the mother's side when the father "misbehaves," i.e., when he is drunk and aggressive.

The danger for the family here is that the mother will consciously or unconsciously engineer a situation in which the father again starts drinking. She says things like, "You can't hold your drink because you are so weak, but I can. . . ." If he takes this up as a challenge, the mother will soon have the children on her side again.

If the therapist were not aware of the power struggle and the role of the children as allies, he could tend to come down fairly hard on the mother, making her feel even more isolated and determined to intensify her efforts to prevent the father/children relationship from improving.

1.7.5 The perverse triad

Minuchin (1974) attributes the processes described above to the "rigid triad." The child takes sides with one parent against the other, passes judgment on both parents, behaves badly or displays other symptoms which stem from the conflict between husband and wife. The more difficult it is to keep the child out of its parents' affairs, the greater the degree of rigidity within the triad. The Jackson family, in which Barry is the "patient," is a good example of this. Barry often sides with his mother against his father, even when the parents are involved in a problem that only concerns the two of them. According to Haley (1967a), where there is a coalition of one parent with a child, and at the same time its existence is denied, we can speak of a "perverse triad."

This can be observed to some extent in the Landman family, when Rick's mother, Barbara, says that she understands Rick so well because she was like that herself as a child. That is why she knows what is best for him. She uses Rick as an ally against her husband, Keith, but not in an obvious way. When the father drags Rick to the car and takes him to school and Rick comes home half an hour later, Barbara pampers him. This makes Keith unsure of himself. He does not know how to react, so he withdraws. He grits his teeth rather than interfere directly with Rick's problems. He, too, however, sees much of himself in Rick. This gives rise to a competition as to which parent Rick most resembles and consequently who is best able to understand him. Both parents are trying to get Rick on their side. Rick's reaction is to build up a good relationship with each parent separately. When his parents are together he withdraws to his bedroom.

CHAPTER 2

The Treatment

Model

2.1 INTRODUCTION

In the previous chapter we dealt with the basic concepts underlying family treatment. Essential within the systems approach which we have adopted is the idea that one is aware of the way in which symptomatic behavior often depends on and influences the prevailing family structures and interaction patterns. By pointing out these influences to the family members, the therapist takes the first step in the direction of actual family therapy. The next step is for the therapist to help the family members to solve the current problems and to instigate new patterns of transactions within the family. For this purpose some basic strategies are outlined in this chapter. These form the framework for the techniques described later (in Chapters 4, 5, 6, and 7) and can be considered as the main themes of directive family therapy.

2.2 THE BASIC STRATEGIES

2.2.1 Basic strategy: increasing problem-solving behavior

The first principle is to consider therapy as a process in which the family members learn to *increase their problem-solving ability* (cf. Epstein and Bishop, 1981). Therapy should not be restricted to solving the current problems of the clients. In general, the goal is only reached when the clients have learned to cope with present and possibly future problems themselves. They need tools for this. The therapist can provide them and can guide them during the treatment so that they can learn to use them better.

The importance of increasing the problem-solving ability in therapy can be supported by two propositions:

(a) Ineffectiveness in approaching problematic situations is often a necessary and sufficient condition for emotional and behavioral disturbances.
(b) It is possible to train clients in general procedures and skills so that they can handle problematic situations themselves.

Based on an extensive series of studies, D'Zurilla and Goldfried (1971) distinguish five stages in the process of constructive problem-solving.

1) There must be a *general orientation*, which implies that problematic situations in everyday life are accepted and that it is possible to deal effectively with them. Furthermore, such an orientation means that problems are recognized as such and that "impulsive" or "doing nothing" reactions are repressed. A main goal of Ellis' rational emotive therapy (cf. Ellis and Harper, 1975) is to change clients in this respect.
2) Once a problem is recognized and accepted, all its aspects must be specified and made concrete. For example, when one family member regularly displays dissatisfaction with another, he will have to indicate in concrete terms what the difficulties are and in which situations and at which times these occur. This is the stage of *describing and formulating the problem*.
3) When a problem is described in specific terms, the *development of possible choices* takes place. The essence of this stage is conceiving a maximum number of possible solutions. This is linked to Osborn's (1963) ideas about "brainstorming." This means that as many ideas as possible are generated in a free-wheeling discussion. The possible solutions may not be criticized in this stage, but an attempt may be made to combine ideas.
4) When several feasible solutions are outlined, the process of *decision-making* follows. The goal is a solution which has an

optimal effect for most of those involved. Each option may be considered employing the individuals' value systems or within the framework of a cost-reward analysis, for example using Thibaut and Kelley's (1959) method.

5) After a solution has been chosen and executed, the effect must be *evaluated*. Were the considerations which led to the decision valid? To what extent have the desired goals been reached? To what extent have side effects (e.g., new problems) come about? Without such evaluations a family may persist with an ineffective solution for a certain type of problem, even though better options are available.

That the stages distinguished here play an important role not only in theory but also in actual mutual relationships is apparent in the study of Lange and Zeegers (1978). They designed a questionnaire that was related to solving interactional problems within a partner relationship. It was completed by 50 couples. In designing the list, they attempted to represent the different stages of problem-solving behavior. A cluster analysis showed that the items which were related to the first three stages came out as three separate, highly reliable indices. The list as a whole also demonstrated a high degree of reliability ($r = .90$). Subsequently, the questionnaire was used in a pre-post design for nine couples who participated in an eight-week course for couples in which the principles of interactional therapy described in this book were studied and practiced. The differences between pre and post measurement were significant for both the separate clusters and interactional problem-solving in general. The repertoire of problem-solving was much more extensive after the course than before.

2.2.2 Basic strategy: increasing (mutual) assertiveness

In psychotherapeutic literature the term "assertiveness" (cf. Bellack & Hersen, 1979; Smith, 1975) has become popular. Training seminars aimed at teaching people to stand up for themselves have become a very frequent phenomenon (cf. Clijsen et al., 1975). We have found that problems with assertiveness can play a role in different complaints. Burger (1976) gives an example of a street phobia which is explained by the fear that the client has of asserting himself with his colleagues at work. Vandereycken (1977) describes how assertive training can be important for patients with anorexia nervosa. In the example of Ray and Sharon in Section 1.5.4, Ray's headaches were related to the fact that he didn't dare to directly ask for the attention and affection which he felt that he needed.

In the Best family, where the husband is the "identified patient" because of his obsessive-compulsive behavior, there are also problems of assertiveness. Mr. Best only asserts himself negatively by sabotaging (with obsessive-compulsive behavior) what his wife wants him to do or, if the repeated criticism gets too much for him, by screaming outbursts. However, when he is asked what his wife or children could do for him, he cannot come up with anything. Mrs. Best also lacks the ability to stand up for herself. Everything she wants from her husband she conceals behind "I don't need anything, it is good for the children." In other words, she does not directly look out for her own interests. When she needs something, she illustrates her demands with proof that her desires are "normal"; she has to *ask* only because her husband is such a horrible person.

When a lack of assertiveness leads to individual problems, individual or group therapy can have a positive effect. However, the influences from the environment can interfere with the therapy and even annul its effects. Suppose that Mr. Best chose individual therapy, and suppose that it succeeded in teaching him a more assertive and constructive behavior repertoire. What would that mean for his wife? It is unlikely that she would react constructively. When the therapist works together with them towards a new range of mutual assertive behavior, the chance of permanent improvements is increased. An advantage of the family or interactional approach is, moreover, that "live material" is available: The non-assertive behavior occurs in front of the therapist's eyes, while the most important persons for the client are involved. Here the therapist's interventions will have more effect than if imaginary figures and role-playing are relied on exclusively. Furthermore, it appears that an increase in assertiveness towards one's own partner usually spontaneously brings about an increased "steadfastness" towards the environment.

All this writing about "assertiveness" and "standing up for oneself" seems to lead to an egoistic therapy model in which everyone is urged to only do what he or she feels like. This would conform to the popular interpretation that assertiveness is equal to the ability to say "no." One forgets that the ability to consciously say "yes," without feeling manipulated, also belongs to the assertive repertoire (cf. Liberman et al., 1975; Smith, 1975). In the family therapy model presented here, the clients are taught to express mutual desires directly, in a constructive manner, adhering to a number of communication rules (see Section 2.2.3).

This, then, is the "input" for new transactions between the family members, where the principles of negotiating and contracts are used.

2.2.3 Basic strategy: applying communication rules

A third main goal is to change the communicative characteristics of the family. In Chapter 1 we discussed a number of related principles in interpersonal interaction, focusing on punctuation problems and confusion about the content and relationship aspect of a message. Both have to do with power struggles and the connected issue of who defines the rules in the family. In problematic families these issues appear to play a very prominent role. Conflicts often escalate because each of the family members keeps looking for the cause in the other (punctuation problem) and/or because one does not want to be the loser and therefore attempts to prove that he is right regarding content (confusion between content and relationship aspect). Such conflict patterns can also arise when family members fear discord and attempt to make any disagreement disappear. Family members can learn a number of skills to enable them to communicate with each other more constructively.

2.2.3.1 Positive criticism

Different therapists, including behavior therapists (Jacobson and Margolin, 1979; Liberman, 1970; Rappaport and Harrell, 1972; Stuart, 1969, 1972a, 1980), representatives from the Philadelphia Child Guidance Clinic (Minuchin, 1974), and Milton Erickson (cf. Haley, 1967b, 1973), have emphasized the destructive element in negative criticism and pointed out the necessity of combining criticism with the provision of alternatives. As an illustration, let us look at an imaginary couple, George and Mary (Lange, 1977a). As any modern couple should, they are struggling with emancipation problems. Mary feels much more responsible than George for all kinds of practical issues in the home and concerning the children. She considers this to be unjust, however, and would like George to increase his share of the domestic activities and pay more attention to the children. George has his job and feels that he already does more than enough; in short, this is an area of conflict.

Talking about the conflict is not effective because they only talk when the conflict seems to get out of hand. For example, Mary reproaches George for never being home, for only thinking about his job, for taking no interest in the children, and for letting her sort out everything. Understandably, she does not want to put up with this any longer. But George does not want to accept that. He tries to prove that he does pay a lot of attention to the children and that he simply has to work hard to earn a living.

A fruitless debate arises, centered around the question of "who is right." Perhaps the discussion would have proceeded differently if both had not tried so hard to "win," and if Mary's wishes had been presented as wishes and not as imperative demands. Especially in a relationship where power struggles and rule problems predominate, demands result in the partner's feeling needlessly attacked and looking for arguments to improve his or her position. Instead of trying to prove that she objectively has a right to what she wants from her husband, Mary could have said something like, "We are in this position now and I'm having a hard time and you could do me a big favor by taking over some of my tasks." The chance that George will feel attacked and react defensively will be much less, and the chance of a subsequent positive interaction chain much greater.

We have intentionally chosen a common and somewhat controversial example. Some women will think: "But damn it, she's right and she doesn't have to beg for that, does she?" Although such a reaction is very understandable, we hope to demonstrate, with this example, that in an interaction process being right is irrelevant. The more one assumes that one is right and that the partner is obliged to do as told, the less the chance that it will actually happen. Expressing wishes instead of emphasizing rights increases the chances of positive interaction sequences and of reaching the goal—in this case more equality between husband and wife.

From the above one could conclude that we assume that no one should ever say to another in a simple way what annoys him. That could be the ultimate consequence of the principles sketched here. Obviously this is not the case. In a "normal interaction process," not characterized by rigid patterns, simple expressions of criticism can be included very well in the total exchange of messages. However, even in "normal" couples it is true that a solution to incidental problematic situations can be found by reformulating the mutual desires in the described way. In more permanent, problematic interaction chains, positive criticism is an essential condition for breaking the pattern and enabling the partners to relate intimately again. Therefore, at the beginning of the treatment the therapist ought to illustrate these principles (see Chapter 5).

2.2.3.2 Talking concretely instead of vaguely

Even when family members say what they want from each other in a positive and outright manner, it can happen that the desired changes do not occur. Suppose that Mary very honestly tells George that she needs more affection and attention. Then there is a chance that George will respond positively. But does George know what Mary means by attention? Does he know exactly what she wants from him? What could he do to give Mary that feeling of affection that she says she needs? Only when George knows all this can he adequately respond to Mary's wishes. Then he will know what the consequences are for himself and whether he wants to invest the energy. Making mutual desires concrete in specific behavior is an essential requirement if interactional problems are to be solved (cf. D'Zurilla and Goldfried, 1971; Epstein and Bishop, 1981; Lange and Zeegers, 1978). Following constructive communication rules not only helps the partner to react more adequately, but also enables the one who has unfulfilled wishes and desires to realize precisely what he/she wants from the other.

In our opinion the therapist should be constantly on the alert for vague terminology and teach the clients to change this. With one couple, the Smiths, this was in fact the main problem. They continuously criticized each other in terms of "lack of spontaneity," indirectness," etc. The therapist proposed that they wipe these terms from their vocabulary, forcing them to state what they meant. The result was that they began to understand each other much better.

2.2.3.3 Omitting the question "why"

In many publications about Gestalt therapy (e.g., Passons, 1975; Perls, 1969, 1970, 1973), the destructive element of questions beginning with "why" is described. Posing such questions is often the cause of endless discussions in which family members justify and defend their actions. Take the example of Diane and Joe. Joe thinks that Diane nags him. He is not satisfied with stating this and expressing his desire that she change in this respect (see Section 2.2.3.1); rather, he persists in asking *why* she nags. Diane commences with an entire series of reproaches which justify her nagging behavior, such as "you never notice anything;

you do everything wrong," building up to another "why" question: "Why do you never pay attention to what goes on in the house?"

The escalation has now begun. Neither one of them will soon be able to break the vicious circle. They will both keep trying to "be right" and insisting that the other admit that he/she is wrong.

The conversation could have proceeded differently. Joe could have said something like: "I don't know why it happens but I'd like it not to happen so often." The emphasis would then shift from "being right" to exploring the possibility of change. The focus is now on the *how* and on the *effect*, rather than on the *why*. Joe and Diane can solve this problem if Diane becomes aware of *how* she nags Joe and the effect this has on Joe, while Joe should become aware of the effects that his negligence has on Diane.

Sometimes the why question is also misused in a somewhat different way. Mr. Butler was referred because of alcohol problems. Between the second and the third session he had a relapse. His wife kept harping about why he had done that. He couldn't give an answer. Her insistence on knowing the "why" of his drinking behavior had a negative effect. He became more and more the pitiful little man and she became more and more the punishing figure. Using the "why" question here continuously confronted him with his failure.

In summary, there are two aspects to asking for reasons and causes (why?) of negatively experienced behavior of the other. First, asking "why" is often used to force the other into the defensive position and to "score" points in an argument. Second, asking "why" often results in nothing but rationalizations and counter-accusations—precisely the opposite of what was initially intended.

It is important to point out that not every why question is of the nature described here. Why questions may, naturally, be used to obtain factual information. For example, when a man comes home from his work later than usual, in most cases the obvious question is: "Why are you late?" However, when the why question is used to express and support negative feelings, those involved should be cautious.

2.2.3.4 Statements instead of questions

A related principle, derived from Gestalt therapy (Levitsky & Perls, 1970), concerns another type of destructive questioning—questions that are, in fact, veiled statements. An example from ordinary, domestic life is given by the father who says to his son, "Don't you think that it's about time to get a job?" A more direct manner of talking would have lead to a remark such as: "I think that you should get a job." Another example can be seen with Mark, who asks his wife, "Don't you think you're an asshole to always go out at night?" The following would have been more honest and direct: "I don't like it when you go out so often at night."

In general, posing such questions results in the asker's remaining uninvolved. He only expresses his own opinions and feelings when he thinks it is most opportune, forcing the person being questioned to take a defensive position.

2.2.3.5 Not talking about the past

Talking about the past often has the same function as asking why questions. Events are used from the past to show that statements, questions, or other messages of the other are incorrect. This leads to "debating" instead of discussing more deeply what the other wants (cf. Naranjo, 1970). For example, Bernice tells Tim that she is not able to work on their shared administrative jobs at home. The children demand too much of her. Tim responds by pointing out that when they got married she had clearly said that she saw the business as a joint venture for which both of them would be responsible. Tim's reaction is not constructive. He does not respond to Bernice's message but starts a debate to prove that Bernice, on the grounds of past statements, has no right to express such desires now. It would have been much more positive if he had asked what Bernice's concrete proposal was, considered what that would mean for him, and indicated to what extent he could comply with her wishes.

Holding the other to previously made statements or behaviors can also be destructive in another way. Consider the following case. Father finds it difficult to accept that his 18-year-old daughter is going her own way more and more by, for instance, not saying where she is going in the evenings. He checks up on her everywhere without, however, exercising authority over her. After the therapist confronts him with this, he comes to the realization that he will have to change. At that moment his wife says, "You'll never be able to manage that anyway because you always enjoyed going everywhere with her." Here the woman (not necessarily on purpose) uses the past to prevent possible changes occurring in the present and the future. Merely by expressing the expectation of her husband's failure she increases the likelihood that he will actually fail. A process of "self-fulfilling prophecy" (Merton, 1957) is set in motion. Such a process often occurs when clients begin to work on changes.

Another example is the alcoholic who has developed a strategy with the therapist to keep his drinking behavior under control. At that moment his wife interrupts with, "You can't do that anyway—that has never worked with you."

From the above it might be concluded that during therapy sessions the past is never considered, so that current communication problems can be dealt with. However, when the "here and now" principle leads to the therapist's not paying any attention to past experiences of the clients, this can have dangerous results. Often something that apparently belongs to the past is not really "past." It is still so vivid for one or more members of the family that, cognitively and emotionally, it belongs to the present. In Chapter 7 this issue is dealt with extensively. There an example is provided of a therapy that was about to fail because the therapist focused for too long on only the interactional problems between the partners.

2.2.3.6 Speaking for yourself and not for the other

In marital therapy Connie emotionally expressed the following complaint: "Robert is so irresponsible. He goes to bed much too late, drinks too much, and smokes. He is wrecking himself. This is very bad *for him*; he must feel dissatisfied about that." Although Connie's reaction might be understandable, the therapist recognized dangerous elements. It seemed as if she wasn't asking anything for herself but was only concerned about Robert. In reality the situation was much more complicated. She wanted something from Robert that was important for herself, while Robert didn't feel at all like going to bed earlier and drinking less. Connie's speaking for Robert resulted only in useless discussion about whether or not Robert's behaviors were harmful. Only after Connie—with the help of the therapist—had come to a reformulation in terms of her own desires regarding Robert, could a constructive conversation take place between the two of them.

This way of talking occurs frequently. All too often it is felt that a desire cannot be expressed without adding something to make it appear that fulfilling the desire would be beneficial for the other. This is often seen in parent-child relationships. Remarks such as, "Oh well, John would really like to go to the other school," are common in some families. We can only assume that the parents want John to want that. Apart from the regressive effects of this type of talking, it makes an honest discussion between John and his parents very difficult. A therapeutic goal is to teach clients to indicate clearly what they themselves would like from the others so that the others can respond accordingly.

2.2.3.7 No mind reading

Another destructive way of not speaking one's own mind is described by Lederer and Jackson (1968, pp. 224-5). They give the example of Sam who, upon his arrival home, hears from his wife Sue, "Oh darling, you look so tired!" Sam feels somewhat disarmed, sits down, and lets her pour a drink for him. "Darling, you're angry about something," Sue continues. "Yes, you are," she goes on before Sam has the opportunity to answer. "Sue, I don't know what you're getting at. I am a little tired. I am not angry," says Sam a bit irritated. "All right, if you won't say. I don't see why you can't share anything with me anymore. I just wanted to help." "Damn it, I don't need help. I'd like to listen to Miles Davis and relax a bit before dinner. Is that asking too much?" "Well, I like that! You're mean and nasty and I'm getting sick and tired of it." She flees to the kitchen, rattles the pans, leaving Sam to wonder how they got into this argument.

This interaction deteriorated because Sue did not accept Sam's expression of his own feelings. Even if she had been right—and Sam was in a bad mood (which may not have been true at all)—it would have been useless to force him to admit that she was right. It would have been better to go along with Sam's description of his own situation. If this description were incomplete, Sam could perhaps have expressed his feelings of dissatisfaction later. Of course, this game of mind-reading could also have happened the other way around. Sam might have come home and said, "Boy you look really depressed. . . ." "No, I'm not." "But I can see that something is bothering you."

2.2.3.8 Direct versus indirect language usage

When Mary asks George why he has not said anything all evening (informative question), George answers, "Maybe I think that you won't listen anyway." This is a typical example of indirect language usage (Conville, 1974; Mehrabian, 1966, 1967; Wagner and Pease, 1976). Words such as "maybe" and "possibly" are often indicators of not openly expressed hostility. George blames Mary for something but does not dare state this firmly. The same applies when words such as "someone," "people," and "they" are used instead of naming the specific, intended person(s). For example, Mary says, "If someone immediately starts to shout there is nothing more to be said." It would be more honest and direct to say: "If George immediately. . . ." or "If you immediately. . . ." Epstein and Bishop (1981), when assessing family structures, strongly emphasize the need to identify this type of masked aggression. Bandler and Grinder (1975) even base a whole elaborated therapy model on the relationship between psychological well-being and language usage.

A special case of indirectness arises when words such as "one" or "you" are used when the self is intended. Especially in the Gestalt literature (Greenwald, 1975), much attention is given to this.

In Section 2.2.4 on restructuring, we will deal in detail with several aspects of language in the therapeutic process.

2.2.3.9 No debating tricks; responding to the message

In Section 5.5 we will show how essential it is for family members to be able to indicate *what they want from each other* in a simple, straightforward fashion. Often this is very difficult because the expression of mutual desires easily results in debates. One spouse feels that it is necessary to prove that he is entitled to the fulfillment of the desires, while the other is concerned with showing that the desires of the partner are unfounded. Linguistic tricks are often used which would not be out of place in a political debate. As the partners in such a relationship get caught up in a spiral, it becomes impossible to simply express and fulfill each other's desires. In this section a number of these frequently occurring destructive tricks are discussed.

In 2.2.3.5 we showed how *events from the past* are sometimes used to get the better of one's partner. Instead of responding to the question concerning current desires, one partner uses arguments like, "You never used to say that," or, "You used to do this yourself," to demonstrate that the desires of the other are not valid.

Extensive discussion of one irrelevant point which is not quite correct frequently occurs. A woman reproaches her husband for hardly ever being home and for spending so little time with the children. She would like him to come home earlier from work. To support her case she gives some examples of evenings when, according to her, this would have been possible. Unfortunately, one of these examples is badly chosen—that night her husband had a very important business appointment. The husband grasps at this mistake and ends in a debate in which the wife's wish is no longer central.

Adam and Miriam, a dating couple, illustrate the *reversal trick*. Miriam relates that she finds it hard to tolerate Adam's going out with other women. She doesn't want to force him to stop this but would still like to see some changes in the present pattern. Before Adam exactly finds out what this will mean for him, he says, "But I don't ask you not to go out with other guys." This is an irrelevant point that sets off a fruitless debate. What Miriam needs does not have to be important for Adam and vice versa. It would have been much more constructive if Adam had asked what the consequences of Miriam's wishes would be for him. After that he could have indicated—not in terms of being right—to what extent he would oblige, to what extent he was prepared to do things differently for Miriam's sake. A discussion about this could perhaps have led to a compromise. Or it might have led to Adam's stating that he had no desire to restrict himself in this respect. Even the latter would have been more constructive than avoiding the issue by using irrelevant debating tricks.

This discussion of communication rules is by no means exhaustive. We could give many more examples of destructive interactions. However, here we only want to emphasize that the therapist should not allow destructive communications to pass unnoticed. We will discuss a number of relevant intervention techniques in Chapter 5. For extensive descriptions of frequently used "quarrel tricks" in families, the reader is referred to Lederer and Jackson (1968) and Bach and Wyden (1968). Bach and Wyden (p. 63) underline the destructive element of quarreling techniques as described here by pointing out that if the one wins and the other loses there are in fact two losers.

In conclusion, we would like to point out that "debates" are not always started by "number two." The one from whom something is desired is not always the first to open the debate. Often the demander will begin with criticism and defense, for example, "you are never home," "you take no interest in the family," "the children suffer because of this," etc. More constructive would be: "I'd like it if you were home more often so that I could go out more in the evenings."

2.2.4 Basic strategy: restructuring and
relabeling

In the previous sections several principles were outlined which serve
as a basis for what could be postulated as goals in directive family
therapy. In the following sections some basic strategies and principles
are sketched which are available to the therapist in attempting to help
the clients reach these goals. One of the most important strategies concerns restructuring, which ought to be a part of every therapeutic approach and, in particular, of family therapy. In family therapy two
related components can be distinguished in restructuring. The first
concerns changing the structure of the family. The second, cognitive
restructuring or reframing, implies that the therapist places certain actions of one or more family members in another light.

2.2.4.1 Change in family structure

Minuchin (1974) emphasizes structural change in the family. For
example, he describes a family in which an asthmatic girl was the
"identified patient." During the initial interview the therapist shifted
his attention to the problems of a second child, who was extremely
obese. By considering both children as problematic, he opened the way
to change in the structure of the family.

Minuchin accentuates structure by strengthening the boundaries between subsystems. According to him, the parental subsystem should
also be the authoritative system in relation to the child system. With
a family where it appears, for instance, that the oldest child exercises
a strong control over the younger brother, the therapist confronts the
family with this situation; he makes sure that authority is taken over
again by the parents.

Restructuring is also necessary in families where there is a lack of
privacy and intimacy for the parents. In that case one can hardly speak
of a "married couple system" in the family. This subsystem must be
strengthened (Aponte & Hoffman, 1973). We see an obvious example
of this in Chapter 4 with the Spitz family. The O'Brien family, which
we will deal with more extensively in Chapter 5, also provides a good
illustration. During the first two sessions the therapist noticed that the
parents constantly addressed each other as "mama" and "papa." They

even used these terms when they were talking about each other to the therapist. The therapist considered this indicative of the lack of privacy that the parents had together as husband and wife. Also, with each other they only functioned as "upbringers." The therapist convinced them to call each other by their first names during the sessions. He also gave them "homework" that was meant to give them more privacy from their children.

Changing the structure may be done at the outset in choosing the issues to be dealt with. When the therapist decides to pay attention to the problems other than those concerning the "identified patient," this can lead to a change in the structure of the family. In Section 6.5 about treatment contracts we show that sometimes the therapist should leave the existing structure intact for the time being because of tactical considerations. Restructuring may also take place due to changes in affection and power patterns in the family. This can be related to the positions of the parents, such as in the example described above, or to the position of one parent or one or more children.

2.2.4.2 Cognitive restructuring based on attribution and self-perception theories

In modern behavior therapy more and more attention is being given to the client's cognitive processes. Thus, it has been realized that some problems stop being problems when the problem-carrier does not experience them as such anymore. In this case the client's objective behavior does not need to change. Ellis's rational-emotive therapy (Ellis and Harper, 1975) is based on this line of thought.

Interest in cognitive factors is based, for the most important part, on two theories which were developed by social psychologists and tested in laboratory experiments: attribution theory and self-perception theory.

Attribution theory

Attribution theory states that people are continuously finding certain causes for their emotions and behaviors. The causes to which they ascribe their situation in turn influence the nature of the emotion. Positive experiences and desired behavior may be preferably ascribed to external factors instead of to the self. On the other hand, as Valins and Nisbett (1972) demonstrate, many psychological problems arise because negative experiences are completely attributed to one's own shortcomings instead of also taking the environmental influences into consideration. The feelings of inferiority and tension that arise can, in turn, produce new negative experiences, which contribute to a circular process from which escape is difficult. This reminds us of the principle of "self-destructive prophecies"—expectations about failure (cognitions) result in actual failure. It goes without saying that there are many cases where therapeutic intervention ought to be specifically aimed at breaking through the inclination to label the self negatively.

For example, Johan, age 13, is referred because of a school phobia. Although he is a good student in many subjects, his achievements give him no satisfaction or self-confidence. He attributes his success to luck, help from his classmates, or extra attention from the teacher, etc. That his classmates apparently like him a lot does not contribute to his self-confidence either. They're friendly, he says, not because he's such a great guy but because they pity him. In addition to exploring how Johan acquired this pattern of attribution, changing it will be an important goal of therapy.

Attribution theory can be especially useful when clients have vague (physical) complaints, increased "arousal," or unfocused "anxiety," for which they themselves have no clear explanations. As Schachter (1971) has shown in a series of interesting experiments, in such situations the client is highly susceptible to suggestions from the environment which can lead to explanations (cognitive coding of the arousal). If one is successful in finding an acceptable, nonthreatening explanation for the client, then negative emotions will be prevented and the condition of the increased arousal will gradually decrease. The "negative placebo effect"—where placebos introduced as drugs result in the feared symptoms (Davison and Valins, 1969)—is based on this process.

Knowledge of attribution theories leads therapists to pay attention to the labels that clients give themselves in certain situations. Does the client see himself as "stupid" in school, or "clumsy" in sports or a "failure" at his job? Often the therapist will attempt to get clients to see their emotions and symptoms in another perspective by giving interpretations. So-called *positive labeling,* an important variant of interpretation, results in the clients' viewing their own behaviors in a more positive context so that they are not bothered as much by them and can work on changes more easily.

For example, a couple was being seen in a sex therapy program based on Masters and Johnson (1970), where very small steps were taken. The therapist had given stroking assignments as homework. During the next session the woman said, when asked, that she had hated it. The therapist asked her exactly what it was that she had experienced so negatively. In tears the woman said that she had found it repulsive to stroke her husband's back. The therapist asked whether there were still other unpleasant things regarding stroking and what she thought of being stroked herself. Everything was all right except stroking her husband's back. The therapist asked her to relate what she didn't like about that. After listening to her complaint that it was distasteful to her, the therapist was silent for a long time. Then he said the following: "What I am about to say might sound strange, but I'm actually very glad about everything that you've just said. One of the most important things in a sexual relationship is not that you should like everything that the other does but that you can talk about it—that you can say what you like and what you don't like. With that you have made a beginning which gives me much hope for the future." The woman was noticeably relieved. The attribution of "see, I'm not normal and it'll never be right" was changed into "actually it's good not to like everything and I am normal but we must still work hard before we will really enjoy having sex together."

In the above example the therapist influenced the self-attributions of the client by telling her his view (or rather, his attributions of her behavior). Cognitive restructuring often takes place in this way. Almost every interpretation and summary of the therapist can subtly influence the self-image of the client.

Self-perception theory

A second method for leading the client to new self-opinions is based on Bem's self-perception theory (1972), which proposes a cause-effect relationship which is opposite to the one used in "common sense." One does not behave as one feels but feels as one behaves. According to Bem, we constantly observe our own behavior and draw conclusions from this about our own personality and qualities.

Self-perception theory assumes the following circular sequence in a person's thought pattern: (a) I do something→(b) I perceive that I am doing it→(c) why do I do that?→(d) because I am such and such a person →(e) if I am such and such a person I should act like that too, etc.

Self-perception theory has led to many interesting hypotheses and experiments (Laird, 1974; Lepper et al., 1973). The major conclusion is relevant to therapy: Through specific assignments clients can be taught to display new behaviors which, in turn, lead to a new, more positive self-image.

The Morris family is an example of this. Father, the identified patient, had phobic complaints that prevented him from working and was very isolated in the family. He was convinced that everything in his life had failed and that he could not develop a good relationship with anyone. The oldest son, Eric, also had problems at school and could not get along very well with his brothers, who accused him of verbal and physical aggression.

Part of the treatment involved teaching Mr. Morris to change his son's behavior by using contracts and selective reinforcement techniques. Although he initially thought that he could not do this at all, he was successful (using the assignments from the therapist) in bringing about drastic changes in his son's behavior. This success had a great influence on Mr. Morris' self-image. It shifted from "I am completely ineffectual" to "If I dedicate myself to something, I do this completely and then there's a chance that the problems will be solved." Such a change in self-image can be considered as a shift from external to internal locus of control (cf. Lefcourt, 1976).

Sometimes changes in clients' self-image can be achieved or strengthened simply by teaching them to address themselves in a new way. In Mr. Morris's case, the therapist suggested that he write a sentence expressing his new, more positive self-image on a note card. Every time Mr. Morris had the urge to take on a weak attitude again, he reached for the card and read it out loud. For more extensive consideration of such techniques, see Meichenbaum (1974) and Lange (1976).

2.2.4.3 Restructuring and language

The self-perception theory states that our behavior influences our feelings and the opinions we have about ourselves. A special variant of behavior is speaking. The way in which we speak, the choice of words, has an influence on how we feel. A frequently occurring example of this is the wrong usage of the verb "can." Peter, who is being treated for his fear of social situations, repeatedly says, for example: "I can't go there." After hearing this a few times, the therapist interrupts the conversation. He points out to Peter that "I can't go there" is an incorrect formulation. He doesn't go there, he finds it difficult to go, or he doesn't want to go. It is agreed that Peter will wipe the words "I cannot" from his vocabulary.

The intention of this assignment is based on the self-perception theory. As Peter hears himself say, "I don't want this or that," or "I find it difficult," rather than "I can't," a change takes place in the self-conception. In the beginning Peter sometimes forgot this agreement, so that the therapist gave him a signal every time he said, "I can't. . . ." Soon this was not necessary.

Such linguistic interventions take little time and effort but can result in a breakthrough in therapy. In Peter's case the phobic complaints were no longer directly worked on; however, attention was paid to increasing his assertive behavior, especially in relation to his girlfriend. After about five sessions Peter began to report changes in his pattern of going out. Apart from the changes in associating with his girlfriend, the changes in his vocabulary were, according to him, an important contribution to his improvement.

Another example of the effect of linguistic interventions is described by Lange (1976). In the couple therapy discussed there, the male partner is directed to stop using the word "depressed" to describe himself—he wasn't depressed anymore but a "nuisance." This term provided a more workable situation and offered more possibilities, since it referred to his attitude regarding his wife. It would not be correct to attribute the visible changes in this man entirely to the new label, which he began to use very consistently; however, it is probable that this contributed to an improvement of the situation.

Bandler and Grinder (1975) illustrate in detail how the choice of linguistic formulation is, on the one hand, influenced by certain thought processes, but, on the other hand, also influences those processes. They describe how the use of nouns, where actually verbs ought to be used, leads to distortion of the message. They give the example of the client who says: "I regret *my decision* to go home." According to Bandler and Grinder, this sentence indicates that there is no longer an ongoing process in which the client can intervene. The client has given up control and made himself helpless. If, instead, the client says, "I regret that I decided to go home," then there is a process that he can still influence. According to Bandler and Grinder, therapists should help clients in these instances to choose that process formulation by which they will attain a less helpless attitude. Although their examples and position are somewhat extreme, Bandler and Grinder have certainly contributed much to the ideas about the influence of linguistic issues in psychotherapy.

2.2.4.4 Relabeling and interactions

In the previous section some general principles of cognitive restructuring and change in the self-image were discussed. In this section we stress the importance of these principles with regard to family therapy instead of individual therapy. In family therapy there is an essential form of relabeling where the therapist rewords or reframes a so-called individual problem as an interactional problem.

Suppose Brenda says that her husband is a terrible, selfish man who never wants to talk to her. This is an individual label: Peter, her husband, is like this or like that. The therapist can reframe this, however, in terms of different needs. Brenda has more need for conversation than Peter. Now Peter is no longer the focus of treatment; rather, they can work on the differences in need for conversation, which provides many more possibilities for solving the problem. A golden rule in family therapy is: *Whenever possible, change the individual labels which family members place on each other into interactional, more workable labels.* This applies to the relationship between adults as well as to the relationship between parents and children. Thus, John not only is a difficult child but also has problems with the way in which his parents want to teach him their rules. John and his parents have problems with each other.

As another example, consider Keith, who complains that there is a lack of emotion in his relationship with his wife, Emily. She never tells anything about herself and never responds to what he says. Emily confirms this but does not know why she acts this way. While they are talking about it together, the therapist notices that Emily makes an anxious impression. He asks whether this impression is based on reality and of whom she is frightened. In tears Emily says that she is afraid of Keith. He always overwhelms her with his verbal aggressiveness. After allowing Emily to talk about this and seeing Keith's reaction, the therapist summarizes the problem. He puts the emphasis on the interactional element. They reinforce each other in precisely that which they do not want. Keith wants Emily to talk more about herself and to speak up more for herself, but by the way in which he attempts to force her he actually pushes her to withdraw further. Emily's withdrawal, however, results in an increase of Keith's verbal dominance, etc. Such an interpretation of the problem makes it easier to manage. It is no longer a static problem (a quality of Emily or Keith), but has a dynamic nature and can probably be solved by small changes from both sides.

In family therapy the role which restructuring plays is possibly even greater than in individual therapy. Clients receive a new coding not only of their own behavior but also of the behavior of the other family members. Mr. Petersen nags his wife when she has done something wrong in the upbringing of the children. Mrs. Petersen labels this as "splitting hairs" and teasing, by which her husband tries to play the boss. The therapist can now go two ways. He can select the negative side (playing the boss) and make this the subject for intervention. This will sometimes be necessary. A more positive approach, however, will often yield better results; in this case, for instance, the therapist might point out that Mr. Petersen is apparently a considerate father, which is to be highly valued. Unfortunately, his opinions deviate somewhat from those of his wife, which should be an area for discussion in therapy. When the intervention is formulated in this way, a new self-image is created for Mr. Petersen and his behavior is placed in a more positive light for his wife, so that it becomes easier for her to respond constructively.

During a family therapy session the therapist often has to choose between negative and positive interpretations. A general guideline cannot be provided. In some cases it is necessary to urge a client to explicitly speak up for his own needs and to not diminish the differences between him and one or more other family members. Then a negative interpretation may be appropriate. However, an experienced therapist will often be able to give even this a positive sway (see Section 5.10 about confrontation and support). In many cases it is fruitful to directly emphasize the positive elements which cling to the negative behavior so that negative self-fulfilling prophecies can be broken in favor of positive interaction chains. Van der Velden et al. (1980) give a number of guidelines for the use of positive labeling.

No matter what direction therapists give to their interpretations and recodings, it is essential that they remain conscious of the effects on the family members and that they ask themselves to what extent "the family members can do something with it."

2.2.4.5 Restructuring by interactional assignments

The idea that behavior change often precedes a change in feeling is of utmost importance in family therapy. Mrs. Watts had big problems with her oldest son, Jim, age 12. He was aggressive (both verbally and nonverbally), disobedient, etc. The therapist observed clear signs of a power struggle. Instead of sharing these observations with mother and son, he asked them to have a contest lasting one week. Whoever did the most pleasing things for the other would be the winner. Each of them would write every day, on a large piece of paper on the wall, every positive action which had been especially done for the other or negative actions not done. Ordinary routines such as cooking, etc., were not to be included. After a week it appeared that Jim had won the contest, but mother had also done very well. However, most important was the fact that a number of self-conceptions and conceptions of the other had changed. Jim noticed that he had actually liked doing things for his mother. His self-image was changed, but his ideas about his mother had also been altered. He now had more understanding of what she wanted from him. A similar process had happened to his mother.

From this brief example it does not become clear which assignments must be given in what cases. However, this case does illustrate the essential idea that directed assignments can lead to new images regarding all family members, through which new and often more constructive interaction patterns become possible.

2.2.5 Basic strategy: applying learning principles

One of the most important characteristics of directive family therapy is the integration of the systems approach and learning theory principles. In behavior therapy literature the learning theory concepts are applied mainly to changing the individual. But important behavior therapy techniques like "shaping," which implies teaching individuals to make fundamental changes in small steps, are also applicable when *the interaction pattern between two or more people is the unit of treatment*. A husband and wife who are continuously at each other's throats do not benefit from an assignment that would imply that they must all of a sudden act like turtledoves. This request would be too difficult. However, they can be asked to fulfill one small wish of the other (see Chapter 6 on contracts). Thus, the "shaping" principle is applied to changing an interaction pattern. This can also hold in the application of selective reinforcement techniques. When the therapist consciously rewards some transactions between the partners while others are ignored, the unit of treatment is again not the individual but the interaction between the individuals.

To a somewhat lesser degree this is also the case when clients are taught how to apply certain principles of selective reinforcement regarding each other. In families with problems, one often sees that there is an exclusively negative selection in reinforcement schemas between the family members. The punishment of undesired behavior is present but the more important component of rewarding positive behavior is lacking. This is usually related to the power struggle and rule problems described in Section 1.5.1. Therapy can here be aimed at leading the family members to more positive behavior.

Mapping of existing patterns must precede the instigation of new patterns of reinforcement. Just as in individual behavior therapy, it is desirable and very well possible in family therapy to make a functional analysis at the beginning of the treatment, in which the way in which various (symptomatic) behaviors are reinforced in the family are systematically studied.

It is not our intention to discuss learning principles exhaustively and extensively. More examples can be found in Section 2.2.2 (about assertiveness) and in Chapter 5 (about techniques). It is remarkable that many behavior therapists, who from a learning theory framework ought to be able to recognize the importance of environmental factors, still hesitate to consider the interactions between the identified patient and the relevant environment as a unit of treatment.

2.2.6 The judo approach

Most of the basic strategies described in this chapter are founded on a rational problem-solving approach. The core of this is that, together with the family members, the therapist establishes various goals for therapy and discusses how they can work towards these goals in small steps. This "clean" approach, based on the question, "What do you want?", is not always possible. Some clients do not know what they want—and don't want to know either. Their symptomatic behavior meets a demand so that they will not be willing to give up their symptoms just like that.

Robert and Danielle are an example of this. Robert was referred because of depression and apathy. The pattern between the couple soon became clear. Robert was not used to directly requesting attention for himself. He "didn't need anything." However, he did need care, attention, and sympathy. He received these—but only when he felt "depressed." Danielle then tried to help him in every possible way. He always brushed off her attempts with comments such as, "I can't be helped anyway." Since she then began questioning him with "Is it this or that?" or "Shall I do it?", he received maximum attention, which he could maintain by sabotaging any offers of help. In short, Danielle's questioning reinforced Robert's symptomatic behavior.

This pattern occurs in many marital relationships, as well as in relationships between some clients and their therapists.

Various authors point out that in such a situation the therapist must not immediately attempt to give the clients insight into the nature of the complaints and to convince them of the necessity of directly working on the interactional pattern. Such an approach would only lead to debates and reinforce the symptomatic behavior. A "judo approach" (Lange, 1976; Mandel et al., 1975; Minuchin, 1974), which is based on the therapist not forcing the client to change, is then more effective.

The judo principle is elaborated further by Rubinstein and Van der Hart (1977). They remark that judo, as a sport, is based in large part on the application of the *ju* principle. The literal meaning of this term is "flexibility and pliability." In practice the *ju* principle consists of two components. The first is *going along with*. This means that the attack of the opponent is accepted instead of directly resisted. In the judo sport this can be translated into: If he pushes then pull and if he pulls then push. The second component concerns the *counterattack*. Going along with the force of the opponent is transformed into an active taking over. Now one's own strength is used, along with, at the same time, the strength of the opponent, who is concentrated on his own attack. If the opponent pushes, one must pull harder and if he pulls, one should push even more. This causes the opponent to lose his balance and he can then "be thrown."

An important part of the therapy with Robert and Danielle was based on these aspects of ju and judo. Opposing Danielle, the therapist went along with Robert in his description of the problems. He made it clear that while he understood how difficult it all was for Robert, unfortunately he could not help him. That would only be possible if Robert himself would supply the material. This type of interaction occurred a number of times. One time the therapist even carried on a long discussion with Danielle about totally different issues, ignoring Robert completely. Another time the session was terminated after five minutes. In all cases the message to Robert was: "I'd like to help you but you'll have to do something for it. If you don't, it doesn't matter, but then I can't do anything either." This aspect of the judo approach, going along with instead of resisting, was also conveyed to Danielle. If Robert displayed his apathy at home she was allowed to ask him once whether she could help and what he wanted from her. If she did not receive a positive reply, then his listlessness was resolutely but kindly ignored. Danielle had great difficulty with this assignment but complied anyway.

Robert's "moods" decreased in frequency and intensity while he expressed his needs more and more directly.

In this therapy the therapist's judo approach consisted of not confronting Robert with his weak attitude (which would have only lead to a fruitless discussion) and not continuously offering solutions and reasonings which Robert could then reject. He went along with Robert's description that his situation was very difficult. Furthermore, he began a counterattack at certain times by purposely ignoring Robert or by giving him assignments in which his symptomatic behavior was actually prescribed (see Section 5.13).

A judo-like attitude by the therapist can be important in both individual (Mandel et al., 1975) and in family therapy. From the example presented here it is clear that in family therapy the "modeling" function (see Section 5.9) that the therapist's "non-resistance" has for the other family members is influential.

Another example is found in the treatment of the Burger family. The referral was partly based on "intractability" and aggressiveness of the two sons, 14 and 15 years old. During the first session the oldest, Ron, left little doubt about the fact that he thought it was nonsense to come along. Accompanied by deep sighs, he continuously looked meaningfully at his watch. The therapist then told him, in a friendly way, that he could easily understand that Ron found it awkward and would rather leave. To go along with him he proposed that Ron should check the time so that the session would at least not run overtime (Van der Velden, 1976). Ron thought this was great and from then on participated actively. He did not show up for the next session; he had remained in the car. His parents wanted to go and get him. The therapist advised them not to and ensured that they had a session in which a good behavior contract was made for Ron's brother, Tom, and his parents. At the end of this session he asked the parents to specifically tell Ron that he should only come when he felt like it, that he (the therapist) would not be angry at all if Ron didn't come along. Nothing useful could be accomplished anyway if he came against his will. Here too the judo approach of the therapist was a model, especially for the mother who found it hard not to argue with her children and not to "pull them."

Judo is often useful at the beginning of family therapy when there clearly is an "identified patient." Suppose that a family enters therapy because the oldest son is in continuous trouble with the police. Apart from that there is "nothing wrong" in the family. Even if the therapist suspects that there are certain other problems in the family, he must avoid expressing this too soon. It is better for the therapist to initially go along with the description that the family members give of the problems and their concern about them. Only when a suitable opportunity arises and the family is ready can the discussion begin about other problem areas, such as the parental relationship or relationships between the parents and the other children. By the way, in such a situation—which often confronts many therapists of child guidance centers—"going along with" should be demonstrated very carefully. If the therapist only supports the rest of the family, there is the chance that the "identified patient" will be driven further into a corner and that the therapist will not establish the necessary contact with that person. Tact and nuances are very important.

It is not possible to give a summary of all the types of situations in which the judo approach, described by Sherman (1968) as "siding with the resistance," is necessary. As a rule of thumb, the judo approach is appropriate in those cases where the therapist notices or suspects that the clients are not (yet) inclined to accept his view of the nature of the problems and the suitable approach. Although in this respect the judo strategy is contrary to a rational congruent approach, it is not the same as a paradoxical strategy (cf. Selvini Palazzoli et al., 1978), which implies prescribing symptoms as homework. Judo might be seen as a therapeutic attitude which can be followed by congruent or paradoxical assignments when resistance is broken. The choice in that respect is determined by the kind of problems presented.

In conclusion, therapists must be aware of their responsibility towards the family members and tune the strategy to their special characteristics, their interaction patterns, and the relationship that they have with family members. Sometimes this can imply that the first impulse to "directly" convince the family or couple must be discarded in favor of a more indirect approach (Van der Hart & Rubinstein, 1977) that leads them to change themselves.

2.3 STAGES IN THERAPY

In this section we describe the different stages which can be distinguished in the process of family therapy.

2.3.1 The first stage: assessment

Section 3.3 deals in detail with the following question: "Who should be invited to attend the first session?" Using various considerations and examples, we reach the conclusion that the therapist must always make a conscious choice in answering this question; the therapist should not feel obliged to accept a configuration which is apparently being forced upon him by the referring person. As a rule of thumb, for a first session the largest possible unit of directly involved and/or living together family members ought to be invited.

When it has been decided who will be involved in the first stage of the therapy, the treatment can commence. The first stage consists of assessing the family situation. In Chapter 4 we describe in detail how the therapist in the first sessions brings the specific problems to the surface, gains insight into the various aspects of the family structure, observes the style of communication, and makes an inventory of the strong points. Necessarily, first sessions are also characterized by "coupling" (Minuchin, 1974), as the therapist works to win the confidence of the family. This can be done by displaying interest in other areas, such as work and hobbies, and by making it clear where he himself stands or setting out his principles. This stage is more or less terminated by a "preliminary treatment contract."

2.3.2 The second stage: choosing issues for treatment

In the second stage, the issues to be treated are selected. From the wide range of problem areas which have come out in the first session(s), some areas are chosen which will be worked on first. In general, the choice is determined by two factors, which can sometimes be in contradiction: feasibility and relevance for the family members. The second factor hardly deserves explanation. Naturally it is desirable to begin work as quickly as possible on the problems which are the most urgent for the clients. This, however, is not always possible. Sometimes problems are so inaccessible and embedded in other problems that the chance of immediately tackling them is very slim. This applies, for instance, in the case of sexual problems. Janet and Murray provide an example of this.

Sexuality was such an immense problem for them that Janet cried about it in the first session. Murray was her first and only lover. During intercourse Janet had never experienced an orgasm. She saw this as a failing on her part, while she had the idea that Murray had had satisfying sexual relationships with other women. She even thought that he still had them. This caused violent feelings of jealousy which, for that matter, did have a real basis. Murray, too, experienced their sexual relationship as dissatisfying. Although this problem area was very important for them, the therapist felt that it could not be worked on immediately. It could only happen when they, by solving a number of other problems, became closer and trusted each other more. Therefore, the first seven sessions of treatment were dedicated to learning to express irritations, to negotiate differences, to listen to each other, and to enter minor behavior contracts. Sexual contact was forbidden during this period. Only after this approach had led to rather major positive changes in their relationship was a sex therapy program following the Masters and Johnson model (1970) initiated.

If the chance of successfully working on a problem seems slim, it is best to start with a simple, related problem. The successes acquired in one area can form the foundation on which more important and difficult problems can be tackled later.

After the first goals are determined, they are approached in small steps. The therapist asks clients to describe their problems as specifically and concretely as they can; "monitoring" often serves as an important aid here (see Section 5.3). Later, changes are created by using techniques such as "immediate feedback," behavior exercises, modeling, symptom prescription, contracts, etc. A number of these techniques are described in Chapters 5 and 6. After approximately four sessions, a joint evaluation follows of this first stage of treatment. The therapist then has data for a more extensive functional analysis (Kanfer and Saslow, 1965). The therapist has been able to see how the clients react to this approach and how they carry out their homework. Based on this, he can now give a more exact prediction of what is and is not feasible and how long therapy will take. Also, at this point the clients have more information about the therapy than directly after the assessment session(s). All of this makes it possible and desirable to establish a second, more definite treatment contract at the end of the first treatment stage.

2.3.3 The third stage: consolidation and (possibly) new issues

In the third stage new problem areas may arise. They also can be worked on using the above-mentioned techniques and those described in Chapters 5 and 6. Furthermore, the therapist now concentrates more on the *way* in which the family members approach their problems than on the provision of concrete solutions during the sessions. During the sessions the therapist stimulates family members to come up with solutions on their own. Instead of eliminating problems, the therapist strives to increase problem-solving ability in this stage. In addition to these general differences between the first and second stage of treatment, there is still one specific difference. This is related to therapies involving judo. If judo is needed, this will be evident in the assessment sessions and will greatly influence the strategies used during the first and second stage. If these stages proceed successfully, a more direct style can be used in the third stage of treatment.

2.3.4 The fourth stage: transfer of change, generalization

The main goal of the last stage of treatment is to help clients learn to generalize what has changed in the sessions to other situations. They must cut themselves loose from a therapy in which they have received many guidelines and feedback about their own functioning and about their mutual communication patterns. It is not always easy to maintain improvements without the therapist. During this stage the therapist should keep a number of principles in mind, which are briefly described in Section 5.16. For a more extensive description see Goldstein et al. (1966) and Rose (1977).

2.4 SCHEMA AND CONSIDERATION OF THE TREATMENT MODEL

In Figure 2.1 the course of directive family therapy is schematically presented. The successive steps are linked to the stages and principles described in this chapter. Furthermore, several techniques and principles are placed in the schema which will be discussed in detail in Chapters 4, 5, and 6.

The treatment model, as it appears in the schema and the above sections, must be considered as an ideal type. It offers a framework which can be used in structuring and building up family therapy. However, the stages in this model cannot always be strictly followed. Even in a first assessment session summarizing and structuring have an intervening value. Thus, assessment could be considered as a first stage in treatment. On the other hand, working towards specific goals and interventions, in the second and sometimes also in the third stage, can again provide new information about the family and its possibilities, leading to reassessment.

The process of detachment is especially emphasized in the last stage. Nevertheless, it is sometimes already necessary in the assessment stage to prepare clients for the fact that treatment will have to be terminated at some time (Lange, 1976; Rose, 1972). On the other hand, it is not always possible in the last stage to maintain the "transfer of change" principles which are described in Section 5.16. Sometimes a new prob-

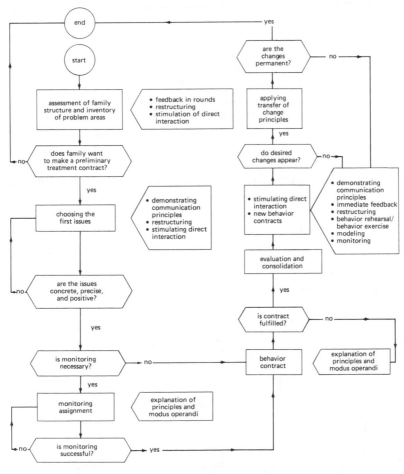

Figure 2.1. Schema of the treatment model.

lem comes up which requires a structuring intervention by the therapist.

The model reflects a direct, rational, problem-solving approach, where recognition, concrete formulation, negotiation, conscious choice of solutions, and adherence to a number of communication rules are important principles. However, therapy often consists of more. In particular, the indirect judo-like approach is sometimes a condition for being able to use this model successfully. When, for example, family members show resistance or receive significant secondary gain from their symptoms, a direct start only results in fruitless sessions which, moreover, hinder a more judo-like approach in a later stage.

For example, Jacob and his wife Teresa were referred to a family therapist. He had been treated for paranoia and depression for a number of years. Another therapist had worked with him in a direct way by teaching him the techniques of rational emotive therapy (Ellis and Harper, 1975). This had been partially successful, but the depressions, feelings of inadequacy, etc., had remained. During the assessment stage it became clear to the new therapist that Jacob very much enjoyed describing himself as "a hopeless case"—his own words. The therapist also saw that by using this tactic Jacob received much attention from Teresa, who kept on providing "solutions."

The therapist decided not to fall into this trap. He "went along" with the helplessness. He underlined the fact that he saw quite well that it might not be successful. However, an attempt could be made, but then maybe Jacob would have to do a few strange things and the therapist wondered whether he would want that. When the intervention was formulated in this way, Jacob was eager to go along. The suggestion of the therapist was as follows: Jacob should immediately write down every negative feeling that came up in him during social situations (e.g., fear that others would talk about him or think badly of him). On top of that he should attempt to exaggerate the feeling, to try to imagine, in as extreme a way as possible, what the horrible thoughts were that others had about him. He should take 15 minutes each time for writing down this exaggeration of the negative feelings. This assignment was presented to him with the statement that change would only be possible if he consciously experienced what usually came to him unconsciously.

In addition, the couple was strictly forbidden to discuss Jacob's problems together. There was a time established every evening (from eight o'clock until quarter past) when Jacob could relate the awful things he had experienced. Teresa would listen and then give a summary in her own words of what he had said. To react (helping him) was not allowed, but it was at least clear that she knew what he was going through. This part of the assignment was also provided with a motive: Jacob had a right to his own problems. Making these conscious had always been hindered by Teresa's attempts to help (with good intentions, of course). The intervention was designed to break through the patient-nurse pattern that characterized their relationship because of the extra attention Jacob received when he was "depressed." Furthermore, Teresa would receive the opportunity to learn how to stand up for her own needs instead of always thinking about Jacob's needs.

After a few sessions the relationship between Teresa and Jacob had changed drastically. Jacob began to behave more independently, while Teresa could detach herself much more easily from Jacob's problems. The next stage in therapy was characterized by making unfulfilled needs concrete and working on remaining irritations. This became possible due to the growing equality in their relationship.

This example is included here, since the treatment deviated from the stages outlined in this section. The main problem was immediately tackled without using small steps. An indirect judo approach was necessary here. Not until the third stage of treatment could a more rational, problem-solving method be used. Another order would have had little chance of success in changing the pattern that Teresa and Jacob displayed at the outset of the treatment.

Besides deviating from the stages of the treatment model, in some cases the therapist cannot apply certain basic strategies, such as the principle of the "small step" described in Section 2.2.5.

An example came up during the fourth session with the Burger family. Intractability of the two boys was the initial complaint for which treatment was requested. The therapist suspected that small steps (à la Patterson, 1971) would not help. The boys would think this was silly and sabotage the therapy. Instead, he introduced a dramatic, difficult contract. During the week the boys would not allow themselves to be provoked in any way and they themselves would annoy no one at home, except during one-half hour per day at a time established during the therapy. Then they would produce as much noise, swearing, etc., as they could.

They were to decide themselves at the end of the week whether they had stuck to the agreement or not. If so, then father would give them each $10 (an amount chosen by them) at the next therapy session. The contract was solemnly written and signed by everyone. While formulating it the therapist stressed the difficulty of the agreement and said he could understand that it might not be successful. This was too much for the boys' honor. Their honor was also stimulated by the therapist's showing his trust in them by letting them decide what the reward would be. The following week it appeared that the agreement had been precisely kept. An unknown peacefulness had prevailed in the Burger home. The boys themselves were flabbergasted. Father cheerfully handed out the $10. The boys understood that they could not enter such contracts for money every week, and certainly not for such a large sum. Consequently, they agreed to follow the assignment for a week but without a monetary reward, if father and mother would also be prepared to alter certain behavior. This appeared to be possible. In the following weeks various small irritations from both sides were worked on. The small steps which seemed initially useless came in this case after the first big step had already led to changes.

The model outlined in this section can serve as a basis for treating families and other natural groups. Small and sometimes large deviations from this model are no exception, however. In the example cited above, an initial dramatic change was necessary in order to involve the children. For various reasons the therapist thought this was feasible. First, mutual positive emotions were present in the family. If the difficult interactions had been paired with ill-feelings or negative affects, then the "big step" would probably have been impossible. Second, the therapist thought that both the children as well as the parents were capable of displaying the requested new behavior. An important link here was the children's strong sense of honor.

In general it can be stated that, in case of deviations from the model, it must be clear on what grounds these occur and what the chance of success is for the other approach. Decisions in this regard will partly depend on the experience and style of the therapist.

PART II

Practice

CHAPTER 3

Intake and

Preliminary Information

3.1 INTRODUCTION

Mrs. Jackson telephones a family therapist requesting couple therapy. Her husband regularly assaults her and recently the beatings have been so bad that she has become desperate. She says that he is a beast who demands sex with her every night, which revolts her. The therapist asks how long this has been going on and whether anything has ever been done about the situation. She tells him that her life has been hell for ten years. Eight years previously she had turned to a social worker for help, but she has not had any contact with the bureau for the past year.

After obtaining Mrs. Jackson's permission, the therapist contacts the social worker, who tells him that several other therapists also worked with the family (husband, wife, and two children, aged 11 and 12) for several years. They tried everything—family therapy, couple therapy, and individual counseling with Mrs. Jackson. Every time it became clear what the root of the problem was and what changes were necessary, the therapy broke down because the family would no longer cooperate.

Mrs. Jackson complains about her husband constantly, but is not prepared to do anything to change the situation. The husband and wife are very different in many respects. He is an unskilled worker, a rather coarse, dull individual, who did not finish primary school. She comes from a fairly affluent middle-class background and has a high school education. His "crudity" annoys her intensely. His preoccupation with sex revolts her and she despises his "animal mentality," which comes out in his heavy drinking and physical violence.

The social worker supplies the names of a number of therapists who have worked with the Jacksons. They had all encountered so many irreconcilable differences between husband and wife that they could only recommend divorce. The family therapist sees no reason to question their professional judgment and does not feel that he can change or add anything significant to their assessment of the situation. He telephones Mrs. Jackson, tells her what he has heard and says that he cannot do any more for her than the previous therapists have done.

The above illustrates how the therapist obtains information from two sources—Mrs. Jackson and previous therapists—before interviewing the whole family. In this chapter we further examine the process of intake and acquiring preliminary information before the therapist begins to treat the family as such.

3.2 INTAKE

Mrs. Jackson herself presented the family for treatment. She contacted the therapist on her own initiative. Sometimes a member of the family takes this step on the basis of advice from another therapist or the family doctor. Alternately, a doctor or welfare worker can contact the family therapist, pass on information about the family's problems, and ask if the therapist is prepared to take on the case. If a therapist agrees, there are a number of courses of action open to him. He may ask for the family's name, address, and telephone number and telephone them to make an appointment for an assessment interview. This approach is not to be recommended. If therapy has not previously been discussed with the family, or if they are not sufficiently motivated, the therapist's call may seem like an attempt on his part to "sell" therapy to them. It is preferable for the referral source to get in touch with the family and explain why they should see a family therapist. Then the family can contact the therapist.

Sometimes one member of a family will call the therapist for an appointment but say that one or more members of the family do not want to take part in the treatment. This might be the beginning of a struggle about the control over the structure of the therapy. If the therapist agrees to family treatment with only part of the family, he is allowing the family to determine the nature of the first session; subsequently, it will be difficult for him to regain control (cf. Whitaker, in Haley and Hoffman, 1967). In a first interview with a family or couple, therefore, we seldom agree to seeing one person alone or only some of the family members.

The person presenting the family may oppose having the other members of the family attend the first session, or he or she may be pessimistic about the willingness of the others to take part. The therapist will then explain that an introductory session is necessary to enable him to gather as much information as possible. It is always emphasized that agreeing to participate is in no way an admission of guilt. The therapist simply points out that they are all involved in or affected by the situation and that each of them may be able to help solve the problems. If the client is afraid that the therapist will see the marriage itself as the cause of the trouble, the therapist can point out that in fact a partner can provide invaluable support in carrying out therapeutic directives.

This sort of appeal will help most people overcome their reluctance to take part in the first session (cf. Lange, 1981). Once that is over, it is usually not difficult to make a second appointment with everyone involved.

A telephone call is usually the first form of contact between the family and the therapist. First impressions often determine later interaction patterns, and so it is extremely important for this first conversation to be conducted with great care and professional skill (Napier, 1976; Selvini Palazzoli et al., 1978). It is a job for an experienced therapist, not a beginner—a point all too often ignored in mental health institutions.

3.3 WHO IS PRESENT AT THE FIRST SESSION?

There are various opinions about who should be present at the first session. Generally, we apply the following rule, naturally allowing for exceptions: *The first session should be attended by the largest possible unit of people living together or directly involved with one another, regardless of whether the presenting problems are "individual" or "interactional."* The reason for this is simple—having everyone present provides the most information. When a child is the "identified patient" (as in several cases in Chapter 1), naturally the whole family is invited.

A child's problems are usually closely bound up with the way the members of a family, and the parents in particular, relate to one another. Even when an adult is the "identified patient," the therapist is able to form a firsthand impression of the structure of the family if all its members are present at the first session. In this way the isolated position of "problem individuals," as, for example, in the Madder family (Section 1.4.1), the Best family (Section 2.2.2) and the Spitz family (Section 4.2), becomes clear to him.

Even if only the parents request treatment, it is often essential to have at least one assessment session which includes the children to enable the therapist to determine how the relationship with the children influences or is influenced by the tension between the parents.

If a child's problems occur wholly or partly at school, it is useful to involve his teachers in part of the first session. They can then express their opinions directly so that the therapist does not have to act as an arbitrator between the parents and the school at a later stage. It is sometimes possible to involve teachers and even classmates after the first session (Aponte, 1976).

Involving as many people as possible in the first session yields the maximum amount of information. It is also important for the simple reason that it is much easier to reduce a large "treatment unit" than to try and expand a small one, should this eventually prove necessary. For example, if during a first interview it becomes apparent that the children do not play a significant part in their parents' relationship problems, the therapist can easily continue with the parents alone. Similarly, if a husband has been presented because of individual complaints and the relationship between the partners proves to be highly satisfactory, the wife can always be excluded from further therapy. It would be far more difficult if individual therapy were started with the husband and it became obvious after five sessions that his relationship with his wife was giving rise to a great deal of stress, which was a significant factor in his symptomatic behavior. If the therapist then decided to switch to couple therapy, there is a good chance that both husband and wife would feel that there was an alliance between the therapist and the original client, the husband. This would make it difficult to motivate them (the wife in particular) to cooperate in couple therapy.

We should like to make one exception to the above. During intake parents sometimes indicate that their children are totally unaware of any problems in the marital relationship, and that for this reason they are not to be involved. In such cases the wishes of the husband and wife should be respected. The therapist can always mention that it might be necessary to include the children at a later stage.

The children's ages are not necessarily important when considering whether to involve them in a family interview. The way in which parents relate to small children (and even babies) during a session can provide valuable information. Toys and drawing materials should always be available so that children do not have to sit still and listen for long periods. Creating a more natural situation for children during a session increases the chances of behavior corresponding more closely with what happens at home.

Finally, there are some couples whose problems can be traced back to conflicts with their parents or families of origin. If this is obvious before the first session, Whitaker (Whitaker and Keith, 1981) and Peck (1974) try to involve as many members of both families as possible in the first interview. We prefer to start with the couple and their children alone, but at a later stage of the treatment we do sometimes ask one of the partners to arrange for his/her parents, brothers, and sisters to come to a session (cf. Framo, 1976). In Chapter 7 we describe other ways of working with parents or the family of origin.

3.4 PRELIMINARY INFORMATON

Before the first assessment session the therapist is often supplied with information about the family and its problems. This can come from the member of the family with whom he makes the first appointment, a previous therapist, or the person or organization who has referred the family to him. In Rick's case (Section 1.2) the family doctor offered some information, but the family therapist also contacted Rick's teacher before the first session.

Although there are advantages to having preliminary information from certain sources, there are also some drawbacks.

3.4.1 Preliminary information from one of the members of the family

Often the member of the family who first calls the therapist will try to present his version of the problems. The therapist must be extremely wary of this kind of information for it can have a detrimental effect on the therapy.

3.4.1.1 Biased observation

Naturally, people see problems from their own point of view. When two people are quarreling and blaming one another for their difficulties (cf. Section 1.5.1), the first telephone call to the therapist might consist largely of telling him how unbearable the other party is and assigning blame for all the family troubles to one member. For example, Mrs. Jackson talks only about her husband's "revolting animal mentality" and his violent behavior, never about her own contribution to their problems. She is clearly biased. She never says anything about her own role. The risk here is that the therapist will have formed certain preconceptions by the time he speaks to all the parties. He may tend to see Mrs. Jackson as an "innocent victim" and Mr. Jackson as an "animal," which will render him incapable of judging the contribution of each of them to the problems they share.

3.4.1.2 Taking sides

The member of the family who provides the therapist with preliminary information will sometimes see the therapist as an ally during the first session. He/she will then see it as the therapist's job to help fix the "guilty" partner. If the therapist has allowed himself to be put in this position, he will find it difficult to extricate himself from the coalition which has been imposed on him. Even if he remains impartial, the other members of the family may still think that he has taken sides with the original informant. When such misunderstandings arise, they usually can be cleared up relatively easily by discussing them openly.

The context in which the first appointment is made is important. A family therapist at a psychiatric institution or a therapeutic day hospital will sooner be suspected of taking sides than a therapist at a child guidance center or a family guidance center. At a day hospital the members of the staff, particularly the family therapist, are sometimes seen by the rest of the family as supporters of the "patient." Alternatively, the "healthy" members of the family may consider the therapist as a member of a coalition with them against the "patient." When this happens, it is best not even to ask for factual information before all the people involved have come together. This gives the family therapist the opportunity to dissociate himself immediately from a standpoint that some members of the family hope he might take with regard to the presenting problems. He could start by saying, "Rina, you approached me for an appointment. You told me that you and your husband have problems, but that was all. I don't know anything else about you so perhaps one of you could tell me about the problems." If the therapist does have preliminary information, it is best for him to share it with everyone at the beginning of the session.

3.4.2 Preliminary information from the previous therapist or referral source

Mrs. Jackson took the initiative in telephoning the therapist, who asked for the name of her previous therapist and then contacted him. The information he was given was such that he saw no point in making an appointment with the Jacksons. The danger in adopting this course is that the therapist will miss an opportunity to influence the family in a positive way. Even if he decides to go ahead with therapy, preliminary information from a previous therapist can create problems for him. It can influence the therapy in an unfavorable way, as in the following example.

Psychiatrist A refers the Meyers to a family therapist for couple therapy. Over the telephone he explains some of Hank and Jill's problems—they argue a great deal, seldom if ever with constructive results, and their relationship has degenerated into a "war of attrition." The psychiatrist thinks that Jill starts the quarrels because, he says, "she's a most unpleasant person—between the two of us she's an emasculating bitch." The therapist makes an appointment with the couple and, instead of observing their interactions objectively, "sees" an "emasculating" woman and sympathizes with Hank for having to put up with her. Hank and Jill do not come back. Jill refuses to because of the therapist's hostility towards her. By adopting the psychiatrist's prejudices, the therapist failed in his attempt to help the couple.

3.4.3 Halo effects

According to social-psychological literature (cf. Krech et al., 1962), preconceived ideas such as those described above may lead to "halo effects." When we have a generally favorable impression of someone, we tend to notice his or her positive qualities and ignore or underestimate the less positive ones. The reverse is also true. When a negative impression is formed first, relatively more negative traits will be perceived, ignoring the good sides. In his well-known experiment, Kelley

(1950) demonstrated how strong the halo effect can be. Describing a so-called visiting professor as a "warm person" or "cool and aloof" significantly influenced students' opinions of him.

Kanouse et al. (1972) maintain that negative information influences people more than positive information. When psychiatrist A remarks that Jill is an unpleasant person but that he likes Hank, the halo effect of the negative judgment is probably the stronger of the two.

In our view, the labels "psychiatric patient" and "(mentally) ill" convey information which can lead to a negative halo effect. Farina and Ring (1965) have investigated this. Psychology students who could be expected on the basis of their age and training to have a fairly positive attitude towards the "mentally ill" (Nunnally, 1961) were instructed to perform a certain task with a partner. Half of them were told that the partner was a "relatively normal person," the other half that the partner had twice been admitted to a psychiatric institution "for some sort of nervous breakdown." Compared to the subjects in the first group, the subjects in the second group found that their partners were less able to understand themselves and get along with other people and were more unpredictable. Moreover, the students in the second group felt hampered by their "mentally ill" partners, despite the fact that they had done better (objectively speaking) than the students who had worked with "relatively normal" partners.

Langer and Abelson (1974) showed behaviorally and psychoanalytically oriented therapists a videotape of one of the research workers and a person who was talking about his recent experience when applying for a job. Half the therapists were told that the man was simply applying for a job, the other half that he was a "psychiatric patient." They recorded their responses to the tape in a questionnaire. The behavior therapists saw the man as "fairly well adjusted," regardless of what they had been told. The psychoanalytically oriented therapists who had been told that the man was a "patient" found him significantly more disturbed than those who had been told he was simply applying for a job. They considered the "patient" "dependent," "passive-aggressive" and "extremely afraid of his own aggressive urges." The "man applying for a job" they found "realistic to a certain extent" and "someone who knows how to conform but finds this difficult."

Using psychiatric labels has a detrimental effect, especially at the outset of social contact. It sets patterns of interaction in motion from which it is difficult to eliminate negative stereotypes at a later stage (Farina and Ring, 1965). According to Langer and Abelson (1974), this often leads to a "self-fulfilling gloomy prophecy."

For the above reasons some family therapists do not want to receive any preliminary details. Zuk (1972), for example, generally wants to know nothing except the family's name and whether they will definitely turn up for the first assessment session. Sometimes at the end of the session he compares his own observations with those of the referral source. Kempler (1973b; 1981) does not like preliminary information either, because he wants to meet the members of the family as "living people" and not as "cases."

3.5 ASSESSMENT OF THE REFERRAL SYSTEM

Zuk's and Kempler's strategies are diametrically opposed to that of other family therapists, who prefer to gather as much information as possible before the first interview. The latter consider it inefficient to ignore useful information supplied by others. This does not mean that they are not fully aware of the dangers of bias. Assessing the strong and weak points of the referral source is one way of objectively judging its value. When the psychiatrist who refers the Meyers to therapy remarks that the woman is the cause of the problems, he is in fact revealing one of his own weaknesses as a therapist. He cannot see past certain behavior and this renders him incapable of making an assessment of the pattern of interaction between the husband and wife. For example, he cannot see how some of Hank's behavior evokes a certain response from Jill—that Hank is, in effect, also contributing to the problems.

The ability to evaluate the information and opinions passed on by a referral source is not entirely dependent on the therapist's personal qualities. The policy of the organization to which the therapist is attached is also important. If psychiatrist A, for example, passed on information regularly and his strong and weak points were known, his judgment would be viewed accordingly. In other words, assessing the referral source works most efficiently when the same people are involved all the time.

3.6 INFORMATION FROM THE BROADER ECOLOGICAL SYSTEM

When a child is presented because of learning problems, for example (cf. Rick, Leo, and Frank in Chapter 1), it is not always advisable to start with family sessions. The presenting problem, such as Frank's extreme disobedience at school (cf. Section 1.3.4), should not always necessarily be interpreted in terms of interaction problems within the family. Is the family then the right system at which to aim the interventions? In such cases it is useful to find out what is happening at school before the first family interview. The information obtained from school reports and psychological tests may lead the therapist to the conclusion that interfering in interaction in the family is not appropriate at the outset. Although a child's learning difficulties may indeed be caused by exaggerated negative attention from the parents (as in Leo's case, Section 1.3.1), a change in the latter does not always guarantee improvement in the former.

When the presenting problem is of a psychosomatic nature, the therapist must be certain of the client's medical history. Medical tests before the first interview are therefore advisable in some cases. A therapist who is very strongly against receiving any form of preliminary information can, of course, make inquiries about the medical history after the first session.

3.7 COOPERATION WITH THE REFERRAL SOURCE

As indicated above, it will sometimes be necessary to consult a previous therapist or doctor in order to conduct family therapy in a responsible manner. This can be illustrated by the case of a family referred for therapy by the family doctor. On being told that the doctor feels that the family's difficulties are bound up with the husband's drinking problem, the therapist asks the doctor to prescribe a drug such as Antabuse in order to help him stop drinking. He will then be prepared to work with the family on the next step towards solving their problems.

This sort of cooperation is sometimes necessary during therapy itself. In Section 5.8.3 we describe a case of a husband with a drinking problem who is instructed by the family therapist to record how many drinks he has each day. If he feels he is about to exceed the agreed limit, he is to telephone the therapist. The next day he happens to mention this to his doctor, who says it would be better to stop drinking completely. This creates so much stress over the weekend that he starts drinking and has a serious quarrel with his wife, who accuses him of not keeping his part of the bargain. This naturally did not help him to stop drinking either. Regardless of whether the therapist's assignment was too easy or the family doctor's unreasonably difficult (which was probably the case), the lack of communication between the doctor and the therapist had an unfortunate outcome.

3.8 CONSULTATION RATHER THAN
TAKING OVER THE CLIENT

The family therapist does not always have to agree that the best course of action would be for him to take over the family. Psychiatrist A's referral of Hank and Jill stemmed from his personal problem with the couple—he had taken such a dislike to Jill that he could not get any further. In a situation like this, a consultation session at which the family therapist, the psychiatrist, and Hank and Jill are present might be helpful. Attention would then focus on the system formed by the psychiatrist, Hank, and Jill, and the family therapist could try and help the psychiatrist to see the Hank/Jill dyad in a different light. This would enable new interventions to take place. The more experience family therapists gain and the more other therapists, social workers, and doctors start thinking in terms of interactional problems, the more such consultation sessions will form the first stage of therapy.

After clients present themselves, the family therapist has to estimate within which system the major problems lie—if they are individual problems, or whether they relate to the couple, the family, or the family in relation to the outside world. Sometimes the best solution lies in advising the person already working with the family, rather than taking over therapy completely. In its manual for therapists, the Chedoke Child and Family Center, a progressive institute in Hamilton, Ontario, Canada, issued the following guideline: "Wherever possible, community personnel are invited for the assessments of referred cases and referral is made back to the community with the necessary continued consultation provided. In this way the services are delivered with an important educational component. It allows for the strengthening of community resources and skills and provides us with an understanding of strengths, gaps and needs in the community." Such advice could naturally be extended to other professionals in the therapeutic field, such as social workers, psychiatrists, psychologists, and adult education workers. In the future, "front-line" workers such as family doctors and clergymen should be included as well.

CHAPTER 4

Assessment in

Family Therapy

4.1 INTRODUCTION

To devote a whole chapter to assessment might suggest that assessing the situation in a family constitutes a separate phase of treatment, which is only partly true. There is likely to be more emphasis on listing and assessing the problems in the first few sessions of therapy than during later stages, but this is very much a question of degree. The therapist should be on the lookout for new problems and fresh insights at all stages of treatment. In this respect, therapy is one extended process of assessment. Some therapists, on the other hand, intervene with a view to producing changes right at the beginning, sometimes even during the first session. The clients' reactions to the interventions then provide the therapist with an understanding of the strong and weak points of the family system. Minuchin (1974), for instance, says that it is not always important for clients to carry out directives. The way in which they deal with them provides information about their interaction with one another.

In this chapter family assessment is treated separately in order to explain it more clearly as a stage which receives a great deal of attention, particularly at the outset (cf. Epstein & Bishop, 1981). Some of the questions we pose are:

1) How much time should be spent on assessment?

2) To what extent should interventions aimed at bringing about change be introduced in the assessment phase?
3) To what should the therapist pay special attention during assessment?
4) Which principles and techniques are at his disposal during assessment?
5) What kind of aids are at his disposal?
6) What should his aims be, besides drawing up an inventory of the problems?

In Section 4.2 we describe the first session with a family of four, and chart its progress, explaining as we go along the options open to the therapist at each stage. In Section 4.3, using this session as an example, we present a number of general principles important during assessment.

4.2 A FIRST ASSESSMENT SESSION

The Spitzes have been referred to a family guidance center by their doctor. The father, who has recently spent a week in a psychiatric clinic, is the "identified patient." The therapist opens the session with a few short remarks about himself, his job, and what he already knows about the family. His first question is something like, "Who would like to tell me why you're here?" From that point on, he has to observe carefully, paying attention not only to what is said, but to who says it and how. An experienced therapist will be able to tell a great deal from the last two aspects. The mother, Nel, answers the opening question with factual information about the family, which consists of the children, Larry, 11, and Michael, 12, her husband, Alex, who is a building contractor, and herself. She used to be a professional potter, but pottery is now a hobby.

The therapist then asks each member of the family to explain his or her own reasons for being at the session: "Why in your view are you here?" This question has two purposes. It will probably reveal a first problem area and it makes clear that each member of the family should speak for himself/herself, a point which will undoubtedly come up again. While this type of intervention has a function as far as assessment is concerned, it also has a modeling function. It clearly illustrates that the way in which assessment is structured depends partly on the therapist's objectives. We share the views of Eisler and Hersen (1973), who plead for a behavioral change approach to "family crisis intervention." Most important to them is the development of new "problem-solving" behavior, which enables members of a family to deal with their problems satisfactorily (cf. Section 2.2.1; Epstein and Bishop, 1981) instead of perpetuating a destructively antagonistic spiral.

The first step towards achieving this is when clients learn to say specifically and precisely where their problems lie. The therapist sets the tone by refusing to accept vague descriptions. When Mrs. Spitz starts to explain in vague and general terms that there are problems, "which is hardly surprising after 16 years," the therapist asks her to be specific. She answers, "Sometimes there's something wrong with me, and sometimes it's him" (indicating her husband). The therapist continues with the same line of questioning: "When there's something wrong with you, what is it precisely?" Again, without explaining exactly what the matter is, she advances all kinds of theories about the influence of the past on her present troubles. The therapist takes her up on this to illustrate two important principles—first, that he wants to work in the present with the problems she is experiencing here and now, and second that he does not want to get "bogged down" in searching for possible causes. They are often less important than the way in which a certain type of behavior manifests itself and the effect it has on the rest of the family.

Within an interactional system, "reasons" for one's behavior are usually only a means of justifying it. This is often a way of rationalizing it that leads to punctuation problems (cf. Section 1.5.1.2). By demonstrating certain principles in the early stages of therapy, the therapist has three closely related objectives. First, he makes his own position clear and indicates the sort of therapy his clients can expect. This makes the drawing up of a treatment contract a sincere and meaningful matter (cf. Section 6.5). Second, he teaches his clients different and more constructive ways of dealing with one another. He "rewards" precise and specific references to mutual problems and desires and "punishes" rationalization aimed at self-justification. (In Chapter 5 we deal more thoroughly with the importance of this principle.) Third, this sort of intervention "protects" the therapist from being pinned down to one particular subject. It gives him the opportunity of quickly assessing the problem areas. At this stage he deliberately avoids advancing possible solutions—an extremely important principle in assessment. He is, in fact, demonstrating one of the first steps towards developing problem-solving behavior (cf. Section 2.2.1).

Problems should first be described in terms of behavior, without going into possible causes. Avoiding talking about causes facilitates the transition to the next phase, which D'Zurilla and Goldfried (1971) call "brainstorming." This involves setting out without challenging all the possible solutions, of which the best can subsequently be used as and when necessary.

Let us now go back to the Spitz family. After the therapist's intervention, Mrs. Spitz says that she suppresses many of her feelings because of her concentration camp experiences. The therapist wants to know how this creates problems for her at the moment. She answers with difficulty, after which the therapist sums up as follows: "You find it hard to discuss painful and unpleasant matters with your husband, but you wish you were able to." He then checks to see that this definition of the problem is accepted by Mrs. Spitz, which it is. She does not like this interactional approach, however. She says that it is her problem: "Alex has completely different problems, but he must talk about them himself."

The above interaction between the therapist and Mrs. Spitz illustrates several important assessment principles. The therapist persists with his questions until the problem has been formulated in terms of behavior. He then sums up. The importance of this method is dealt with more fully in Section 4.3. Apart from the restructuring involved, it allows the therapist to sum up the problem in a way which gives it a new, constructive label, making it easier to solve. This is a specific type of intervention known as "relabeling" (cf. Section 2.2.4). The therapist does not believe Mrs. Spitz when she says the problem is hers alone. He sees this statement more as an accusation of her husband, but chooses not to say so. His reasoning is as follows: However she "punctuates" the problem, she is implying that she would like to talk to her husband about certain matters more often. It is therefore important to pick out the interactional element and place the emphasis there.

In this way the therapist subtly sets an example for the rest of the therapy. He formulates the problem as a desire on the part of Mrs. Spitz (rather than an accusation against her husband) for more of a certain kind of interaction between them. This is preparation for therapy designed to teach Mr. and Mrs. Spitz to express what they want in terms of requests or wishes rather than accusations. Once this has been achieved, the clients can learn to negotiate in order to have their wishes carried out. This is described in more detail in Chapter 6.

Once "problem number one" has been summarized and rounded off, the therapist directs his attention to Mr. Spitz. His wife has mentioned that he, too, has problems. Mr. Spitz says that these are primarily work problems. He is self-employed and is involved in different kinds of projects. Often they are irritating, but he needs them to earn a living. He expresses his frustration about his work when he gets home in the evening. The therapist asks him to be more specific: What exactly are the problems at home? In what way is he irritated, and how does this come out? Mr. Spitz begins to talk about an uninteresting job a while ago, which had rather thrown him off balance. The therapist interrupts by asking how this manifested itself. Mr. Spitz gives specific examples of experiences he had had immediately before he was admitted to the psychiatric clinic. He does not get very far before his wife says, "Your behavior was very strange. You were apathetic about your work, completely shut off, with a wild look in your eyes. I knew what was going to happen, I could see it coming with someone like you. . . ."

This presents the therapist with a dilemma. During the first ten minutes of the interview the structure of the family seems to have emerged clearly—the father is the identified patient who is weak and unreasonable and the mother is the "strong" person who always sorts things out. The way the mother looks at the children when talking about her husband also indicates that she regularly encourages her sons to form a front with her against the father. At this point the therapist could intervene and confront her with the futility of her last remark, which crushes her husband just as he is beginning to talk about himself in a meaningful way. He chooses not to do this, but to go on with listing the problem areas instead. He feels certain that the mother's behavior will provide enough opportunity for interventions later, when they will be more effective.

Without confronting Mrs. Spitz directly, the therapist interrupts by saying, "Someone like. . .?" She does not respond, and so the therapist turns to the children and asks, "How do you see this?" He does this for two reasons: First, it is important to involve the children during the early stages, and second, their answers will provide more information about the balance of power, coalitions, and the affective relationships—in other words, about the structure of the family. Larry (the younger son) replies quite vehemently, "When he's at home, it's awful. He keeps shouting at me." The therapist now slips in a few questions about how the boys are getting along and getting on in school ("joining"; cf. Section 5.1). The therapist then goes back to their relationship with their father. He asks them how often they find their father annoying (being specific). He consciously makes the children talk *about* their father instead of *to* him.

This requires further explanation. In many cases it is important to stimulate the family members to talk to each other—this is often what is so difficult for them, so they would rather express their complaints, desires, and requests through the therapist. In the early stages it is often best simply to accept this situation, especially at the beginning of the first assessment session, which is primarily devoted to evaluating the problems. The therapist asks for information which the clients supply. It would be unnatural for the clients not to reply directly to the therapist, even though this is like talking about someone (the father in this case) as if he were not present. Once the therapist has decided to tackle a particular problem, the members of the family will have to address one another directly. We shall see examples of this later in the session.

Let us now go back to the therapist's last question. Michael says that his father is not annoying all that often and, when he is, Michael goes off to play football. The therapist is not satisfied. "How often is 'not all that often'?" he asks. Michael finds it difficult to be precise, but what it boils down to is that when the father is on a big job there are no problems; the trouble starts only when he has little jobs on his mind. Then he quarrels with the mother. The therapist detects the mother's influence in the way the children, particularly Michael, talk about their father. They express themselves in the same way and have the same opinions as she does. This comes out in quite a subtle way in the emphasis of Michael's remark: "Then father quarrels with mother."

Once again the therapist decides that he should not deal explicitly with the question of coalitions at this stage. He indicates in an indirect manner that the situation has not escaped his notice by asking, "And doesn't mother ever quarrel with father?" This is a way of showing that he does not agree with the one-sided presentation of the interactional difficulties between the husband and the wife. Larry now confirms the therapist's impression. Using his mother's phrase, he repeats that his father does indeed have problems with his mother, but that he will have to solve them himself, because "we can't help him with that kind of thing."

The therapist then sums up by pointing out that tension increases when the father is having difficulty at work and by restating the wish of both children that father be less irritable with them. He, furthermore, points out that they will have to talk in more specific terms if they are to clear up their annoyance with one another. For the time being, however, this is a full enough description of one problem area.

When the therapist asks if there are any further problems, Mrs. Spitz mentions her husband's drinking: "Sometimes he's pleasant when he's been drinking, but sometimes he's just awful. And I'm not the only one who thinks so, am I, boys?"

The therapist decides once again not to confront her with her let's-close-ranks-against-father behavior. The session has not even been in progress for 20 minutes. He first wants to hear more about Mr. Spitz's drinking habits and how he himself assesses the situation. Mr. Spitz starts defending himself—talking about things he should reorganize at work and how he wishes he had more self-discipline. The therapist interrupts him and points out that he is now trying to find solutions for the work problem they talked about earlier. Even though he is being constructive in that respect, that subject is not under discussion now. They will come back to it, but must first find out more about the drinking problem. It may then be possible to establish links between the various problem areas.

By saying this, the therapist achieves two things. By using positive labeling he shows support for the husband who occupies a weak position in the family. At the same time he prevents repetition and is furthering the discussion of the concrete aspects of the drinking problem. He asks Mr. Spitz if he regards his drinking as a problem. Mr. Spitz hesitates and Mrs. Spitz breaks in by saying that it creates awful situations. The therapist does not repeat his question to Mr. Spitz, but instead asks her, "What sort of situations?" She cannot really add much, except that it affects the children. She asks them what they think of their father when he has had too much to drink. Larry says, "It's awful; he acts very peculiar." She goes on, "He's not himself," and Larry adds, "He always wants to drive home when he's drunk."

The above interaction illustrates the structure of the family. The mother and the younger son join forces in a coalition in order to dispose with the father. The therapist does not intervene. He waits for the father's reaction. The latter makes a feeble attempt to defend himself by saying that things are not all that bad. "I do drink from time to time. . . ," he says. "From time to time. . . ," Larry repeats sarcastically and then Mrs. Spitz joins in, "You get so drunk, you don't know what you're doing. I've never seen anyone behave like he does when he's drunk—he goes completely berserk."

The therapist now has several options. He can either confront Mrs. Spitz with the way she squashes her husband, embedding the confrontation in support by making positive remarks, for example, about how much she obviously cares for her family (cf. Minuchin, 1974). Alternatively, he can simply go on gathering specific details of the problem, such as how much the father drinks and when. With drink problems in particular, it is useful to know the exact quantities consumed and in what circumstances. The therapist, however, does not choose this course of action. After all, Mr. Spitz has said that he does not consider his drinking to be a problem. The therapist does not wish to continue using the terminology of the mother and sons or become part of the coalition against the father, thereby helping to reduce him to the status of a patient. Another possibility is to confront Mr. Spitz with his inability to defend himself—he takes their accusations as meekly as a lamb. The therapist decides, however, that it is too soon to deal with the father in this way, since the session has only been going for about 20 minutes and father is constantly being "given hell" anyway. He is aware though that this will have to be done at some stage.

He eventually decides to support Mr. Spitz directly so that he can later confront him with his "weak and pathetic" act. The therapist says, "In your place I wouldn't know what to say—I wouldn't react either." Mr. Spitz perks up—he has found a friend. "Well," he replies, "that's probably a bit of an exaggeration, but you're right."

A short discussion between husband and wife ensues in which Mr. Spitz tries to explain that, even though he is in the wrong in certain respects, he has tried to improve. For example, he now drinks much less than he used to. His wife has a much more negative label for this: "When I first knew you, you were a complete alcoholic," she says, "You were paralytic every single day." Larry joins in with the accusation: "Sometimes you work at home for months; then you go to town once and get drunk, even if we're with you." The therapist asks Larry if he has ever talked to his father about this. It turns out that he has not, confirming again the therapist's suspicion that Larry is only echoing and supporting his mother and suggesting also that he is unable to talk about it to his father. Probably both impressions are true.

The therapist decides to change the subject. He sums up as follows, emphasizing the interactional aspect: "Mrs. Spitz, you feel that your husband drinks too much and you, Mr. Spitz, do not agree. I think we should come back to this later so that each of you can say what you regard as excessive and see if you can reach some sort of agreement."

He then asks if there are any other problems, and receiving no response, he asks them to tell him about the positive aspects of their family life. Mrs. Spitz says, "He's such a nice man, we wouldn't know what to do without him." This provides an opportunity to tackle Mrs. Spitz about the way she reduces her husband to a patient and mobilizes her children against him. The therapist addresses Mrs. Spitz: "What strikes me is that you keep talking about 'we.' " The three of you form a front, which you, Mrs. Spitz, are not doing anything to counteract—quite the reverse in fact. I would find it very unpleasant. . . ." Instead of challenging Mrs. Spitz, the therapist could have confronted the husband with the fact that he accepts everything so easily. This would have had the advantage of not sorting things out so neatly for Mr. Spitz, and Mrs. Spitz would still have got the message. The therapist does not do this, as he feels it is too early in the therapy to deal so harshly with the husband, who is in such a weak position. He receives his fair share of criticism as it is. Since he lacks self-confidence, the first step is to make him more sure of himself.

The therapist's support has the desired effect. Mr. Spitz immediately takes his cue and explains how the other members of the family constantly confront him with his failures and never listen to his opinions. Mrs. Spitz and Larry try to break in. The therapist stops them by saying, "Let's not get bogged down in accusations and denials. You've had your say; now it's your husband's turn. I'm not interested in who's right, or in convincing the other person that he's wrong. First we have to find out exactly what you want from one another."

The therapist goes on to tell Mrs. Spitz that she excludes her husband from the family circle and treats him like a patient whose case needs to be discussed. She objects, but the therapist goes on, pointing out that she continually mobilizes the children to take part in the operation. Mrs. Spitz then explains why she and the children are drawn together and the therapist uses this opportunity to point out once again that it is not the reason for a certain type of behavior which is important, but its effect. "What is happening in the family now, however understandable, is making it very difficult for your husband to change his behavior."

A discussion then follows between Mr. and Mrs. Spitz in which he complains about the other members of the family—they are always leaving the lights on and spending too much money; in other words they are generally wasteful. Mrs. Spitz does not take him up on this but instead goes on about her husband's "illness," asking him, "Don't you feel I'm any help to you at all?" The therapist says, "I don't think your husband is talking about help, only about certain wishes on his part—how he'd like to see certain household matters organized." The therapist purposely refers to "wishes," using a positive label (cf. Section 2.2.4.3), instead of talking about complaints or accusations. This links up with what is most likely to be his strategy in future interventions. Mrs. Spitz remains noncommittal and says, "The atmosphere in the family is entirely dependent on how Alex is feeling at a particular time."

The therapist does not take this up, as he has already made his point. If his remarks are important enough they will have an effect on her sooner or later. It would be a serious mistake to force his opinion on her in a debate. During his summing up he explicitly mentions this and, by so doing, once again serves as a model for the type of behavior which is not very much in evidence between the husband and the wife in this family: A difference of opinion does not have to end with one of them being in the right. When both parties try to prove they are in the right, they often get lost in a maze of punctuation and content/ relationship problems (cf. Section 1.5.1).

After the therapist's summary, the conversation turns to the children's friends, who are often not allowed to come over to play because "Dad is at home." Mr. Spitz says that such remarks hurt him. It seems that in many instances communication between the father and the children takes place through the mother. When the father is working at home, the mother tells the children that they have to play outside because "he does not like being disturbed." The therapist asks Larry, the more outspoken of the two boys up to that point, if he would rather his father said this sort of thing to him himself. When Larry replies that he would, the therapist asks him to say so to his father. This gives rise to a constructive conversation between Larry and his father. Mr. Spitz admits that he takes the easy way out by having his wife speak to the children on his behalf. He does not object to the children's playing at home when he is working, although he would sometimes appreciate less noise. He resolves to speak to them himself in future when this sort of situation arises.

When the therapist asks Larry and Mr. Spitz how they feel about the talk they have just had, they both say that they have enjoyed it, and that it would seldom if ever have taken place at home. The therapist once again emphasizes the importance of listing the problems and of being specific about the aspects of the other person's behavior which are irritating, without looking for reasons, but in a way that can lead to new arrangements.

The therapist then asks the parents about the sexual side of their relationship—a subject which people do not often discuss voluntarily, but which frequently gives rise to problems. Mrs. Spitz says that their sexual relationship is excellent; there are no problems on that score. Mr. Spitz agrees. The therapist is not entirely convinced and asks if they mind discussing the subject in front of the children. Mrs. Spitz answers first, saying, "Not at all, we're quite open about sex at home." They also say that they sometimes show physical affection in front of the children. As time is almost up and the sexual relationship does not seem to be an immediate problem, the therapist does not ask them to explain what they mean by this. Instead he goes on to the preliminary treatment contract (cf. Section 6.5). He asks all the members of the family if they now have some idea of the way he works. He explains the most important principles of his method once again and summarizes the points brought up during the session. He emphasizes the importance of "homework assignments" and of sticking to agreements (cf. Chapter 6). Mr. Spitz says he is fully prepared to work in this way, as do the children. Mrs. Spitz is a little hesitant at first, and again mentions her husband's drinking problem. The therapist says he realizes that this could be an important problem area and that it will certainly be given priority. Mrs. Spitz then consents to work as proposed. It is agreed that there will be at least four more sessions, after which they will be able to draw up a more definite treatment contract (cf. Section 6.6).

In conclusion, the therapist gives each of the parents a copy of a questionnaire (see Appendix 1) on which they can indicate where they think the problems lie. The questionnaire is an important aid to therapy. Stuart (1972a, 1972b) designed one which he sends to clients before the first session to save time. This approach is not appropriate with our questionnaire, which is based on that of Knox (1972) and Herbst (1952). Our experience has shown that knowledge of the therapist's methods, together with an explanation by him of some of the questions, increases the reliability of the clients' answers.

In the case in point, the therapist asks the parents to fill in separate questionnaires—without consulting one another—and to send them to him before the next session. This is their "assignment" for the coming week. Sometimes "monitoring assignments" (cf. Section 5.3) are given to one or more members of the family during the first session. On this occasion assessing the problem areas has taken so long that there is not enough time to work out an intervention of this kind.

4.3 REVIEW OF THE FIRST ASSESSMENT
      SESSION

The above session illustrates a number of principles which are important in assessment. We shall now deal with each of these separately, making frequent reference to other chapters in which related points are examined more closely.

4.3.1 What does the therapist take into account during assessment?

4.3.1.1 *Individual problems versus interactional problems: relabeling*

The therapist oberves the family in several different ways, picking out both individual problems (such as Mr. Spitz's work) and interactional problems (such as the complaints made by Mrs. Spitz and the children about the father). Assessment should be geared to both. "Individual problems" cannot always be understood as *intrapsychic* problems. One important task for the therapist is "relabeling" such problems. Instead of calling the husband's drinking "his problem," it can also be seen as the wife's problem or an interactional matter.

Minuchin (1974) relabels in the following way: He turns around the remark "Johnny has a problem" so that it becomes "you have a problem with Johnny." From here he could go on to say, "You (the parents) have a problem between the two of you as regards Johnny," which could lead to the conclusion: "You (the parents) have problems between the two of you." Relabeling takes place during the first stage of assessment, but it is important not to go too far at the outset. In the case of Mr. and Mrs. Spitz, the problems of which they were aware were set out first. The therapist very carefully formulated Mrs. Spitz's problems (the difficulty in talking about painful subjects) in terms of: "I'd like to talk about that sort of thing more often with my husband." This does not constitute a dramatic change, but the slight interactional emphasis makes it easier to come to grips with.

Generally speaking, in the beginning of family therapy interactional problems are expressed in the form of accusations. It is vital that the therapist deal with these "mutual desires" one by one, without using the wording of the accusations and the punctuation of the family members themselves. When mutual sources of irritation do not emerge spontaneously, the therapist should explicitly ask about them—for example, if a family contends that the only problem lies with the identified patient.

This latter point can be illustrated by reference to another example, the Hollis family. The "identified patient," the youngest son, was described by the parents as their "only problem." The boy was at a school for children with educational and disciplinary problems and was not doing very well. His extreme nervousness was evident in the fact that he trembled almost constantly. According to the medical reports, there was nothing physically wrong with him. The therapist asked if there were any other problems within the family. At first the parents maintained that there were not, but later they admitted that there was serious tension and resentment between them. Kempler (1973a) has an effective intervention for families who blame everything on that "one problem." He says, "So if it wasn't for Pete, your marriage would be 100% perfect?" Naturally, this is denied, "No, not 100%, but 90% perfect." Kempler then says, "Fine, let's not talk about the 90% for the moment, but what about the other 10%?"

Erickson (cf. Haley, 1973, p. 204) used a similar but no less effective approach: "If you were a less tolerant woman, and you a less tolerant man, what do you suppose would be the things you would disagree with your spouse about?"

With the Spitz family, the therapist succeeded in discussing a number of individual and interactional problem areas, each of which could serve as a "target" (Stuart, 1973) or as a "working point" (Kempler, 1973a) in the next stage of treatment. Should all the parties agree, they could work on changes with regard to these problems.

4.3.1.2 Positive aspects

The therapist focuses attention on problems in the family, but also on its positive aspects. This provides valuable insight into the structure and problem-solving capacity of the family (Epstein and Bishop, 1981; Epstein et al., 1968). It can also be an important aid to later interventions (cf. Kanfer and Saslow, 1965). For example, in Chapter 6 we shall be looking at several of Liz and Paul's problems. Halfway through their therapy, the therapist started linking "rewards" to "difficult" assignments. The "rewards" took the form of doing something together, such as going out for a meal or a long walk. During the first session they had described this type of activity as "positive."

4.3.1.3 Coalition structure

During the assessment the therapist must come to some conclusions about the structure of the family. The Spitz family exhibited a striking power and coalition structure (cf. Section 1.7). Mrs. Spitz was firmly in charge and had formed a strong coalition with both children (with the younger child in particular), to whom she constantly turned for support.

Minuchin (Minuchin and Fishman, 1981) devotes a good deal of attention to the coalition structure during both assessment of the family and during interventions. When the parent dyad is relatively weak compared with several parent-child relationships (cf. Camp, 1973, and Section 1.7.5 on the perverse triad), he speaks of "enmeshed families." His "structural family therapy" is mainly aimed at rearranging the boundaries between these subsystems. The marital subsystem is strengthened and clearly separated from the parent/child and sibling subsystems.

During the first session with the Spitzes, the therapist saw clear indications that the parent system was weak in relation to a strong mother/children subsystem, and that the division between the subsystems was extremely vague. One sign of this was the proud announcement by the parents that the children knew exactly what was going on in the parents' sexual relationship. This could imply that here as elsewhere the parents do not function as a separate unit and cannot or do not dare demand the privacy to which they are entitled.

Aponte and Hoffman (1973), in a fascinating and detailed account (appropriately entitled "The Open Door") of one of Minuchin's therapy sessions, describe how he emphasizes this point. He tackles the family on the lack of privacy, in particular that of the parents, whose bedroom door is open day and night. As mentioned in Section 4.2, the therapist had reasons for not going into this issue during the first session with the Spitzes. It did, however, contribute to his assessment of the family and would be dealt with at a later stage.

4.3.1.4 Symptomatic behavior, secondary gain, and maintaining a system

In Section 1.5.4 we examined symptomatic behavior in detail and considered the role it plays in maintaining a system. We saw that Ray became dizzy and nauseous whenever guests called and that his symptomatic behavior reinforced the myth in his relationship with Sharon of him as the weak and pathetic patient and of her as the reliable and noble nurse. Without the myth, it would be difficult to maintain the relationship. It might then emerge that Sharon is the kind of person who finds it difficult to stand up for herself and therefore needs Ray to be sick in order to disguise this fact. Another way of approaching this situation—which runs parallel to the above—would be to examine what Ray gains by exhibiting symptoms of dizziness and nausea (cf. Kanfer and Saslow, 1965). What happens if he is not dizzy? Does he then have to do all kinds of tedious jobs or conduct boring or even threatening conversations?

Liberman (1970) describes a case of couple therapy where the wife was the "identified patient." For more than 10 years she suffered from migraine attacks nearly every evening. Many medical investigations did not reveal somatic causes. Apparently the headaches were her only way of gaining her husband's attention. In other words, every time she had a headache, she received a reward. The objective of the therapy was to get the husband not to pay any attention to her when she had an attack but to give her more attention at other times. According to Liberman, it took five sessions to reverse the pattern of reinforcement, which led to complete elimination of the headaches, as established in a follow-up eight months later.

Another aspect which the therapist can take into account during assessment is the extent to which symptomatic behavior on the part of one member of the family is functional for the rest of the family. To what extent do the others benefit from the deviant behavior of the patient—for example, by being able to say and indeed believe "except for the one problem we are a happy family" (cf. Selvini Palazzoli et al., 1978)?

4.3.1.5 Relationship between the family and the environment

In Section 1.3.4 we described the assessment session for Frank, who was referred to therapy by his school because of aggressive and disobedient behavior. There were no real problems at home and the therapist concluded that Frank was hostile and aggressive mainly at school. Clear discrepancies emerged between standards at home and at school which resulted in an antagonistic relationship between the two. In response to this situation the therapist brought all the parties together—Frank's teacher, his headmaster, and the family. The lesson to be learned from this is that the family therapist must be aware not only of interactions between members of the family, but also of the way in which members of the family relate to individuals or organizations in their social environment, if there is an indication that such relationships have a bearing on the problems at hand. With the Spitz family, for example, this meant that the therapist had to consider the way in which Mr. Spitz dealt with his business contacts and how this involved Mrs. Spitz.

4.3.1.6 Aspects of communication

In Section 1.5 we discussed the importance of a number of "communicational rules" which usually characterize interactions between members of a family. Bearing these in mind, it is essential during assessment to observe the way in which people talk to one another, as opposed to the content of their remarks. In the above we saw how the therapist demonstrated a number of these principles in the first few minutes of the session—for example that there is no sense in talking in terms of the causes of a problem (punctuation problems). Another aspect of the way in which people sometimes talk to one another is "inconsistency." In Section 1.5.3 we examined contradictory messages in some detail—that is, for example, when the nonverbal message is negative, while the content of the remark is friendly, and vice versa. We also looked at commands which are contradictory in terms—for example, when a person is asked to do something spontaneously and ordered to enjoy it at the same time. Another type of communication problem which is not quite as obvious, but which the therapist should nonetheless carefully look out for is related to what we described in Section 1.5.1.1 as confusion about the "content" and "relationship" aspects of messages. The fact that the therapist is aware of the existence of such a situation does not necessarily mean that he has to introduce it into the discussion there and then. We will deal with this kind of dilemma in Section 4.3.4.

4.3.1.7 Sexuality, children, money, and autonomy

In addition to general problems of communication, the majority of "problem families" have difficulties which relate to sex, children, money, and autonomy. Problems involving autonomy occur when no satisfactory solution has been found concerning what the family members should do together and what each of them may do alone. This can give rise to serious friction, which is often suppressed. In many problem families, one or more people have a need for some independence, while other family members regard any form of independence as a threat. The reverse can also occur, when, for instance, parents can keep their marriage intact only by never doing anything together. They each lead completely separate lives and come to resemble guests who happen to be staying at the same hotel. Clearly this sort of situation also creates a good deal of friction. We therefore feel that Epstein and Bishop (1981) are right to devote considerable attention to the autonomy dimension during the assessment phase. In the case of the Spitz family, there were so many other subjects to be discussed that autonomy was not dealt with during the first session. It did, however, come up later on. Money problems sometimes go hand in hand with autonomy problems. With Liz and Paul in Chapter 6, Liz wanted access to their bank account so that she would not have to go begging to Paul for every last cent. Money problems may also surface between one or more members of the family and their social environment rather than on an interactional level between the members of the family themselves.

Where bringing up children is concerned, parents often have completely different attitudes which give rise to enormous friction. They find it difficult to adopt the same approach and each accuses the other of inadequacy (cf. Sections 1.2 and 1.3). The children are often involved in the power struggle between the parents. For example, Frances reproaches her husband for not paying enough attention to the children, that being one of the few areas in which she can really "needle" him. But if he pays them too much attention, she immediately sabotages his efforts because she is afraid that her husband and children will become too close.

If no one in the family volunteers information about any of these kinds of problems, the therapist should ask explicitly about them. This is what happened with the Spitz family regarding their sexual relationship, which turned out to be no problem. Quite often the sexual relationship is not discussed during the first assessment session, since many clients, rightly, regard this as a private topic which they would rather not discuss in front of the children. For this reason it is a good idea to have a follow-up discussion with the parents by themselves. This makes it easier for them to talk about sex or other intimate matters. This also applies to their affective relationship, to which the therapist should be extremely attentive, as we describe in Section 4.3.1.10.

On some occasions the therapist might even decide to see one or both spouses separately during this phase of therapy. When this occurs, it is usually at the request of one partner, who wants to inform the therapist about "private" matters like extramarital affairs. There is no clear rule for dealing with such requests, although the following precautions should be taken:

- One should not see one spouse before there has been one or more sessions with both of them.
- The individual session should only be held if the other spouse agrees.
- From the outset the therapist should state explicitly that by coming alone the spouse takes a risk: If secrets are conveyed that hinder the therapist in his functioning toward the couple, the client will have to choose between unveiling the secret or stopping therapy.

Lange (1980) shows that it is not always best to share all the secrets with the patient and even with the therapist. He describes a marital therapy in which the wife did not express any sexual interest in her husband. The therapist approached the problem in a judo-like fashion (cf. section 2.2.6). At the end of the first interview he told the couple that affection in general, and sexual affection in particular, is a problem which cannot be worked on for change to happen. It would be para-doxical to try and be affective on command. He therefore forbade them to have sexual contact for the following months. In the meantime they could discuss some minor problems between them. In this way he dealt with the resistance of the wife and cut short the unsuccessful attempts of the husband to get sexual intercourse, which made him only more unattractive to his wife.

After two sessions the wife called the therapist to ask for a separate interview. The therapist agreed in principle but warned her about the risks. After a couple of days she phoned to say that it might be better to postpone the separate interview. The couple therapy continued suc-cessfully. Six months after terminating therapy the wife called the ther-apist to tell him why she had wanted to see him alone in the beginning of the therapy. At that time she had had a lover of whom her husband did not know. She had ended that affair during the therapy. The ther-apist was glad that he did not have that information during the therapy, for he realized that he probably would have been much less effective with the couple if he had known about the affair.

This example does not imply that the therapist should always stay out of secrets. Sometimes the therapist might even offer a separate interview because he suspects there is a crucial information which he needs in order to proceed with the therapy. The example only underlines that much care should be taken in these sensitive matters.

4.3.1.8 Methods of behavior control

Behavior control refers to the way in which the family ensures that what they regard as accepted standards are adhered to. This type of problem is particularly important in relation to children. How do parents ensure that what they consider to be fundamentally important is passed on to their children? Are their standards the same or do they fight about differences of opinion over the heads of the children (e.g., the Spitz family). Even if parents do agree on what they expect of their children, they are often unable to convey their views adequately. In Section 1.2 we saw how Rick's parents frequently disagreed about the strategy to be used to persuade him to go to school. It is important for the therapist to examine this type of situation carefully with a view to intervening at a later stage. The literature of learning theory and behavioral change devotes a good deal of attention to this type of problem (cf. Patterson, 1971).

4.3.1.9 Problem-solving ability

There is one element in all of the potential problem areas described above to which the therapist must be responsive, namely, how and to what extent the family resolves whatever interactional problems they may have. That is to say, has the family come to terms with the existence of problems or are the majority of problems regarded as threatening and therefore denied? Once people accept that they do have problems, the next question is whether they can express them clearly and precisely. Then there is the question of whether other ways of solving these problems have been considered—"brainstorming," for example, to use the terminology of D'Zurilla & Goldfried (1971). There are also a number of other questions, such as "Who decides?" and "Do the solutions take all the parties into account?" (cf. the "quid pro quo" idea of Lederer and Jackson (1968), as described in Section 6.2). In their approach to assessment, Epstein et al. (1968) and Epstein and Bishop (1981) emphasize—albeit in a slightly different way—the problem-solving ability of the family. In our approach, these kinds of considerations during assessment tie in with the objective of therapy, which is not to solve the family's problems on their behalf but rather to present them with a model which they can use to solve existing and future problems themselves.

4.3.1.10 Expressing affection and affective involvement

We have described the cognitive and behavioral aspects of which the therapist should be aware during assessment, including the views the members of the family have of themselves and others and *the way in which they express them*. Equally important, though often more difficult to assess, are the nature of the emotional relationships between members of the family and the way in which these are expressed.

Epstein et al. (1968) emphasize in their assessment scheme the extent to which members of a family share in positive or negative exchanges of emotion and the extent to which they are capable of responding in appropriate emotional terms (both in quantity and quality) to stimuli which evoke an emotional response. The therapist may, for instance, ask, "How do you show that you're angry?" or "What does your husband do when he's angry with you?" An open and direct way of expressing anger is to say to the person concerned, "I'm angry with you." A slightly more veiled but equally direct way is to say to the person who is provoking the feeling, "I don't like the way you do your hair," or "You look a mess." It is not veiled but it is indirect if you say "I am angry" to the "wrong" person. Finally, it would be both veiled and indirect if someone were to vent his exasperation with his wife by saying, "All women are lazy."

Perhaps even more important than the way people express their feelings is the *extent to which members of a family or husband and wife are involved* with one another. There is not much point to couple therapy which aims to improve the communication structure within the family if the partners do not really care for one another. In such cases, maintaining the status quo is the most that can be achieved, but since that is rarely the purpose of therapy, it may be best to simply terminate treatment. It can, however, be useful for the therapist to explain the options open to clients in these circumstances. They can intensify their relationship, maintain the status quo, or phase out their relationship. If they both opt for the first alternative, then they may still feel some degree of affection for one another which would warrant an attempt to improve the relationship. If there are children involved, it is certainly worth trying this approach. If both parties opt for the status quo, there is not much point to continuing with therapy. If they both decide to end the relationship, the therapist can help them do so in a way which is acceptable to both of them, although this is hardly couple therapy in the normal sense.

If the *emotional involvement of the parties is excessively one-sided*, then couple therapy may serve no purpose. When Van Dijck et al. (1980) analyzed seven unsuccessful treatment cases, four were found to involve an imbalance in the degree of emotional involvement.

The extent to which couples or families are emotionally involved with one another comes out in a variety of ways. The therapist can ask them directly in the assessment session how much they love one another. However, he should not jump too rapidly to conclusions on the basis of their verbal response. Clients often find it extremely difficult to say what they feel about one another. Nonverbal signs of affection, indifference, or ill feeling can, therefore, be even more revealing during assessment.

Van Ree (1977) also emphasizes the nature of the emotional relationship in family situations. He describes how inappropriate expressions of affection (such as masking affect), the absence of involvement, or symbiotic over-involvement may lead to the appearance of psychiatric symptoms.

If the therapist comes to the conclusion during the first assessment session that the emotional involvement of the members of the family with one another is somehow disturbed, it is often best to make this a subject for discussion. In so doing he will be tackling the real problem rather than talking interminably about other subjects which are much less important.

The second session with the Green family illustrates this point. The presenting problem was the relationship between Mr. and Mrs. Green. The whole family—father, mother, and three children—had attended the first session. It was agreed that Mr. and Mrs. Green would then return by themselves for the second session, so that they could talk freely about their sex and affective relationship. During the session Mr. Green attacked his wife on every front. The expression on his face as he spoke was one of pent-up hatred. The therapist began to wonder if there was any point to couple therapy when their relationship was characterized by such condescension, animosity, and apparent indifference to one another. The therapist confronted the couple with this reading of the situation and informed the husband that in his wife's place he would not speak to him anymore. He asked the husband why he bothered to attend the therapy session if he hated his wife. As a result of the confrontation, the husband broke down and began to unload all the resentment he had bottled up over the years about how his wife had failed him. He realized that he felt something approximating hate towards her but felt this could be cleared up if he could do something about the grudge he bore for her past failures. Clearly, in this example, the husband had more positive feelings than was originally supposed, although they were hidden behind a mask of indifference and resentment. After his outburst and the ensuing positive reaction on the part of the wife, it was possible to work successfully towards deepening and intensifying their relationship.

The above shows how important it is to assess carefully the affective basis of a relationship. If Mr. Green had reacted indifferently to the confrontation and to his wife, further therapy would probably have been pointless. The therapist could then only have provided the couple with guidance on the most satisfactory way to end their relationship.

The degree to which the parties are emotionally involved with one another and the nature of that involvement are not just important with couples; both factors play an *essential* role in therapy with children or where one of the parents is the "identified patient."

The behavioral problems of children are often the result of emotional neglect. If either or both parents find it difficult to show affection for the "disturbed" child, this obviously has implications for the type of treatment chosen. For example, in such cases it would not be appropriate to teach the parents strategies for behavior modification in children (cf. Patterson, 1971). To do so would mean that the therapist was siding with the parents against the child. It hardly needs emphasizing that it is extremely difficult to make decisions on this type of problem during the initial phase of therapy. When is it safe to conclude that parents do not feel any affection for their (difficult) children? In our view, such a conclusion should only be drawn when there are very clear indications to that effect—it is always best to give the parents the benefit of the doubt and to label their concern and response to the child, however clumsy, as positive (cf. Section 2.2.4). If this approach is adopted, there is a chance of a favorable self-fulfilling prophecy, whereby positive feelings towards the child will be reinforced.

When a child is presented for therapy, the relationship between the parents needs to be assessed, as well as their degree of affection for the child. The Sanders family was referred to therapy because of the learning and behavioral problems of their middle daughter, Beatrix, age 16. She had spent a considerable time in individual therapy and her last therapist had come to the conclusion that there was a good deal wrong within the family. This resulted in the Sanders being referred to a family therapist, who quickly became convinced during the first session that Mr. and Mrs. Sanders no longer felt anything for one another. Both of them admitted as much. They did not really quarrel any longer; they left one another completely cold. Their attempts several years previously to remedy this situation by means of couple therapy had been unsuccessful. The therapist asked them if they were still interested in reviving their relationship. They both said they were not. The husband, in particular, said he had absolutely no doubts, even after the therapist had given him two weeks in which to reconsider. He was categorical—he was unwilling to expend any more energy on the relationship.

The therapist's conclusions from these remarks affected the treatment contract he was thinking of offering the Sanders family. He considered that it would be pointless to try to bring about changes in Beatrix's behavior if Mr. and Mrs. Sanders were both determined to maintain the status quo. Their cat and dog relationship was an unsatisfactory basis on which to bring up or act as a model for their 16-year-old daughter. She would be better off in individual therapy, which could help her to detach herself from the family. If the parents decided to separate, the therapist could provide them with guidance on how to go about this and continue the family therapy with the remaining members of the family with whom Beatrix was still involved. Eventually this course of action was adopted.

The three situations described in this section are all very different types of cases. The first example involved couple therapy, while in the other two children were the identified patients. Of course, many more examples could be cited, such as a family in which one of the parents is the "identified patient" or where there is such an imbalance in the emotional involvement of the parents with one another as to make treatment in the family context impossible (cf. Van Dijck et al., 1980). We hope, however, that the examples we have described will suffice to show that, although assessing the affective relationships within the family is one of the most difficult tasks of all, it is absolutely essential in drawing up a meaningful treatment contract.

4.3.1.11 Contraindications

Family therapy is not always the appropriate course of action. We have just seen that there are sometimes indications that the emotional relationships within a family are such that treatment of the family would serve little purpose. There are also other reasons for not starting or for discontinuing treatment involving the whole family. Some clients have individual problems which are difficult to relate to a wider social context. There are also problem areas which are better dealt with on an individual rather than a family basis. For example, individual behavior therapy seems to produce reasonable results with autistic children (cf. Nordquist and Wahler, 1973). In this area, not many positive results have been recorded with family therapy (Minuchin, 1974).

Zuk (1972) feels that virtually all problem areas can be treated by family therapy. However, treatment is difficult if families do not consult a family therapist of their own free will. This happens when, for example, they are ordered by a juvenile court to undergo therapy. In this type of situation the parents often think it is to their advantage to gloss over all the problems in the family in order to dispense with the "inconvenience" as quickly as possible while still complying with the instructions of the court. According to Rose (1972), group therapy is an excellent alternative to this type of laborious treatment. He describes in a lively fashion how a therapist can motivate a group of adolescents (including delinquents) for treatment and bring about changes in their behavior. Another factor which may work against family therapy is the concurrent participation of one or more members of the family in individual therapy. For example, a married couple consulted a therapist because of problems in their relationship. When it emerged that the wife had been in psychoanalysis for five years, the therapist refused to treat them. He felt that the two different approaches could conflict with one another. The emphasis on the wife's individual problems in psychoanalysis could conflict dramatically with the family therapist's interactional approach. Moreover, the wife would always have someone else she could turn to in conflict situations demanding joint efforts. This had, in fact, already happened in the past. It was decided that the wife would first complete her analysis and then both of them would start couple therapy.

The following example illustrates how this type of duplication can simply waste the time of all the parties concerned. A therapist took on a family for treatment because of difficulties with one of the children. The father was already being treated individually by a different therapist for "personal problems." The family therapist discovered serious conflicts between the father and the mother. The family at first appeared to be willing to work towards a solution, but immediately prior to the second session the father telephoned to say that the stress was too much for him and that in any case he was receiving sufficient help from his own therapist. This meant, of course, that there was no possibility for discussing the problems between him and his wife.

4.3.2 Structuring and being concrete in an assessment session

We saw with the Spitz family how right from the very beginning the therapist had great difficulty getting them to talk about their problems in specific terms. He refused to accept remarks such as, "I used to bottle things up from the past." He wanted to know if Mrs. Spitz still found certain things irritating or difficult, exactly what they were, and how they irritated her. This ties in with Kanfer and Saslow's (1965) comprehensive description of all the different aspects of "behavioral diagnosis." They show how a therapist can conduct a functional and specific assessment session on the basis of certain specific points. They do not deny that events from the past can play an important role—but only if they are still relevant to the present.

On a number of occasions in the interview with the Spitz family we saw the therapist accept fairly vague answers or descriptions of problems—for instance, in relation to the drinking problem of the father. He did not ask questions about the quantities or the precise situations in which alcohol was consumed. This would appear to contradict what we have previously outlined about being specific, but this is not necessarily the case. One thing was expressed quite clearly: Mrs. Spitz wanted her husband to drink less. Mr. Spitz had other views. If the therapist had wished to tackle the drinking problem head on, then further specification of the kind outlined above would indeed have been necessary. He had not reached that stage, however, because to have adopted this approach immediately might have created the impression that he, too, was turning Mr. Spitz into a "patient." All he had done to begin with was to list the problems and listen to what each of the parties expected of the other. At this stage, therefore, the therapist may accept less precise descriptions. This does not mean, however, as we saw in the interview, that he is prepared to be fobbed off with vague answers. In other words he is seeking a compromise.

We saw in the above session how the therapist summarizes the subject which has last been discussed in terms which are as specific as possible and then checks to see whether his interpretation is accepted by the others. This being the case, he then announces that they can move on from that particular subject to see where other problems lie. He makes it quite clear that when it comes to working on the specific problem, much more detailed information will be essential. We call this *assessment in rounds*. The first round consists of a large number of short rounds which are distinct and explicitly separate from one another. In the subsequent round, one or more areas which have come to light during the first round are worked on in depth in an attempt to create the possibility of change there. The second round may sometimes come up during a first session, depending on the nature and the extent of the problem areas which emerge during the first round.

The structured approach to assessment described above has numerous advantages. For one thing it provides for reflection at regular intervals; also both family members and the therapist know exactly where they are in their discussions.

Inexperienced therapists often say that assessment sessions are "absolute chaos"; they cannot get a word in edgewise, the clients constantly interrupt one another, and the discussion ranges over a wide variety of subjects without dealing with any of them satisfactorily. One way to avoid getting bogged down in the information the family is providing is for the therapist to summarize each series of interactions before proceeding to the next topic or before examining the same topic in greater detail.

Figure 4.1 is a diagram of the structure of an assessment session. We should now like to discuss those aspects of assessment which appear in the diagram and which have not already been dealt with.

4.3.3 Other objectives during assessment

4.3.3.1 Relabeling

In Section 4.3.1.1 we described how summarizing problems can be a subtle way of redefining them. One of the therapist's key objectives during assessment must be to describe problems which emerge in such a way that they can be tackled effectively. We have already seen a good example of this when Mrs. Spitz's expressed inability to talk about painful memories is reformulated by the therapist as "a desire to talk more often to her husband about her problems." It is important for the therapist to be aware of the effect of this kind of interpretation.

4.3.3.2 Modeling

Structural assessment based on encouraging clients to be as specific as possible sets an example, as we saw with many of the therapist's interventions with the Spitz family. The first steps necessary to resolve their problems satisfactorily (cf. Section 2.2.1) are shown to the family.

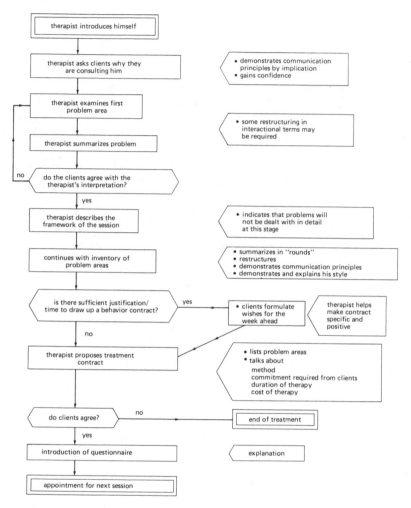

Figure 4.1. Structure of assessment session.

The therapist demonstrates the importance of an inventory of the problems which is both specific and objective and indicates how this can be made. At the same time, he gives the family members an opportunity to practice doing this themselves. In other words, here again, assessment is more than simply assessment—it is also a first step towards change. This is equally true when the therapist demonstrates a number of important principles in the light of what comes up during the session (cf. Section 2.2.3)—the necessity of talking in the here and now, of not asking "why" someone else's behavor is like it is but, rather, realizing the "effect" of one's own behavior on other people, and of talking in terms of wishes and requests rather than accusations. All this is part of a process of change which aims to help the members of the family get along better with one another. The way in which the family members react to the therapist's interventions gives him an idea of their capacity to work along the suggested lines. It also enables him to see where the major problems can be expected.

4.3.3.3 New experiences

From the outset, an assessment session involves new experiences for the clients, simply because they can see and feel that things are changing and that alternative patterns of interaction are possible. This increases their motivation to work with the therapist. This is achieved either by immediate feedback or by practicing new types of behavior. Towards the end of the session with the Spitz family, the therapist had the father and the youngest son talk to one another in a "new" way. In some assessment sessions, this type of exercise results in a first behavior contract (cf. Chapter 6), which means that the family can start working on changes at home immediately after the first session.

4.3.3.4 Winning confidence

The therapist gains the confidence of his clients by holding a structured assessment session during which principles designed to effect change are demonstrated. A relationship with the clients will be built up more quickly if the therapist clearly indicates his position instead of doing nothing but asking questions.

It might be concluded from the above that the therapist's interventions will constantly involve him in confrontation with the clients, but this is not so. The therapist can provide support in many ways, both verbal and nonverbal, even when he is giving feedback on unconstructive forms of interaction between the members of the family (cf. Minuchin, 1974).

4.3.3.5 Power struggles

Structured assessment with the kind of interventions we have described is also important in terms of power struggles. The question of who defines the rules and who is in charge is as important in the relationship between the therapist and the family as it is in the clients' relationships with one another. Although it may sound unpleasant, it is essential that this type of issue be resolved as quickly as possible in the therapist's favor. A constant struggle between the therapist and members of the family to gain the upper hand could seriously impair the effectiveness of treatment. This does not, of course, mean that the therapist should adopt an authoritarian or omniscient attitude, but it does mean (see Minuchin, 1974) that he should operate as a sort of director who, by virtue of his professional expertise, has the last word on what takes place. The elusive matter of the therapist's style is dealt with in more detail in Section 5.20.

4.3.3.6 Preliminary treatment contract

After a session of the kind described in Section 4.2, therapist and clients know a fair amount about one another. The therapist knows the family's problems and the position the individual members occupy in the family system. Family members have become acquainted with the therapist's approach and style and have observed him define the problems and explain the options open to them. When the therapist has asked the family at the end of the session if they wish to proceed further on this basis and explained precisely what this will involve, a meaningful treatment contract (cf. Section 6.5) can be drawn up.

4.3.4 Dilemma: intervention or assessment?

The Spitz family presented the therapist with a dilemma on several occasions. The session had barely begun when Mrs. Spitz began to talk to and about her husband in a disparaging way. The therapist chose not to respond with interventions at that point, because by doing so he would have been diverted away from the immediate objective of assessment. However, by remaining silent he risked appearing to condone the destructive behavior in question and failing to make his own position clear. This is a recurrent dilemma, both during assessment and at subsequent stages.

Kempler (1973a) sees this as the therapist consciously choosing his working points at every stage. In other words, as each subject comes up, he must decide whether it is worth dealing with at that stage or whether to let it pass. He could decide that it will undoubtedly come up again when it will be less disruptive. This is, of course, a highly subjective area and one where opinions will vary; one therapist will say to himself, "I can't possibly let that go," while another will do no more than make a mental note of the problem with a view to coming back to it at a more suitable time.

In our view, the therapist's decision must be based on the importance he attaches to what he sees and the extent to which intervention would deflect him from his objectives. For example the Carson family had problems bringing up their children. The husband in particular seriously neglected his responsibilities. After the problem had been discussed at some length, Mr. Carson said he was prepared to try and approach his children in a different way. His wife interrupted him immediately and told him he was incapable of doing so because "he has always done it wrong in the past." Although the therapist was working with the father and daughter and wanted to carry on with them, he felt he could not allow such a destructive remark to go unchallenged. He therefore turned to Mrs. Carson and confronted her in no uncertain terms with what she was doing. He then returned to Mr. Carson. In Section 5.10 we describe how this type of confrontation can be embedded in support, which is likely to increase its effectiveness.

The type of intervention outlined above is important at every stage of therapy. Failure to deal with an extremely destructive remark will serve to reinforce it, while dealing with it immediately involves relatively little time and effort.

In this chapter, we have attempted to describe the key principles of assessment mainly in relation to a first session, but, as we pointed out in the introduction, the process of assessment is by no means confined to one or a limited number of sessions. In a sense, the entire treatment could be described as a constant process of assessment of the problems and the positive aspects in a family. New problem areas and insights can emerge at any stage during the therapy. On the other hand, there is a clear difference of emphasis between this type of ongoing assessment and listing the problems in a structured fashion during the initial phase. The difference is possibly best expressed by the decisions the therapist takes in choosing the working points.

This was clearly illustrated within the framework of the first session with the Spitz family. To begin with, the therapist was so concerned with making an inventory of the problems that he allowed important destructive interactions on the part of Mrs. Spitz to pass without comment. After half an hour, when a number of problem areas had been touched on and the therapist had a better idea of the overall situation, he began to deal with these comments more forcefully. He chose the least drastic and time-consuming interventions. In a later stage of treatment, he might have asked the husband to respond to his wife's comments or he could have asked Mrs. Spitz, after confronting her with her behavior, to reformulate her views in a more positive way. At the end of the session, he devoted more time to interventions aimed at change. He had the father and the youngest son conduct a conversation with one another in a "new" way. In view of the fact that the therapy was at a relatively early stage, he did not draw up a behavior contract, although he might very well have done so.

One session is not, of course, sufficient to provide a thorough assessment, but it is often enough for a preliminary contract to be drawn up. After several sessions, a clearer picture emerges and the therapist has had the opportunity to try out interventions aimed at change. The reactions of the members of the family to the latter have diagnostic value; in this sense, assessment and working towards change go hand in hand.

After roughly four sessions it is time to scrutinize the preliminary treatment contract more closely to answer such questions as: Does everyone still have the same attitude to treatment? Does the therapist think his own approach will work or should he refer the family elsewhere? Now that the clients are more familiar with the therapist's approach, do they think it will do them any good? If the answers to these questions are in the affirmative, treatment can proceed and an estimate of the number of sessions likely to be involved can be made. At this point, the treatment contract adopts a less provisional character.

CHAPTER 5

Techniques and

Interventions

In this chapter, we describe some of the techniques available to the therapist during treatment and illustrate these with examples. Several are touched on only briefly, as they are dealt with more fully in other chapters. Various assessment techniques and the treatment contract, for example, are the main subjects of Chapters 4 and 6 respectively.

5.1 JOINING WITH THE FAMILY

5.1.1 "Tracking," "mimicry," and "support"

It is important for the therapist to establish a relationship with the client family, particularly during the first stage of therapy. There are several ways in which he can do this. Minuchin (1974) describes three techniques: "tracking," "mimicry," and "support." By "tracking" he means picking up points raised by members of the family and responding by asking a series of related questions. For example, if the man mentions his job, the therapist can show his interest by asking him questions about it.

By "mimicry," Minuchin means adapting to the family's style; the therapist will speak to university graduates in one way and to a couple with minimal formal education in quite another. Different clients have different expectations—using an informal form of address almost immediately will put some families at ease, while with others it will contradict their expectations of a relationship with the therapist and therefore have precisely the opposite effect. A further aspect of mimicry is adapting to the various subsystems. In the last chapter we saw how during the first session with the Spitz family the therapist suddenly focused his attention on the two sons, asking them how they were getting on at school and if they liked their teachers. By doing this he was trying to put himself in their position and looking for subjects important to them.

The third term used by Minuchin, "support," is more difficult to define and contains elements of both mimicry and tracking. Apart from the usual ways of showing support, such as listening, expressing interest, asking questions and adapting, there are several essential strategies in family therapy which facilitate joining with the family. These are described below.

5.1.2 Accepting the problem presented by the client

In Section 2.2.1 we saw that accepting a problem is the first step towards solving it. For this reason and also because of the element of support it involves, the therapist should illustrate this principle in his own reaction. He must show that he understands the problem and not make it in any way ridiculous or attempt to minimize it. It may also be essential for the therapist to identify the member of the family whose problem requires the most explicit acceptance to begin with. However, acceptance does not mean that the therapist cannot subtly restructure the problems while he is summarizing in order to make them easier to tackle.

Take the following example: Mrs. Cohen was an inmate of a concentration camp during the Second World War. She now suffers from psychosomatic headaches and feels a constant need to talk about her war-time experiences. Her husband and daughter find this intolerable and have been trying to persuade her to put the past behind her. The first therapist who treated the Cohens began by adopting the attitude of the rest of the family and tried to convince Mrs. Cohen that her problem was largely imaginary. He suggested various ways of dealing with it, none of which worked. A second therapist was brought in and soon realized that Mrs. Cohen's desire to talk about her war-time experiences was so obsessional that she must be allowed to do so. As he saw it, the past was alive for her in the present, and that was the problem on which she would have to work. It meant talking about the past to her husband and children. He even went as far as giving her the assignment of thinking about her ordeal even more than usual during the coming week, writing down her thoughts and talking about them with her husband for an hour every evening. This case also illustrates the judo technique described in Section 2.2.6 and the timing problems outlined in Section 5.17.

Similarly, Minuchin (1974) cites an interesting case of a therapist failing because he does not accept the client's problem. An elderly lady moves to an area where she lives alone and fairly soon starts exhibiting symptoms of paranoia. The first therapist simply prescribes psycho-pharmacological drugs and recommends admission to a hospital. The second therapist, on the other hand, says that he fully understands the problem: It is quite normal for someone her age to feel vulnerable after moving to a new neighborhood. He describes her as a snail without a shell and discusses with her what she can do to create a familiar environment for herself once more. Accepting the presenting problem in this way not only strengthens the bond between client and therapist, but also restructures the problem in a subtle way (cf. Section 2.2.4). The problem has not changed yet, but it has been made more accessible.

5.1.3 Acceptance by means of positive labeling

In Section 2.2.4 we wrote about the importance of positive labeling, particularly during the initial stages of therapy. Selvini Palazzoli et al. (1974) say that positive labeling is an excellent technique the therapist can use to show that he accepts the family with all its problems and conflicts. It may sometimes appear that in so doing he is entering into an alliance with the forces in the family who wish to preserve the status quo (cf. Section 1.6.1), but, in fact, he is establishing a basis for change. Selvini Palazzoli (1974) consistently uses this approach in treating families with an anorectic daughter. She begins by describing the girl's refusal to take food in positive terms by saying something like "She is so sensitive and generous that she cannot help sacrificing herself for her family." She then does the same for the behavior of the rest of the family, however destructive it may be. The primary concern of the family members is, after all, to maintain unity and stability within the family.

An example from our own experience is provided by the Baker family, consisting of Mrs. Baker, a 45-year-old divorcée, her 35-year-old boyfriend, Jonathan, and her 16-year-old daughter, Gillian, the last of her children still living at home. The family, if one can call it that, considering its constantly changing composition, has had a difficult and chaotic past. Mrs. Baker has been admitted to psychiatric institutions on a number of occasions. All the children, including Gillian, have spent part of their lives in institutions. One of the current problems is that Gillian cannot get on with her mother's boyfriend. They have fearful quarrels during which she screams and shouts; he usually says nothing, but is nevertheless plotting all sorts of complicated ways of getting back at her. For example, he keeps the front door locked at night because she keeps threatening to run away from home.

After a tense initial assessment session, the therapist knows he has made a bad start. He has tried to create order from chaos but without success. Gillian seems more determined than ever to leave home. He realizes he must devise a completely different strategy for the second session and decides to describe Gillian's difficult behavior in positive terms. He therefore suggests to the family, when they next assemble, that in constantly feuding with her mother's boyfriend, Gillian is in fact doing something extremely positive. She is ensuring that she does not come between Mrs. Baker and Jonathan. By being so aggressive she keeps him at a distance, guaranteeing that she does not compete with her mother and thus making her own contribution towards keeping the family together.

The therapist waits for a response. To begin with there is stunned silence. Jonathan looks at him in complete disbelief. Then the mother says that the therapist is absolutely right. She had always thought that herself. Gillian says, "My God, first everything I did was wrong and now suddenly I'm the one who's keeping the family together."

The therapist continues this line of approach by pointing out the positive aspects to the serious conflicts within the family: "All three of you are sincere and honest people who fight and argue openly. All families have problems but many are incapable of facing up to them and they keep festering away beneath the surface."

Positive labeling here formed the basis for the subsequent more congruent approach in which the therapist was able to help Jonathan and Gillian and her mother look after their own interests and negotiate satisfactorily with one another (cf. Sections 2.2.1 and 2.2.2).

5.1.4 The interactional aspect of identifying problems

By accepting and supporting one member of the client family, the therapist may be rejecting another. It is, therefore, vital that he should be constantly aware of the interactional aspect of problems (cf. Section 2.2.4.4). This requires a great deal of flexibility on his part. With the Cohen family, for instance, it would not have been sufficient simply to accept the mother's problems. The therapist devoted attention to the rest of the family and showed his understanding of the problems they were having with Mrs. Cohen. We shall deal with this more fully in Section 5.10.1.

In conclusion, let us offer a word of warning: There is more to joining with the family than giving support and accepting their problems. Clients are entitled to a substantial amount of information about the therapist's role in the proceedings and should be given a clear idea of what he stands for. He should not go against his principles for the sake of showing support—quite the opposite in fact. We shall discuss this in greater detail in Section 5.10.

5.2 TREATMENT CONTRACT

In Chapters 4 and 6, which are about assessment and contracts respectively, we outline the importance of treatment contracts. Without dealing with them in any detail here, we should like to stress how important such contracts are at the outset of therapy. The contract has a "joining" function in that it clarifies the position of the therapist, the goals of therapy, and what the therapist expects from his clients. Usually families respond positively to this, having had virtually no idea in advance of what to expect. The first treatment contract often rounds off the first stage (assessment) and clears the way for the second stage, working on specific problems.

5.3 MONITORING/SELF-REGULATION

Often the first step in working on problems is to collect as much information as possible in order to provide a specific description of them. One appropriate approach involves systematically recording the problematic behavior. Monitoring, as this is called, often yields clear information, but there is a reactive side to it as well (cf. Kazdin, 1974; Nelson et al., 1976). Observing behavior, whether this is done by a client himself or by others in the family, often leads to a reduction of symptomatic behavior. Below we describe a number of types of monitoring which have varying degrees of immediate impact on the behavior in question.

5.3.1 Simple recording of behavior

A client says that she frequently suffers from an inexplicable feeling of tension—she finds it difficult to describe and has no idea where it comes from. This is a situation that calls for *monitoring for information purposes*. The client should record exactly where and when she has these feelings and how long they last.

The Butler family provides an example of a different kind. Mr. Butler was the identified patient because of his excessive consumption of alcohol. The first step was to get him to write down details of his drinking habits. This is not as simple as it would seem. Certainly a drink is a drink, but there are a number of potential sources of misunderstanding which should be removed from the outset. Do, for example, beer and scotch both count as one drink and does a sherry mean a large or a small glass? It was even more difficult with Liz and Paul. Liz was to monitor how much time Paul devoted to the children. Was she to include mealtimes? Did watching television together count? Before monitoring of this kind begins, potential sources of misunderstanding should be cleared up and unambiguous arrangements made.

If the type of behavior being recorded occurs very frequently, it is best to sample it, that is, to agree on fixed times when monitoring will take place. As a rule, we use the following guideline: *The more general the behavior and the more often it occurs, the smaller the intervals at which it can be recorded.*

One final point on this subject—cards or forms can make monitoring behavior much easier. Obviously these should match the clients' specific needs so the therapist usually will have to design them himself.

5.3.2 Monitoring and reflecting on the complaints

The above examples are mainly concerned with recording how often a certain type of behavior occurs. Sometimes, however, it is useful to link this approach to an assignment in which the client is asked to *reflect* on his behavior as well as record it—not simply to provide more information or clarify matters. Being asked to reflect on one's behavior can become an extra burden which makes having complaints less attractive.

The assignment might consist of asking the client to go into another room or to sit down at a table every time he experiences a certain feeling and then attempt to write down exactly what he is thinking and feeling for a set period. The length of time can vary from ten minutes to as much as an hour. Sometimes, as illustrated in Section 2.4 with Jacob, the client will even be asked to increase the feelings of tension deliberately so that the period of reflection takes on still deeper significance.

This type of assignment is particularly useful in treating clients who are suffering from depression, are listless and apathetic, and feel that life is pointless. The reduction of symptomatic behavior which this assignment produces can be explained in two ways. By changing his physical surroundings, the client subjects himself to different stimuli and at the same time punishes himself. This is particularly important if, as in the case of Jacob and Teresa, an arrangement which minimizes the secondary gain of symptomatic behavior is linked to the monitoring assignment (cf. Section 2.4).

The type of assignment which links reflection to monitoring should not be used with clients who are in the habit of writing down their feelings in detail, in a diary for example. Lange (1977b) cites the case of a client for whom keeping a diary was more of a reinforcement than a punishment. Before giving an assignment of this kind it is wise to find out whether the client in question is already in the habit of keeping a record of feelings or thoughts.

5.3.3 Observing specific relational problems

Clients' complaints often center on their husband or wife or another member of the family. People often make remarks such as "she is so unfriendly," "he makes me feel that I can't tell him anything," "he never listens to me," or "he never does anything with the children." The vaguer the complaints, the more important it is to start by recording them—for instance, by jotting down a few lines every time a partner makes the other person feel a certain way (see Appendix 4). If need be, reflection assignments can also be included, particularly if the client puts his or her partner under excessive pressure.

If the client has to sit down for half an hour and write down why the other person is annoying him so much, it takes the pleasure out of complaining. Usually it is agreed that the therapist will not see the written text—it is intended only for the writer's personal use. This also applies to the variation described in Section 5.3.2. The advantage of this is that there is absolutely no chance of the client's receiving any reinforcement for what he is doing, while the need for reflection on his own behavior is considerably underlined.

5.3.4 Monitoring general relational complaints

This involves the *recording of irritation* assignment. Both partners write down everything they find irritating about the other, in the widest possible sense, as and when it happens. This may include something the other person does wrong but it could equally be something he or she fails to do. When introducing this assignment, it may be best to avoid using the word "irritation" and instead to ask the couple to record what each of them wants of the other at a given moment. This is important because many clients are embarrassed about mentioning small points as sources of irritation, with the result that they do not talk about them, while they still play a role in determining their relationship with their partner or the rest of the family. This type of assignment is especially useful if clients have escalating quarrels or if they never quarrel at all. When introducing this assignment, as with the previous ones, it is a good idea to emphasize the need to develop greater self-awareness, particularly as far as the pattern of mutual irritation is concerned. For a detailed description of this, see Appendix 2.

5.3.5 Less precise monitoring of mutual complaints and mood; the "mood meter"

Writing down everything you find irritating about someone else without comment at the time it happens is a precise and a somewhat contrived kind of task. There is nothing wrong with it at the outset of therapy; however, bearing in mind the "transfer of change" principles (Section 5.16), it would be wrong to continue it for too long. A technique which can be used to supplement it or even replace it is what we call the mood meter. Clients are asked to draw two axes on a large sheet of paper, one representing the days of the week numbered from 1-7 and the other representing their state of mind from 1-10 (see Appendix 5). Clients are then asked to record their moods each day—the higher the number, the better the mood. It is necessary to agree in advance that the graph will be filled in at the same time each day; otherwise it can be systematically distorted by one or both of the clients waiting until they are in a good or bad mood before filling it in. The therapist should also be aware that there may be confusion about the period of time to which the number relates. If, for instance, the graph is to be filled in at 9 p.m. every evening, should the number reflect the client's mood throughout the rest of the day? In practice this does not work very well; it is preferable to ask the client to record his or her mood at that very moment, even if it was completely different half an hour previously.

Of course, all kinds of variations on this basic theme are possible. For instance, the accent can be placed on the relationship, in which case the "score" relates to one's mood in relation to the other person. In most cases, however, it is best to think in more general terms. If someone is walking around with a long face because of something which has happened at work, it is vital to allow this to come out; otherwise the other person will be likely to think that he or she is to blame.

5.3.6 Self-monitoring versus monitoring by others

Carla O'Brien, age 12 (cf. Section 5.10), was referred to therapy because of her abnormal eating habits. She was almost twice the average weight for her age and height. Part of the treatment was based on asking Carla to monitor her own eating habits. Rose (1972) and Patterson (1971), both of whom describe in considerable detail the monitoring techniques which can be used with children, place the responsibility on the parents, whose job they feel it is to record and chart the child's problem behavior. In our view this is not desirable in family therapy, since it only makes the identified patient more of a patient and reinforces the existing system. The parents get off scot-free.

In some cases, however, self-monitoring is impossible because the person concerned is simply unaware of his or her behavior. For instance, Monica wanted Tim to stop bossing her about so often. The therapist first asked Tim if he was prepared to work on the problem and Tim said he was. The therapist then asked if he would agree to having Monica monitor his behavior. In couple therapy, it is essential to ask permission first if one person is going to monitor the behavior of another. By giving his consent, Tim made it clear that he was prepared to work on changing the behavior which Monica found so unpleasant. Since he had committed himself in this way, there would be less chance of irritation on his part when he saw her writing things down. This type of monitoring sometimes forms part of a behavior contract (cf. Chapter 6). In that case, Tim would be entitled to ask Monica to work on changing an aspect of her behavior which he did not like.

5.4 COMMUNICATING THE INFORMATION OBTAINED BY MONITORING

In both family therapy and couple therapy, it is useful and sometimes vital for the clients to pass on to one another information they have obtained by monitoring. Sometimes, however, clients get nowhere because they find it difficult to talk to one another. It is then necessary for the therapist and his clients to agree on an exact procedure for discussing their observations. We describe a number of ways of doing this below. Some of them are used in combination with a certain type of monitoring, but strictly speaking, this is not absolutely necessary. Other combinations are also possible.

5.4.1 ABA conversations

Written monitoring of irritation (Section 5.3.4), the aim of which is to avoid discussion or debate, is often accompanied by an ABA conversation. The partners take turns reading out loud something they have written down. The person reading is A; the other person, B, may respond to what he or she hears, but only once. A is then allowed to come back and round off the topic. Appendix 3 describes the procedure in detail. ABA is not necessarily the best sequence—A, AB, or ABAB will sometimes be better. The essence of this technique is that one is entitled to know what one's partner finds irritating without having to admit being in the wrong. Clients experience the fact that being right or wrong is less important than being able to identify frustrations and negative feelings. The form the therapist chooses, ranging from A to

ABAB, will depend on how articulate the clients are and the extent to which there is a danger of escalation as the sequence goes on.

ABA conversations can also be linked to specific monitoring assignments (see Sections 5.3.1 to 5.3.3). If Norma writes down the number of occasions on which her husband, David, does not listen to her, she can tell him what she has jotted down that evening using the ABA technique. She is then A only and he is B only.

Whatever the subject matter of the ABA conversations, it is important that there should be no confusion about when they are to take place. This can be avoided by making *one person responsible* for suggesting when the session should be. The same person should not be responsible all week; the partners can take it in turns. Who will be responsible on the first day can be decided during the therapy session. In some cases it is useful to give one person permanent responsibility, for example, a spouse who is hostile towards therapy or the weaker party in an unbalanced relationship.

5.4.2 The interview

The mood meter described in Section 5.3.5 provides clients with an aid which they can use every day to convey their moods to each other. This is bound to provoke questions from the other person. After they have both recorded their scores, therefore, a conversation should take place, possibly using the ABA technique. The disadvantage of this is that it is highly artificial and represents a step backwards at the stage of therapy at which this assignment is usually introduced. It is much more appropriate for the clients to interview one another. Here, too, the accent is on communicating information, rather than on being right or wrong. The object is for the interviewer to use questions to establish the occurrences which have contributed to the score. The interviewer must, however, be careful not to ask leading questions and to refrain from passing comment on the answers. This ensures that debate does not ensue (Truax and Carkhuff, 1967). As most clients simply do not have the skill to carry off this type of Rogerian exercise effectively, it is sensible to practice it first during the therapy session. The big advantage of the interview technique is that it has lasting value. Quite apart from the score aspect, it is useful to be able to stimulate one's partner to talk about himself or herself without immediately responding.

Responsibility for the interview can be agreed in the same way as for ABA conversations.

5.4.3 The hidden signal

So far we have described techniques which involve communicating the information which has been accumulated as a result of monitoring at a later stage. Sometimes, however, it is necessary to inform the other person more or less immediately of what one has observed, while at the same time making sure that a discussion does not ensue. It is therefore a good idea to agree on a sign which the observer can give the other person whenever a certain type of behavior occurs. The parties can agree on an unobtrusive sign which can even be used in the presence of other people.

Teresa and Jacob used this technique. Jacob had a habit of saying, "I feel guilty," when what he really meant was "that really annoys me"—not a particularly assertive attitude. After immediate feedback (cf. Section 5.7), he and the therapist agreed that the word "guilty" would be banned. Teresa would try and help him by making a sign with her hand every time he used it. Lange (1976) writes about another couple who used this system. Danielle accused Robert of showing indifference towards her; he did not know what she meant. It was agreed that Danielle would put up her hand whenever she felt that Robert was being indifferent. Robert would do the same if he felt that she was being domineering in the presence of other people.

In the first of these examples, the object of the sign is to help an individual; in the second it is simply to convey information. In both cases it is essential that the therapist should emphasize the subjective nature of the exercise. When Danielle puts her hand up, Robert knows that at that moment she feels that he is behaving indifferently but that she need not necessarily be right. It is not a question of right and wrong but of finding out what the other person is thinking and feeling.

5.5 BEHAVIOR CONTRACTS

In Section 2.2.2 we discussed constructive assertiveness and remarked how many relationships are characterized by the inability of the partners to express their desires and needs in relation to one another in a direct and undisguised fashion. We also saw in Section 2.2.3 how people attempt to prove that their mutual desires and needs are justified and that this can stand in the way of functioning properly in interactional terms. This was illustrated by the example of the woman who told her husband that he should go to bed earlier because he was working so hard. The discussion centered around whether this was, in fact, the case and was predictably inconclusive. The real point was that the wife *wanted* the husband to go to bed at the same time as she did, but she seemed to be incapable of saying so. She had to *prove* that her demand was justified; she had to prove that she was *right*.

In some couples, this type of interaction pattern leads to recurrent struggles in which the original points of dispute are rapidly forgotten. The problem of who defines the rules, as well content and relationship aspects (cf. Section 1.5.1), plays a role here. In other couples, these processes prevent anything from being discussed. It is simply not worth it and neither spouse dares to make any demands. These are the type of people who solemnly maintain that they never quarrel. In fact, however, there is a significant undercurrent of disagreement, but they are unable to convey it explicitly to one another and instead resort to such tactics as sulking and sarcastic remarks. In families which fight constantly and "silent" families which perpetuate the myth of having no problems, these signals are highly destructive. They either create confusion in the minds of the people for whom they are intended or put them on the defensive so that there is no chance that they will react positively to them. In an interactional system where there are few rewards, where the struggle for power is all important and where people rarely if ever show their vulnerability, there is little likelihood of members of the family indicating to one another in clear and simple terms what they want the other party to do. This is usually done in a roundabout and threatening way, so that the other person's response is either not explicit (in the silent families) or is negative (in the families which constantly fight).

In Chapter 6, we describe in detail how behavior contracts can be used to combat escalating quarrels. Such contracts can also be useful in families which maintain that they do not have any problems since they can form a simple and "safe" alternative to the discussion which everyone fears. However, it simply is not possible to go through a course of therapy, much less the rest of one's life, settling differences of opinion only by means of contracts. Practicing behavior contracts, however, results generally in an easier way of formulating one's wishes with regard to the other person. This, in turn, makes it possible for one to stand up for oneself in a constructive manner. Instead of negative criticism and discussion, one learns to indicate in a specific way what one wants from the other person, who is then able to respond more adequately. People know where they stand with one another. The therapist has to supervise this process by having the clients practice using such expressions as, "I want you to. . ." or "I would like you to. . ." (cf. Section 5.14).

5.6 TALKING DIRECTLY TO ONE ANOTHER

People with problems in their relationship often find it difficult to talk to one another; they either say nothing or talk through a third party. By forcing the clients to address one another directly, the therapist is breaking down the existing system and providing the clients with the opportunity to practice this skill. Kempler (1974) calls this the "no gossip" principle. If someone wishes to say something about someone else, he has to say it to that person and not to the therapist. In the early stages of therapy, there is often resistance when the therapist asks the parties concerned to address one another directly. In general (we shall discuss the exceptions later), the therapist should not allow himself to be put off by this.

Kempler (1973a) quotes the case of a young man who complained that he could not talk about certain things to his father. Kempler therefore asked him to discuss this with his father. The following case is from our own experience: A married man is having an affair and is in a dilemma. His relationship with his wife is unsatisfactory; however, although there are no children, he does not want to leave her. The therapist asks him to tell his wife what attracts him to the other woman. He says he cannot. The therapist then asks him to tell his wife that he finds it difficult to talk to her about this; the result is a highly significant conversation.

Some clients will respond to being asked to tell another person something directly by saying, "He already knows." The therapist should not allow himself to be deterred by this type of remark. Even if the other person has a good idea of what is coming, it can be very important for the parties to address one another directly rather than communicate through the therapist.

Minuchin (1974) describes a number of techniques which the therapist can use to encourage the parties to do this. One simple method is to repeat the request. The therapist can also make it more difficult for the clients to address him by pushing his own chair back or by facing the opposite direction. He can also refuse to answer if they speak to him. Sometimes indicating by a gesture of the hand that the speaker should be addressing someone else will be sufficient. The therapist can even leave the room and observe the family from behind the one-way screen. Once techniques of this kind have been used on a number of occasions, it will be an accepted rule that the members of the family speak directly to one another.

The advantages of talking directly to one another rather than addressing other members of one's family through the therapist are as follows:

(a) The "here and now" is central. The parties discuss a topic which is important "now."
(b) The parties are forced to respond to one another—often a *breakthrough* from the usual pattern of not talking directly about certain subjects.
(c) The therapist can provide them with *immediate feedback* (cf. Section 5.7) by indicating where the conversation is going well or badly.
(d) Partly because of point (c), the parties get good practice talking and are provided with a model for how they should deal with one another at home.

We have said in the above that, notably in the early stages of therapy, situations may arise in which the therapist will allow someone to talk about another person. We cite examples of this in Chapter 4 on assessment. Talking about other people is also acceptable when the therapist has asked the family for information and the information supplied is known to the various members of the family but the therapist does not want to examine it in more detail at that stage. If a wife, for example, says she finds it intolerable that her husband always makes her look after the children, the therapist need not insist that she says so to her husband. He is more likely to summarize the problem and then let the husband respond, particularly during the assessment phase. The conclusion of a behavior contract (cf. Chapter 6) will often take place through the therapist, particularly during the initial stages. It makes the negotiations easier and increases the chances of success.

In certain families, often those with serious psychiatric problems, talking directly to one another is either impossible or fails to produce any positive results. In such cases, the circular interview technique described by Selvini Palazzoli et al. (1980) may be the most appropriate.

The relationship between the family members is then examined by means of questions to a third member of the family, as follows: "Your mother said that Marco has always been a difficult child. But according to you, did your mother and brother fight more before or after your father got sick?" (p. 10).

In summary, it is often preferable for the parties to talk to one another directly. If the therapist allows the discussion to take place through him, this must be a conscious decision on his part and not something he does out of carelessness, negligence, or laziness.

5.7 IMMEDIATE FEEDBACK VERSUS
ANALYSIS OF THE "SPOKEN WORD"

Immediate feedback, a term we have taken over from Eisler and Hersen (1973), means that the therapist responds to verbal and nonverbal interactions which take place during the session instead of commenting on the specific content of what has happened in between the sessions. According to Haley (1970), one of the major differences between the experienced and the inexperienced therapist is that the latter will become deeply involved with the content of what is said, whereas the experienced therapist will be more likely to respond to what he sees and hears. Several examples will serve to illustrate this.

During the first session with the Jackson family, the mother, Ann, accused her husband of failing to deal with important matters. She had to assume all the responsibility herself, a state of affairs which she did not regard as acceptable. In the ensuing discussion, she spoke very patronizingly to her husband, using such phrases as, "What do you know about it?" or, "I'll explain it to you later." The therapist observed that the tone of these remarks did not really suggest that she wanted her husband to assume responsibility for important matters. In such circumstances, this type of comment by the therapist is likely to produce better results than asking, "What is it exactly that you want your husband to do?"

Minuchin (1974) gives a similar example. Mrs. Smith complains that her husband hardly ever says anything. However, every time he tries to speak, she interrupts him. By drawing attention to this (through immediate feedback), the therapist is working on an important point more effectively than he would be doing by responding to what Mrs. Smith is saying about her husband.

In the case of the Jacksons, the therapist deliberately chose to work on the interaction which was taking place at that moment, rather than responding to the situation at home as described by the wife. This approach is usually the right one, since it means the therapist is responding to what he himself has witnessed. Moreover, the interactions themselves are likely to be more representative of what happens at home than the accounts of one or more members of the family. Another advantage of immediate feedback is that it has much more effect on the clients than comment by the therapist on something that happened several days previously.

This is confirmed by a comparison of the following situations. In situation A, the wife complains that her husband constantly demonstrates that he has no confidence in her. The husband defends himself by saying that his wife approaches many things in the wrong way and gives several examples. The therapist develops this theme and shows the couple how they are both reinforcing a vicious circle. By making it clear to his wife that he expects her to do everything wrong, the husband is increasing the chance that she will in fact do so (self-fulfilling prophecy—cf. Merton, 1957; Watzlawick et al., 1967). By failing, the wife decreases the likelihood of her husband having any confidence in her ability in that particular area in the near future.

In situation B, the couple has just discussed the problem in question. The wife has indicated that she intends to approach it in a different way in future. The husband interrupts, saying, "You've always done it wrong and I don't see how you'll ever change." The therapist intervenes and points out the destructive effect of a comment of this kind (see situation A). Clearly, the immediate feedback from the therapist in B links up much more closely with firsthand experience and will mean much more than the therapist's interpretation of the same theme in example A.

Another way of providing immediate feedback is to record therapy sessions on videotape. A destructive interaction can be played back on the spot and comes across much more forcefully than if it were described by the therapist (cf. Bodin, 1969; Eisler and Hersen, 1973).

It would appear from the above that immediate feedback always involves confrontation and is therefore negative. This is by no means the case. Responding to positive exchanges and complimenting the participants is very much a part of immediate feedback too.

In sum, immediate feedback makes it easier for the therapist to concentrate on the here and now, which means that more essential themes surface than if he were simply to interpret what the clients have told him. Immediate feedback also has a considerable effect since it means responding to things as they happen. In the following section, we should like to discuss a technique which gives the therapist additional opportunities to employ immediate feedback.

5.8 BEHAVIOR REHEARSAL AND
BEHAVIOR EXERCISES

5.8.1 An example and a description of the
process

Tim and Monica began the third therapy session with an account of a fierce argument they had had two days earlier. The therapist interrupted and asked if they had settled the quarrel in a satisfactory way. They said they had not. The therapist then asked them to concentrate for several minutes on that particular situation and, once they had done so, asked them to act out their quarrel. This is an example of behavior rehearsal. Inexperienced therapists will discover that clients are surprised to be asked to act out an experience: "Do you really want us to start quarreling all over again?" they will say, or, "No, we can't, not now." This should not necessarily deter the therapist from persisting with the approach, bearing in mind the following points (which he can also share with the clients):

1) Reenacting the quarrel need not last very long. The essence of a quarrel usually centers on the way people talk to one another and this often becomes clear after a few minutes. Reenacting the quarrel gives the therapist an opportunity to respond to what is happening here and now, rather than analyzing a report of something which happened several days ago. We have already outlined the advantages of this in the previous section on immediate feedback.

2) The therapist should make it clear that he does not want the clients to act out the quarrel word for word. They must start from the same point but the disagreement must take place in the present. Remarks such as, "You didn't say that then," are irrelevant. If necessary, the therapist should interrupt the clients and lead them back to behavior rehearsal.

3) It is important to describe the topography of the situation by asking detailed questions about the physical setting in which

the conflict took place. Where exactly were the people concerned and what were they doing? If, for example, the conflict
arose when A was in the kitchen cooking when B came home,
A should be asked to simulate the situation by taking a part of
the room to represent the stove. B will then be asked to leave
the room and return several minutes later. This gives both
parties time to concentrate on reconstructing the situation. The
behavior rehearsal starts the moment B reenters the room.

Dramatization (cf. Moreno and Kipper, 1971) makes it easier for the
person concerned to relive and demonstrate what he or she was feeling
at the time. We saw a striking example of this with a family in which
there were serious conflicts at meal times. The husband accused his
wife of behaving strangely when he came home from work. They reen-
acted coming home. First the man left the room and came back again
a few minutes later. The therapist was amazed. He had changed beyond
recognition. The expression on his face had become threatening, ma-
levolent, and morose, so that it was hardly surprising that his wife
behaved so strangely towards him. If, instead of rehearsing this situation, there had been a discussion about it, what was going on would
never have become clear. This way the therapist could see it for himself.
Behavior rehearsal is not an end in itself; it is a technique which
allows the therapist to deal with a theme which is important to the
client in the here and now. This can be done in the following ways
(the points below are by no means mutually exclusive):

1) The simplest way is for the therapist to give immediate feedback on what he has just seen. He may stop the rehearsal at
   any appropriate moment and then restart it.
2) If the rehearsal makes the quarrel flare up again, the therapist
   can couple immediate feedback with an assignment requiring
   the clients to approach the problem in a constructive manner.
   When this happens, the partners must make sure that they tell
   one another what is bothering them, but in a way which is not
   threatening to the other person. This is called *behavior exercise*, since it provides clients with an opportunity to practice
   a kind of behavior with which they are unfamiliar.
3) If this succeeds and the conversation proceeds on a different
   basis, the exercise is concluded with a joint evaluation. The
   participants begin by saying in what way they have behaved

differently. There is one danger here of which the therapist should be aware: the participants often claim that discussion is now easier because of the improved behavior of the partner. They say things like "you were much more pleasant and that made it easier for me." This is, of course, simply holding on to the old interpretation of "if something goes wrong, it's the other person's fault" (cf. Section 1.5.1.2), instead of being aware of the effects of one's own behavior on the other person. The therapist should help clients think carefully about what has really happened by telling them what *they* themselves have contributed to the interaction.

The type of punctuation problem we have just described emerges in many other situations—for example, clients report for a session and say that they have had a very good week. When the therapist asks them why, the reply is, "Peter was much nicer than usual," or "Lindy didn't have any bad moods." In such circumstances it is important that each person ask what his or her contribution has been.

4) Often the behavior exercise is unsuccessful the first time—it simply degenerates into the familiar old quarrel. The therapist can either intervene frequently and by means of immediate feedback attempt to help the family use the technique more successfully, or, if that does not work, he can apply modeling. This means that at a certain point the therapist decides to stop the exercise and take over the role of one of the participants—he then becomes the husband, the wife, or a child.

Sometimes it is necessary in couple therapy for the therapist to play the part of each of the partners in turn. Here, the advantage of co-therapy is that the two therapists can act out the behavior of the couple together. It may seem complicated, but a single therapist can also act as model for both partners. It means, however, that he has to keep moving his chair to sit next to each of them in turn in order to act out the role. This requires a certain amount of flexibility, but has the advantage that there can be no confusion about what he is trying to show the clients at a given moment. We discuss the advantages and disadvantages of co-therapy more fully in Section 5.19.

5) After the therapist has demonstrated his model behavior, it is important for an evaluation to take place so that the partners can comment on the difference between how the therapist behaved and how they behaved. Afterwards, they can continue

Figure 5.1. Diagram of behavior rehearsal, behavior exercise, and modeling.

by themselves. The process then starts again at point 2), followed by modeling as and when necessary, and so on. This is set out in diagram form in Figure 5.1.

5.8.2 Immediate feedback and behavior exercise

In the above, behavior exercise was preceded by the deliberate rehearsal of destructive behavior. More often though, behavior exercise is the logical consequence of immediate feedback. If, for example, a husband says to his wife: "You never react spontaneously to me and I find that very irritating," the therapist may intervene and say something to the effect that, as far as the wife is concerned, a negative remark which orders her to be spontaneous (cf. Section 1.5.3) is paradoxical. Often he will not simply leave it there but will go on to ask the husband to express himself differently. He may, for example, ask the husband to tell his wife in precise and specific terms the kind of behavior he wants from her in certain circumstances. This is exercising new behavior. If the wife does not respond constructively to her husband's new approach, the therapist then shows her how to change her response and allows her to practice. This type of exercise can be repeated often and is a powerful instrument for bringing about change.

5.8.3 Behavior exercise and individual therapy

Modeling and behavior exercise are techniques which have achieved recognition mainly through the learning theory (cf. Bandura, 1969) and behavior therapy (e.g., Casey, 1973; Lazarus, 1966). Arguing in favor of behavior rehearsal, Rose (1972) refers to important research such as that of Underwood and Schulz (1960), Goldstein et al. (1966), Sturm (1965), and McFall and Marston (1970). A major premise of all these studies is that exercising new behavior, as opposed to talking about behavior, leads to greater change because it enables both clients and therapists to work on a total response pattern in a live situation.

Rose (1972, pp. 121-2) concludes by saying this (the book is about group therapy with children): "In most instances, children view modeling and rehearsal procedures as enjoyable diversions while they are changing their behavior. For the therapist, however, modeling and rehearsal procedures are central to the whole treatment process." This applies equally to adults. Rehearsing new behavior is often an agreeable experience and one which enlivens therapy. After all, there is absolutely no reason why therapy should not be pleasant some of the time.

Even in couple therapy, it is sometimes necessary to work with individuals. For example, it may be necessary to exercise new types of behavior with a particular individual who has problems asserting himself (cf. Hersen et al., 1973). For example, Mr. Butler had been referred to therapy by his family doctor because of a serious drinking problem. The doctor told the therapist that there were also problems in the marriage. From the outset, the therapist worked with both husband and wife together. On the one hand, he devoted attention to the interactional aspects of Mr. Butler's individual symptomatic behavior (his drinking) partly by examining the role played by his wife. He noticed that Mr. Butler found it very difficult to talk about his problems to his wife. Whenever he tried to confide in her, she went on and on about his shortcomings. As a result, he again turned to drink.

The therapist also worked individually with Mr. Butler in the presence of his wife. He had him develop a system of self-monitoring (cf.

Section 5.3), which meant that every time he had a drink he was to write down the precise circumstances—where, when, what, and how much. The therapist knew from experience that a client's environment often makes it difficult to carry out this type of assignment. Mr. Butler had to be prepared for comments such as, "You do keep going on about it," or, "What difference does it make?" This applied especially to Mr. Butler, since he also had problems standing up for himself. Finally the therapist introduced a role-playing exercise. He asked Mr. Butler to show him what he would do if, as often happened, he were offered a drink at the office. Mr. Butler accepted the drink and wrote down what he was doing in accordance with the arrangement. His wife pretended to be a colleague who started making fun of him, providing Mr. Butler with the opportunity to practice how he would respond to ridicule. This is a kind of individual therapy within couple therapy (cf. Section 1.3) which increases the likelihood that the client will be able to translate into practice what he has learned during the sessions.

5.8.4 Behavior exercise and role reversal

One way of widening and extending the existing "behavior repertoire" of clients is by asking them to exchange roles. If reconstructing a conflict and the subsequent behavior exercise do not meet with any success—for example, because a client does not identify enough with the other person and cannot therefore imagine the effect of his own behavior—this can be an appropriate method (cf. Casey, 1973).

The therapist asks both parties to concentrate once more on the conflict, but this time to reverse roles—to imagine that they are the other person. Any subsequent discussion must then take place with each of them speaking as the other. To increase the effectiveness of role reversal it is useful to have the partners change places with one another. For the ensuing discussion they can go back to their original places. This technique often results in a degree of understanding for the other person which would otherwise have been impossible. To consolidate what has been learned, a behavior exercise may be carried out in which the participants once again play themselves.

A special type of role reversal and behavior exercise consists of one of the parties playing both himself and the other person; in other words, he carries on a conversation with himself. Tim is a good example of someone with whom this approach produced positive results. He could not understand how difficult he made life for Monica by *insisting that she should enjoy* the clerical duties he imposed on her. In Section 1.5.3 we explained the paradoxical nature of this kind of demand. The therapist asked Tim to talk to Monica about this problem and then to play the part of Monica himself. As Tim, he sat in his own place; as Monica, he sat in her chair. It was a very lively conversation which gave Tim the best possible opportunity to experience his demands and their effect on Monica. At the same time, he was able to modify his own behavior when he was speaking as himself.

5.9 MODELING

5.9.1 The therapist as model

Bandura and Walters (1963) and Bandura (1969) show convincingly how important imitation is in the learning process. Given that family therapy may be regarded as a new and constructive way of relating to other people, we should not underestimate the role of the therapist as an example for his clients. Social-psychological studies have shown that people tend to imitate people who are very popular or who are held in high regard (cf. Lippitt et al., 1958). Generally speaking, therapists tend to be popular and respected, making them ideal models. In view of this, it is hardly surprising that many people regard a positive relationship between therapist and client as an absolute necessity for effective treatment.

In Section 5.8.1 we saw how the therapist can operate *explicitly* as the model when new types of behavior are being tried out, but he will often serve as a model for his clients in a more subtle and less explicit way. Whenever he interacts with one of the members of the family and keeps to the communication rules described in Section 2.2.3, he is displaying model behavior. It is important for the therapist himself to be aware of this. A therapist who insists that his clients not express their allegations in the form of questions (cf. Section 2.2.3.3) must, of course, be careful that he does not make the same mistake. This also applies to other communication skills, such as being specific and avoiding vagueness. We would advise anyone practicing therapy to take careful note of how he or she acts as a model in order to make sure that what is usually fairly automatic happens on a more conscious basis.

5.9.2 Other models

It is, of course, possible to have people other than the therapist acting as models. Rose (1972) gives interesting examples of using famous sports personalities or ex-prisoners in treating juvenile offenders.

In family therapy, models of this kind are less likely to be used, but there are several other possibilities. Some therapists have their partners take part as co-therapists and are willing to discuss their own problems when they resemble the problems the clients present. Such interventions should be prepared carefully, since the aim is to display constructive behavior as a couple. Some therapists consider that this type of modeling is a good argument in favor of co-therapy. We will come back to this point in Section 5.19.

During a session with the King family, the therapist confronted the husband with the impossible demand that he was making of his wife, which in brief amounted to the "be spontaneous" paradox. She not only had to take care of an annoying chore for him, but was also supposed to enjoy it. The therapist narrated an anecdote about himself and his wife—how more or less the same situation had arisen, the problems it had presented, and the solution they had managed to find. In another session of couple therapy, the theme was that of the division of roles between husband and wife. At a certain point in the discussion, the man said, "I'm very busy at work; my career is important so you'll just have to fit in with it. You look after the house and kids." His wife, who was keen to work herself, did not respond. She withdrew into her shell and said nothing. At this point, the therapist invoked the figure of his own wife as a model. "If I said that to my wife there would be trouble. We've had arguments about this sort of thing too and she just doesn't take it from me.' The wife looked surprised and the therapist encouraged her by saying, "Go on, tell your husband what you think." In this sort of *covert* modeling (cf. Kazdin, 1976), the therapist's partner who is not present at the session is involved as a model, in addition to the therapist himself.

There are a number of important points to bear in mind in relation to this way of talking about oneself:

1) Talking about one's own problems has a relabeling function with regard to problems in general. The clients see that having problems and being involved in destructive interactions need

not in itself be disastrous. The problems begin to weigh less heavily and are more accessible to solutions. This links up with the first stage of problem-solving behavior described in Section 2.2.1.

Here we would like to refer to Masters and Johnson (1970) who, in discussing various forms of sex therapy, say that therapists must be able to talk openly about their own sexual experiences and problems. The first step in therapy for sexual problems is for those concerned to accept that "problems" are nothing to be ashamed of. The therapists can make this point by talking about problems of a similar nature they themselves have experienced.

2) It has a positive effect on the relationship with the therapist. Clients and therapist become closer without this in any way detracting from the therapist's status as an expert. By being frank about himself and his relationship with members of his own family, he makes it easier for his clients to accept certain interventions.

3) It is often one of the easiest ways for the therapist to demonstrate feedback to clients. This was the case with Mr. King, who initially found it difficult to understand why his demands were so paradoxical. After the therapist's anecdote, everything became much clearer.

4) Talking about his own experience gives the therapist an opportunity to outline ways in which clients' problems could be solved. In so doing, he uses real models, even if they are not always present.

5) The approach suggested by the therapist must not provoke comments from clients, such as "we'll never be able to do that" or "if only we could. . . ." This means that the therapist should not make the distance between himself and his clients too great. The approach he demonstrates must be simple and one with which the clients can identify. They must have the feeling that the goals he sets are attainable.

6) How honest does the therapist have to be when recounting such anecdotes? This is a difficult question. The therapist's most important task is to teach his clients to cope with their problems effectively. In order to function as a model for them, it may be necessary for him to modify his account of what happened. On the whole, however, he is likely to enjoy what he is doing more if he does not resort to tactics of this sort.

A therapist might also be called "dishonest" when he does not describe a personal experience similar to that of his clients because he feels he has not been able to find a satisfactory solution to it within the terms of his own relationship. In such circumstances, he may feel that it is best to say nothing. In our view, however, it is preferable for the therapist to be "free himself" by openly relating that he is experiencing similar problems and has not managed to resolve them. By admitting his limitations, the therapist is again acting as a model and is at the same time free to attempt to guide his clients toward a solution—as long as the roles do not become reversed and the clients have to help the therapist!

To conclude this section, we should like to refer briefly to the opportunities for modeling offered by *groups of couples* (e.g., Nevejan, 1973) or *multiple family therapy* (Laqueur et al., 1971; Leichter and Schulman, 1974). Apart from considerations of efficiency—dealing with several couples or families during the same period of time—it is possible that when several couples work on a specific problem one couple will benefit from the skills of another. For example, one couple could demonstrate a certain pattern of interaction to another. If Mr. and Mrs. A find it difficult to talk to one another in terms of "I want this or that from you," while Mr. and Mrs B find it easy, the latter could demonstrate how to do it. Of course, in such circumstances, the relationship between the couples is also important. A positive modeling effect is only possible when the models are accepted as such (Bandura, 1969; Rose, 1972).

Van den Berg and Van Loon (1976) show that therapy with groups of couples is not necessarily more effective than separate couple therapy. They organized a structured therapy course consisting of 20 sessions, each lasting two hours, with a group consisting of four couples. Before, during, and after treatment they systematically investigated the clients' problem-solving ability and asked them how happy they were about certain aspects of their relationship and with their relationship in general. On the basis of their research, they came to the conclusion that the 40 hours of therapy would probably have been better spent treating the four couples separately. However, it would be wrong to conclude from this that working with structured couple groups is pointless. The composition of the group analyzed here was unfortunate, in that one of the couples taking part came from a much lower social class than the rest. This couple was inhibited about discussing relevant aspects of their relationship in the group.

Kilgo (1975) maintains that it is desirable for the couple group to be heterogeneous. By this he means that the couples should not have problems which are equally serious. This would seem to increase the chances of success. The same cannot, however, be said about differences in social class.

Another difficulty in relation to structured couple groups concerns the necessity of agreeing on a fixed number of sessions. Some couples manage to improve their relationship long before the end of the agreed upon period. Another disadvantage is related to the fact that with some couples discussion about continuing or terminating therapy should be possible in a much earlier stage than at the end of the agreed upon number of sessions. In summary, a structured couple group may be useful if it is homogeneous in terms of social class and heterogeneous in terms of the degree of difficulty of the couples' problems.

5.10 CONFRONTATION AND SUPPORT

Kempler and Minuchin are two well-known family therapists whose approaches differ considerably. Kempler (1974) is known for his confrontational approach. If he does not like what he sees during a session, he says so in no uncertain terms. He operates on the basis that many problems in relationships are the result of the "game of weakness" people play with one another, in which he refuses to take part. He attempts to change this situation by expressing his own feelings of displeasure in an extremely direct way, thereby acting as a model. This often provokes a violent reaction from the members of the client family; this Kempler (1973b) regards as the start of change.

Minuchin does not avoid confrontation but maintains that change cannot take place in an insecure atmosphere (Minuchin, 1974). A confrontation or "challenge," to use his own terminology, ought to enrich the behavior repertoire of the people concerned rather than simply reducing it. The confrontation should, therefore, be embedded in acceptance of the way in which members of the client family behaves (cf. Van der Velden et al., 1980, on positive labeling).

Carla O'Brien, aged 12, the eldest of three sisters, had been admitted to a clinic because of her abnormal eating habits—her weight was almost twice the average for her age. After several interviews with her parents, the doctors decided to recommend family therapy. It seemed that there was serious tension at home and this was apparently having an effect on Carla's eating habits. During the first assessment session, the therapist was struck by the father's domineering attitude. His wife and children could hardly get a word in. Carla was afraid of her father's frequent bad moods and the torrent of words with which he tried to force the rest of the family to do exactly as he wished. The therapist decided that an essential element in any treatment would be to try to teach the father to be less authoritarian and to give the other members of the family, particularly Carla, greater responsibility. He also suggested that Carla should use self-monitoring to work on her weight problem (cf. Section 5.3; Abramson, 1973) and that the parents should try to strengthen their relationship with one another and reinforce the boundaries of the parental subsystem (cf. Minuchin, 1974).

It was, therefore, necessary to confront the father with his overbearing behavior. The therapist turned to the father very seriously and told him how much he admired the concern he exhibited for his family. Obviously he was someone who did not shirk responsibility—quite the reverse. But, according to the therapist, he was also being unfair to himself and his family by behaving as he did. He was entitled to a rest from time to time, but his own attitude made that impossible. Moreover, the therapist went on, constantly pressuring the family to do what he thought best for them was sometimes difficult for his wife and children to accept. By using this method of confrontation ("yes, but. . ." according to Minuchin, 1974), the therapist accepts the father in the first instance in order to propose later that he should change certain aspects of his attitude and behavior. This resulted in the father's being highly involved in therapy and putting a great deal of effort into trying to change.

The "yes, but. . ." technique can be important, particularly at the outset of therapy. This is illustrated by Herbert and his 12-year-old son, Tom. In the first sessions, the therapist pointed out to Herbert on a number of occasions the weakness of his own behavior both in relation to himself and in relation to his son. He thought that Herbert should not play pathetic games but should stand up for himself. Because the therapist had not attached any acceptance to his displeasure, Herbert began to distrust him. He felt that the therapist was showing too much sympathy for Tom. It is by no means certain that another approach would have worked any better, but it is likely that greater use of the "yes, but. . ." principle would have established a better relationship between Herbert and the therapist, as a result of which Herbert would have been more inclined to work on his share of the problems.

Embedding confrontation in support is not as essential later on, when usually enough support has been shown that the therapist is above suspicion. The therapist's confrontations in relation to specific problems are not regarded as threatening because a supportive atmosphere has normally been established by then. It is important, however, for him to continue to be aware of the possibility of bringing about change by adopting the "yes, but. . ." or "yes, and. . ." approach at a later stage.

As with the modeling described in Section 5.9.2, questions could also be asked here about the "honesty" required on the part of the therapist. Here, too, honesty is a fairly elastic concept and is certainly not the therapist's main concern, which is probably efficiency. While the therapist would normally not have disguised his confrontations with Mr. O'Brien so carefully outside the therapeutic context, he is not compromising his convictions by praising him for his sense of responsibility. The latter is an observable feature of Mr. O'Brien's behavior. By emphasizing it, the therapist invokes a realistic kind of restructuring.

As a rule, we would strongly urge that the therapist should try to tie in positive comments with confrontation, certainly in the early stages. In cases where this would be too contrived, it should be avoided, since it would not be effective anyway.

5.10.1 Confrontation and individual versus interactional feedback

During a session, Liz expressed her displeasure with Paul by means of a short, aggressive remark. Then she turned and deliberately faced the opposite direction, clearly insulted. The therapist thought that this was an extremely negative way of expressing herself and wanted to confront her with this view. He showed her what the effect of her behavior was and that it was not achieving anything. However, he said that, in view of the idiosyncracies of their relationship, he could understand that she should seek refuge in this type of strategy. By saying this he made the interaction between Liz and Paul central, shifting the emphasis away from the individual problem and the individual confrontation.

The same principle is exhibited when one of the parties constantly argues during a session in order to prove that he or she is right. This is rarely an individual phenomenon—more usually it is part of the way members of the family deal with one another. It is wise for the therapist to point this out in feedback. He can then show that he is not siding with any particular individual, but is aware of how interactions between members of the family take place. Apart from the accuracy of these observations, they make it easier for the person who is being confronted in the first instance to come along and accept the therapist's feedback.

So far we have described situations in which the therapist can point out that both partners exhibit the same kind of destructive behavior. Often this behavior is also complementary: A tolerates B's symptomatic behavior and even reinforces it by responding with symptomatic behavior of his or her own. Whenever Tim has one of his bad moods and starts shouting, Monica responds like a nurse by making a fuss over him. When Tim is able to stand up for himself again, she withdraws. In his confrontation of Tim, it was essential for the therapist to underline this interplay.

5.11 REINFORCEMENT: REWARD AND PUNISHMENT ON THE PART OF THE THERAPIST

In Section 5.9.1, we discussed implicit modeling by the therapist, i.e., the fact that he often serves as a model for certain types of behavior without being aware of it. We should now like to concentrate on how the therapist consciously and unconsciously reinforces certain kinds of behavior. By nodding, smiling, or responding positively in verbal terms, the therapist reinforces the behavior he has just observed. The reverse happens if he does not respond, or looks or speaks in an unfriendly way. For a detailed description of various forms of reinforcement, see Liberman (1972), Bandura (1969), and Craighead et al. (1976). Here we simply wish to emphasize that the therapist must be aware of the fact that he influences his clients by responding in either of the ways we have described. He should, therefore, use positive, negative, and neutral responses in a *selective* manner, that is to say depending on the objective he is pursuing and the strategy he is employing at that given moment. If he does not do this, there is a danger that he will reinforce destructive behavior and forget to reward constructive behavior.

The O'Brien family provides a good illustration of this. The father constantly does his best, is concerned about everything, and is continually speaking. The therapist may be tempted to respond positively and in an understanding way (by nodding for example) to someone like this who is so willing to talk at length about himself and his family. However, by doing so, he would simply be reinforcing the system and strengthening the existing pattern, in which the father is the central and rather domineering figure. In such circumstances it is better to "extinguish" the father's behavior by not reacting to it (cf. Liberman, 1972) or even to react in a punishing way, for example by means of immediate feedback. The therapist must also be aware of those aspects of the father's behavior which he wishes to reinforce. If, for example, the father sits back and listens to the members of his family without interrupting them, the therapist can reward him by making a friendly remark or simply giving him a friendly glance. This is selective reinforcement. The father's silence is rewarded; at the same time, the therapist might reward the mother for more forceful behavior.

We could quote many more instances of this type of reward and punishment, but the reader will undoubtedly be able to furnish examples from personal experience. Suffice it to say that reward is a much more powerful therapeutic method than punishment (cf. Liberman, 1972). It is far more effective to concentrate on rewarding behavior which the therapist regards as constructive, while responding less to negative behavior, than to attempt to bring about change by frequently punishing undesirable behavior. Patterson (1971) and Patterson and Gullion (1968) analyze this principle in detail and discuss its consequences, for example in bringing up children.

5.12 TOPOGRAPHIC INTERVENTIONS

In the session described in Section 4.2 the therapist asked Mr. Spitz (the "identified patient") to change places with his wife. The position in which he had originally been sitting symbolized his position in the family—or, rather, outside it. By making husband and wife change places the therapist reinforced the restructuring process which was necessary in this family. Minuchin (1974) strongly advocates this sort of restructuring technique, seeing himself as a director continually giving the members of the family instructions on all kinds of subjects, including their physical location.

Erickson (cf. Haley, 1973) had the members of the family change places frequently and sometimes asked some of them to leave the room. This enabled him to work with different combinations of people during one session. He might ask a child to leave the room and tell the mother to go and sit in his place saying, "If you sit in your son's place you will be able to think about him more clearly."

With the Spitzes, changing places highlighted the basic structure of the family; in other situations, it can have significance for less far-reaching goals. During the second session with the O'Briens, the therapist asked Mr. O'Brien to sit next to Carla on the couch in order to reinforce the relationship between the two of them, as we pointed out in Section 5.10. The father went to sit next to her; in the beginning this made him noticeably edgy. The therapist encouraged them to talk to one another and as they did the father's nervousness slowly disappeared. After a few minutes he touched Carla and hugged her, something which rarely happened at home. Figure 5.2 shows where everyone was sitting. To prevent the mother from being literally pushed into a corner on her own, the therapist asked her to sit in her husband's original seat.

Sometimes topographic changes lend an occurrence more impact. When two members of a family are talking, it can be useful to remove them physically from the context of the rest of the family and seat them together. This is, of course, also important in behavior rehearsals and exercises (cf. Section 5.8).

The therapist should not always sit in the same seat either. Sometimes he will need to sit next to a person he is supporting or to pull his chair forward to enable physical contact. The reverse is also true. By pushing his chair back, he can indicate that he does not want to be involved in an interaction, for example, when two members of a family are talking directly to one another.

The way the members of the family choose where to sit often provides information about the structure of the family. As we have seen, the therapist can intervene in this, and the position he himself chooses also influences the situation. When working with a couple he should sit so that he can see both of them easily. In co-therapy, the therapists should sit where they can see one another and communicate effectively.

In conclusion, using topographical interventions implies that the therapist does not take the seating arrangement as a purely coincidental or unimportant detail, but that he carefully considers the role each person's physical location can play during therapy.

Figure 5.2

5.13 PRESCRIBING THE
SYMPTOM—"PARADOXICAL"
ASSIGNMENT

5.13.1 Background to prescribing the
symptom

Prescribing the symptom means that, during a certain period, the therapist asks a client or clients to exhibit or exaggerate the symptomatic behavior over which they have no control and which they wish to eliminate. On an intrapsychic level, prescribing the symptom is indicated particularly in cases where there is a vicious circle: The more a person tries to avoid something, the more it happens; the more effort he puts into achieving something, the more it eludes him (cf. Frankl, 1960). This applies to conditions in which anticipation anxiety plays an important role, for example phobias, or to complaints such as compulsive neuroses, trembling, or insomnia, where the client tries either to suppress spontaneous behavior or to induce it. The more the client tries to avoid the symptomatic situation, the tenser he becomes, with the result that the symptoms escalate. In this type of situation, prescribing the symptom can be regarded as a relabeling assignment (cf. Lange, 1972). By deliberately not trying to fall asleep, the client relabels his insomnia, experiences less "arousal," and therefore finds it easier to fall asleep (cf. Storms and Nisbett, 1970).

Haley (1963) emphasizes another aspect of prescribing the symptom—changing the control function of symptomatic behavior on the client's environment. Steven Best's compulsive behavior, Robert's apathy (Section 2.2.6), and Jacob's paranoia and depression (Section 2.4) are examples of this. Displaying symptomatic behavior becomes considerably less attractive when one is instructed to do so, and even more so if one's partner is not allowed to react, as with Jacob and Teresa. The secondary gain of symptomatic behavior is thus minimized. Relabeling also takes place for the partner. A woman who was greatly irritated by what she felt was her husband's deliberate and malicious use of professional jargon was suddenly much less annoyed by it when the therapist directed him to use it even more. She then saw it as a kind of obedience (Lange, 1972).

Another positive result of prescribing the symptom, in addition to relabeling, is that it is a form of "negative practice" which leads to satiation. The behavior is extinguished because it does not occur at the usual time and the customary "rewards" are no longer given.

5.13.2 Prescribing the symptom, and interactions as a unit

We have described a number of examples in which individual symptomatic behavior (which of course makes itself felt in a relationship) is dealt with by prescribing the symptom in various ways. In family therapy, the therapist may ask clients to exhibit interdependent symptomatic behavior. Bert and Rita had escalating quarrels characterized by two elements: According to Bert, Rita was remorseless in her criticism—she always knew better, she found fault with everything and was permanently dissatisfied. According to Rita, Bert never faced up to his responsibilities, left everything to her, and never took the initiative. The situation had apparently degenerated to the point where small changes or behavioral contracts would not have had any effect. The therapist therefore told them to exaggerate the pattern of behavior they had described as much as possible during the following week. Rita was to nag about everything and Bert was not to take any initiative. The therapist predicted a difficult week, and the couple were also apprehensive, so he explained the reason for the assignment in the following way: Sometimes it is useful to make yourself fully aware of what you are doing by doing it deliberately before trying to change it. Bert and Rita agreed to give it a try. At the next session they reported that they had had a bad week, but the fact that they were able to make their quarrels worse at will showed that they could still exercise some degree of control over them and would therefore also be able to reduce this symptomatic behavior.

5.13.3 Regulation in prescribing the symptom

In the above example, Bert and Rita were asked to exhibit *unlimited* symptomatic behavior. A useful variation on this is to increase the symptomatic behavior at *certain moments* (cf. Van Dijck and Hoogduin, 1977). For instance, William and Mary reported that they shouted at one another too often—they never talked calmly. The therapist wanted to break this pattern quickly and arranged with them that they would vent all their pent-up anger as vociferously as possible at a certain time every evening, between 8:30 and 9 o'clock. This meant "saving up" their irritations and making a note of them (cf. Section 5.3.4). They were not allowed to quarrel at any other time. At the next session they reported having had a quiet, pleasant week. They had tried to fill the half hour with shouting, but had not managed it once. The rest of the time had been extremely peaceful. In consultation with the therapist they decided to reduce the half hour to 20 minutes and to carry on the assignment for several weeks until their pattern of quarreling had been fundamentally changed. The advantage of an arrangement like this is that the symptomatic behavior is confined to a relatively short period. It is easier for clients to control themselves if they know that there is a set time each day when they can give vent to their feelings.

A similar method was used with Mrs. Butler. She conceded that she was unreasonably jealous and constantly imagined that her husband was having affairs. She was instructed to concentrate on her jealousy for an hour every day and to imagine how terrible it would be if it were true. During the last 15 minutes she was to write down everything that had gone through her mind. After three days she stopped because she thought that her jealousy was ridiculous. "I've been cured of that nonsense," she said.

5.13.4 Timing prescribing the symptom

When a therapist instructs clients to overdo symptomatic behavior, he must count on their actually doing so. Prescribing the symptom does not always result in the immediate termination of undesirable behavior. Bert and Rita (Section 5.13.2) had a very unpleasant week carrying out their assignment. If prescribing the symptom is correctly presented, this need not be a problem. By consciously exhibiting symptomatic behavior at set times, clients begin to grasp exactly what they are doing and gain control over their actions. This can then be used as input for the subsequent and more congruent approach, during which small steps are taken in order to bring about change. It would be impossible to prescribe the symptom once the more rational step-by-step approach had failed. If Bert and Rita had tried unsuccessfully to solve their problems by making contracts, it would have been inappropriate for the therapist to switch then to prescribing the symptom. First, the original motive of increasing awareness would not be present and the clients would probably see the move as a last desperate measure. Second, there would be no logical sequel to prescribing the symptom. Generally speaking, it is particularly useful at the outset of therapy and in cases such as the above, where there is anticipation anxiety, a struggle for power, or secondary gain involved in symptomatic behavior.

5.13.5 A note of caution

As we have seen, prescribing the symptom is appropriate when the very thing one's clients are trying to avoid keeps happening, or when the secondary gain of symptomatic behavior enables the person concerned to keep everyone around him, sometimes even the therapist, under control. It is also to be advocated where conflicts have escalated to such a degree that a direct, congruent approach is unlikely to meet with immediate success.

Obviously there are frequent opportunities during therapy to apply this technique. We should, however, like to warn against its excessive use. If it has immediate success, clients tend to regard it as a magic formula. They are overwhelmed by their achievement, without knowing the reason for it. In short, it does not help them to become more skillful in solving problems in general (cf. Section 2.2.1). Whenever possible, therefore, a direct, congruent approach should be used and prescribing the symptom reserved for situations where nothing else is likely to have a reasonable chance of success.

Furthermore, presentation and motivation are even more important than with other types of assignment (cf. Van Dijck and Van der Velden, 1977). The "awareness paradigm" illustrated in Section 5.13.2 is often useful in this respect, particularly since it contains a substantial element of truth.

In conclusion, when the therapist uses the technique of prescribing the symptom as a last resort, it will probably not have the desired effect. It will usually be effective only when introduced at the outset of therapy.

5.14 EXERCISES

The various forms of behavior rehearsal and the exercises described in Section 5.8 all involve the repetition and practice of certain specific behaviors. We should now like to describe more standard exercises.

5.14.1 The "I would like . . ." and "listening" exercises

As we have already seen (Section 5.5), there are many families in which the members find it difficult to say exactly what they expect of one another. It is generally easier to explain what someone else is doing wrong than to indicate exactly what one does want.

The members of some families do not even say openly what is wrong. They all try to hide the fact that there are facets of the others which they do not like. It is impossible, however, for them to keep this up indefinitely and eventually the bottled-up tension comes out in violent outbursts, "breakdowns," or gastric ulcers. It would be much better if each of the parties could use simple signals to let the others know what was required of them at a certain moment. The "I would like . . ." exercise is designed for this purpose.

The two people involved sit facing one another, or back to back if it makes conversation easier. We will use Connie and Robert as examples to illustrate what happens next. Connie and Robert's problems were mainly concerned with inadequate communication. They were used to letting one another know how they were feeling in a vague and indirect way. Once, when this happened during a session, the therapist asked them to sit facing one another and alternately start a sentence with "I would like you to. . . ." At the same time, a listening exercise (cf. Antons, 1973) was to take place. They were to try and make specific demands of one another. Connie began and Robert repeated what she had said in his own words and then told her what he wanted ("You want me to. . ." and then "I would like you to. . ."). The exercise was a revelation to them. In order to consolidate what had emerged, they arranged to write down exactly what they expected of each other during the following week.

5.14.2 The "conducted tour" (nonverbal)

In Section 5.7 we described how Ann Jackson complained that she felt she was responsible for everything. The therapist noticed during the session that she could not delegate responsibility easily and that any initiative on the part of her husband, Peter, to assume responsibility met with her disapproval. The therapist told Ann to close her eyes and allow Peter to "show her around the room," the object being to reverse the existing power/responsibility relationship. Ann would feel what it was like to be at Peter's mercy and Peter would experience what it was like to be able to guide his otherwise dominant wife.

They both found the exercise pleasant and enlightening. Ann realized how seldom she normally left things to Peter, and she enjoyed the feeling, especially as Peter was so concerned and capable. Peter enjoyed having his wife depend on him and saw that his fear of Ann's superiority often made him choose the path of least resistance and refuse to accept responsibility.

5.14.3 Gestalt exercises

One of the important themes of Gestalt therapy (Greenwald, 1975; Passons, 1975) is becoming aware of and integrating various "I's." Perls (1969) describes the dialogue between the "top dog" and the "underdog," both of which may be present in every individual. Such individual exercises are sometimes appropriate in family therapy, certainly in the types of situations described below.

Bernice and Louis are into the tenth session of couple therapy. Bernice, who is depressed, makes very little attempt to talk and Louis is extremely concerned about this. Since Bernice is withdrawn during the session, Louis asks her what is wrong. She tenses up but does not answer, which upsets Louis. This is indicative of what happens at home. In previous sessions the therapist had given them feedback about what he saw happening, but without any sign of positive results. He now chooses a different strategy. He wants to make Bernice more aware of what is worrying her, so he asks, "What are you conscious of at the moment?" After a short silence she answers, "I'm up against a wall."

"And what do you see?"

"Only a wall."

"O.K. Turn around. . . . What do you see now?"

"Louis and the children. . . . They're walking through a park."

After a time, the therapist continues, "And now?"

"I'm with them . . . and Louis and I have our arms round one another . . . the children are walking in front of us. . . . One of them runs to us and pulls Louis' sleeve." Bernice hesitates and starts crying.

The therapist asks her to carry on. She says that the child needs so much attention from Louis because she is inadequate.

The therapist asks her to identify with that child and then stimulates a Gestalt dialogue between Bernice the mother and Bernice the child. She becomes profoundly aware of her need for contact and her grief at the lack of it. As in the role reversal in Section 5.8.4, the exercise is more effective because Bernice keeps changing places, to correspond with which "self" is talking at that moment.

At the end of the dialogue, the therapist asks Louis how he feels. He tells Bernice that he needs her but hardly ever dares show it. She knows what he means: "Sometimes you put your arms around me and I don't dare react in case you reject me." The rest of the session is spent helping them express what they need from one another. During the following session they discuss how they could spend more time together with the children.

A Gestalt exercise such as used by Kempler (1970, 1974) in his approach to couple therapy is described below. At the beginning of Tim and Monica's treatment, the subject of Tim's almost nonexistent relationship with his father came up. The therapist suspected that Tim felt a great deal of resentment, with which he had not yet come to terms, but which was still important to him. When Tim confirmed his suspicions, the therapist suggested that he should talk to his father, whom he had not seen for five years. The therapist would be the father. The "talk" proved to be important to Tim and led to his talking out certain matters with his real father, at the therapist's instigation. Equally important, his relationship with his mother, who had always interfered between Tim and his wife, became clear to him. He was able to "liberate" himself from both his parents. In Chapter 7 we discuss in depth how a therapist can help clients come to terms with unresolved problems from the past.

5.14.4 Discussion

The above Gestalt exercises, particularly the last one, may be regarded as special forms of behavior rehearsal and behavior exercises. We have mentioned them separately, since their origins are slightly different. Of course, they are by no means the only techniques available. They merely illustrate that existing exercises can be useful aids, as long as they are directly related to the problem at hand (cf. Lange and Van der Hart, 1973). Schutz (1967) and Lewis and Streitfeld (1971) provide more information on exercises from encounter groups and Stevens (1971) and Levitsky and Perls (1970) deal with Gestalt therapy exercises.

5.15 SEXUAL PROBLEMS

So far we have cited specific complaints only to illustrate general concepts and techniques. We should now like to make an exception for sexual problems, which play a role with most couples in need of therapy.

5.15.1 Two categories

With most couples sexual problems are a result of difficulties on a broader level of communication. Power struggles or escalating conflicts make a sexual relationship difficult or even impossible.

There are also couples whose sexual difficulties, such as premature ejaculation, impotence, or inability to achieve orgasm, precede other problems in the relationship. There is no difference in principle in the way the two categories are treated. In both cases the couple has to learn to enjoy caressing one another without being too performance-oriented. With the second category, however, the sexual problems should be dealt with by taking very small steps, whereas this is not always necessary with the first category, for once mutual trust has been restored on other levels, the sexual problems often disappear of their own accord. When they do not, several weeks of carefully selected assignments are usually sufficient to restore the balance to the sexual relationship.

5.15.2 Guidelines for treating sexual problems

We should like to deal briefly with some ideas behind the treatment of sexual problems and several recurring steps in the process. More information on this subject may be obtained from Masters and Johnson (1970), Belliveau and Richters (1970), and Kaplan (1974).

1) When clients themselves do not broach the subject of sexual problems, it is up to the therapist to ask them about their sexual relationship. In family therapy, it is useful to have a separate session with the parents so that they can discuss this, as well as other "private" matters (cf. Section 4.3.1.7).

2) The therapist should spend as much time as necessary gathering all the relevant information about the precise nature of sexual problems. He will need to pose such questions as:

- How long does foreplay last and who initiates it?
- How long does intercourse last?
- What do the couple enjoy?
- What is the bedroom like—do the couple sleep in single beds or a double bed?
- What are the lighting and ventilation like? (Often parents sleep

with the door open, which indicates a lack of privacy (Aponte & Hoffman, 1973).

• What time do they go to bed, and do they go to bed at the same time?

If there are specific problems, the therapist should ask when and how they started. He should also ask about past or current relationships with other partners, with a view to discovering if the same problems occur there. Information on masturbation is also important (LoPiccolo and Lobitz, 1972).

Asking for this sort of information is important in order to assess the problem. The way in which the therapist asks the questions—calmly, frankly, and without embarrassment—and reacts to the answers helps him break down sexual taboos. He can point out that people do not have to enjoy everything in a sexual relationship and that they could discuss this. He should use the same terminology as his clients—it is simplest to ask them what they call certain things. If they talk about "intercourse," the therapist should too, and he should also follow their example if they call it "making love" or "fucking."

3) Immediately prior to or at the start of sex therapy, intercourse is usually banned. This is not a crude device to provoke the desire for it, but a way of creating an atmosphere in which there is no pressure to "perform." It ensures that the first assignments have the greatest chance of success. When a couple has intercourse despite the fact that it is not allowed, the therapist should not interpret this as a success, and should certainly not reinforce it. He should ask them to stick to the agreement in future. This, however, does not apply to every case—exceptions are where sexual problems are clearly of a secondary nature (cf. Section 5.15.1) and characterized by anticipation anxiety. Here the mere fact that intercourse is forbidden may lead to one or more satisfying sexual experiences, after which the vicious circle is broken down (cf. Van der Hart and Rubinstein, 1977).

4) People with sexual or relationship problems often go to bed at different times. The first person is already asleep by the time the second goes to bed. They do otherwise only when they intend to have intercourse. This places an unnecessary emphasis on "performance." The first step in changing this is to arrange one or two evenings on which they go to bed early together. They agree on a definite time (long before

their usual bedtime) and the therapist advises them to combine going to bed with pleasant activities, such as a long bath, reading, listening to music, chatting, eating, or having a drink. Neither fondling nor intercourse is allowed. The aim is to make going to bed a pleasant, peaceful activity without any further *obligations*.

5) The next step is to introduce fondling exercises, often starting by stroking each other in turn, everywhere except on the genital organs, during short, fixed periods. This is followed by letting the other person know either verbally or by guiding the hand what is or is not desired. Gradually, the genitals are included and, instead of taking turns touching each other, the partners do it together. The emphasis remains on improving communication as far as sex is concerned and eliminating thinking in terms of performance. For this reason the ban on intercourse stays in effect for a long time. Only right at the end do they work on having intercourse and orgasm; this is then done in a way dependent on the nature of the original complaints.

6) The various steps have been dealt with only summarily. For more detailed information we refer the reader to the literature mentioned earlier. We wish to emphasize once again that the exact way in which the exercises are to be carried out differs from case to case. The degree of caution and patience required will depend on the severity of the case. For example, Mrs. M had had no sexual experience apart from masturbation before she met her husband and she had never had an orgasm with him. In her case the fondling exercises were built up very gradually. Bert and Rita (Section 5.13.2), on the other hand, who had both had satisfactory previous sexual relationships and suffered less from anticipation anxiety, were able to proceed more quickly.

There is no hard and fast rule governing when to start tackling sexual problems (cf. Section 5.17 on timing). When the sexual problems can be attributed to relationship problems which are not serious enough to jeopardize success in sexual assignments, it is best to initiate the above treatment at the earliest opportunity. When clients see that pleasurable changes are possible in their sexual relationship, they may be motivated to work on other problem areas too. Sometimes, however, the sexual problems are partly independent of the relationship problems, and in addition, there are conflicts which are difficult to overcome and which are based on destructive communication patterns and a struggle for power. It is then usually not feasible to start working on sexual problems in the early stages of treatment. Restoring confidence based on success in other problem areas is a requirement which must be attended to first. The therapist should, of course, explain and discuss his strategy with his clients.

7) Treating sexual problems does not always mean working with both partners together. In certain cases it may be useful to teach one person to use masturbation to heighten his or her sexual enjoyment. LoPiccolo and Lobitz (1972) set out a detailed program for treating women who fail to achieve orgasm. The partner is involved only as a kind of co-therapist. Hoogduin (1977a) claims that this method reduces the emphasis on the woman as a "patient," as she has at least become orgasmic during therapy.

We do not agree with these authors. Using this individual approach too readily reinforces the notion that there is an individual problem, whereas the problems often derive from the way in which the man and woman react to each other's sexual idiosyncrasies. Furthermore, LoPiccolo and Lobitz, as well as Garfield Barbach (1975) in her book on group therapy with anorgastic women, overemphasize the importance of orgasm as such. De Bruyn (1973) rightly attacks this type of therapy in which everything centers on orgasm. Her extensive research shows that women experience orgasm in very different ways and that many women have a highly enjoyable sexual life but do not necessarily consider themselves orgasmic. Her criterion is whether the woman herself calls her sexual experience "satisfying." We share these views and consequently aim to help clients build up a sexual relationship which they both find pleasurable and satisfying.

5.16 GENERALIZATION: TRANSFER OF CHANGE, FADING OUT

So far in this chapter we have described principles and techniques which make change possible in the existing family structure. We shall now discuss the kind of strategy which increases the chance of such change lasting and continuing beyond therapy. In the literature on individual therapy, a number of these principles are described (cf. Goldstein et al., 1966; Lang, 1966; Rose, 1972). Those which are important in family therapy shall also be dealt with here.

5.16.1 Change of location

Towards the end of treatment it may be important for a number of sessions to take place outside the confines of the room usually used for therapy, in order to reduce the association of the acquired changes with a particular location. If therapy has always taken place at the institute to which the therapist is attached or at his private office, some of the last sessions can be held at the clients' home. If the sessions have always been in the family's home, the therapist could invite them to his office for several sessions. The transfer of change can be further enhanced by arranging meetings in places such as bars, club houses, canteens, and parks (cf. "park bench therapy" by Goldstein et al., 1966; Haley, 1967b, on Erickson).

5.16.2 Less directive

Directive family therapy makes structural change possible and teaches the members of a family to solve their problems adequately. As with other types of therapy, there is a danger of the clients becoming too dependent on the therapist. In the final stages of therapy, therefore, the therapist will have to disengage, intervening less (cf. Cleghorn & Levin, 1973) and assigning the solving of certain problems as homework, instead of looking for solutions during the sessions.

Chapter 6 on contracts and assignments contains an example of this. During the last stage of a course of therapy the therapist is less directive and specific in giving assignments and in making arrangements with the clients. Assignments and behavior contracts are no longer written down during the session, and if one or more clients fails to stick to an agreement, the therapist does not have to be telephoned.

The clients are given increasing responsibility for everything that takes place during and between sessions, including mistakes. The therapist should, in fact, prepare his clients for new problems. Given that the goal of therapy is to teach the members of the family techniques to enable them to solve their own problems, special attention should be focused on this aspect during the final stage of therapy. This ties in with Lang's principle (1966) that the therapeutic process should follow a sequence from the specific to the general: First, solutions are sought for specific problems and later on treatment is directed towards learning and gaining insight into general mechanisms.

5.16.3 Preparing for resistance to change in the social environment

The smoker who is trying to fight his addiction by applying monitoring procedures (cf. Section 5.3) or the smoker who has already succeeded in breaking the habit will inevitably be pressured by friends and acquaintances, often quite unintentionally, to revert to his old ways. He will have to contend with comments such as, "I don't see what all the fuss is about," or "Just have one, it won't do you any harm." Even when the problem is less obvious than giving up smoking, in individual therapy it is essential to prepare the client for this sort of situation, by role-playing for example.

In family therapy, the above type of danger is less acute, as the most important elements of the clients' social environment are involved anyway. Something would, in fact, be seriously wrong with the therapy if they were not, for family therapy need not be confined to the nuclear family only; its object should be to include all the people who are contributing in a significant way to the existing problematic system (cf. Section 1.3.4). If this is done adequately, the relevant social environment will adjust to the new situation.

On the other hand, if part of the relevant social environment has somehow not been included in the treatment, the therapist will need to consider problems of adaptation. This was true in the case of Mr. Butler (Section 5.8.3) whose relationship with his colleagues at work influenced his drinking problem. The therapist originally considered holding several sessions at Mr. Butler's office and involving a number of his colleagues, but for practical reasons he decided against this. He dealt with the anticipated resistance to change with the help of the role-playing described in Section 5.8.3.

A slightly different example is that of Jackie and William. Jackie had changed a great deal as a result of couple therapy; from being a shy and weak person she had developed into someone who was not afraid to express her own opinion and who had far more self-confidence. Towards the end of therapy this caused problems between Jackie and her husband's family, who thought she was much too full of herself. For practical reasons the therapist rejected the idea of sessions with everyone present. He taught Jackie and William how to react appropriately to William's family by using role-playing.

5.16.4 Reducing the frequency of the sessions

Most therapy sessions take place once a week for an hour. This seems to be a convenient arrangement for everyone concerned, particularly the therapist. We do not believe, however, that there is any point in laying down hard and fast rules (cf. Haley, 1967b, on Erickson). It can be useful to meet more than once a week for different lengths of time—for example when dealing with sexual problems (cf. Section 5.15)—or only once a fortnight. Whatever the case, it is essential to reduce the frequency of the sessions during the last stage of treatment, when the clients have to take on more responsibility and become less dependent on the therapist.

We often use the following schedule. During the first two stages (cf. Section 2.3), sessions are held once a week (about 10 or 15 in all). In phase three sessions are slightly less frequent—for example, three or four at fortnightly intervals. In the final stage they are reduced first to once a month and then gradually to once every three months. On termination of therapy a follow-up session is arranged for six months later and this may of course be repeated.

5.17 TIMING

In this chapter we have dealt with a number of techniques which have a bearing on the treatment model presented in Chapter 2. We wish to emphasize that mastery of these techniques does not necessarily guarantee success. The ability to apply techniques is a necessary prerequisite for successful treatment but by no means the only one. At all times during treatment the therapist must carefully adjust his interventions, keeping his client's needs in mind. Forms of treatment which are indicated for some people at the outset of therapy will not necessarily suit others in this phase of therapy, even if the problems are similar. The relationship between the therapist and his clients is also important here, as we saw with the Burger family in Section 2.4, when the therapist consciously rejected the important principle of taking small steps at a time (cf. Chapter 6). As early as the second session, he introduced a dramatically significant treatment contract between the parents and one of their sons.

In Chapter 4 we saw how a therapist is often faced with the dilemma of whether or not to give immediate feedback during an assessment session. This is a matter of timing. It should depend on the answer to the question of whether the therapist has established a sufficiently good relationship with his clients for them to be able to cope with the feedback or whether it would be wiser to wait for another opportunity. There are no textbook answers to this question of timing—the therapist must use his discretion. There are certain guidelines, however; for example working in a congruent, problem-solving way with treatment contracts and immediate feedback has little chance of success if there is strong resistance to therapy to begin with. A much better strategy then, and one that is more likely to succeed, is to go along with the resistance by giving monitoring assignments (cf. Section 5.3) or even to prescribe the symptom before trying a more rational approach. However, the correct timing of this is at the therapist's discretion and is difficult to lay down in general rules. This applies equally to the right moment at which to start sex therapy. The decision will be influenced by factors such as the seriousness of the sexual problems (cf. Section 5.15) and the extent of other problems. If two people who are constantly at each other's throats report that they have sexual problems, it is best to start by trying to improve their relationship in general. Once a measure of success has been achieved, it becomes possible and even desirable to tackle the sexual problems. The two parts of the therapy will then complement one another. Where sexual problems predominate and the relationship is otherwise reasonable, it makes sense to begin work on changing the patterns of sexual behavior. Once again, phasing and timing take place at the therapist's discretion.

The question of timing also plays a role in deciding whether or not to deal with a client's *past*. This is discussed extensively in Chapter 7, which contains the example of a therapist who keeps focusing on a couple's interactions, while he should also be devoting attention to the wife's resentment towards her father. Mr. and Mrs. Wells provide an example of a different kind. Mrs. Wells, the "identified patient," was "sexually dead." She had not felt sexually aroused for years; she did not masturbate; she had no sexual desires and no fantasies about other men. During the first session she said that 20 years earlier her husband had been to bed with her sister, a fact she had known for certain only for the past few years, although she had always suspected it. The therapist thought that this occurrence was still playing a role in the present and was standing in the way of a satisfying relationship with her husband. He asked her to write about it every day for two weeks. He also had her write to her mother and the sister in question (cf. Anonymous, 1972; Section 7.2). When the two weeks were up, he asked her to make a drawing of the painful event. Husband and wife later buried the drawing together in a field. At the same time as the problem from the past was being dealt with (cf. Chapter 7 on rituals), the therapist was working directly on the patterns of interaction by means of monitoring exercises and contracts. After five sessions therapy was terminated without sex therapy being necessary, as the obstacle had been removed. Even if things had not worked out so well and sex therapy had been necessary (cf. Section 5.15), the question of timing would have been vital. To have started with sex therapy without first banishing the ghosts of the past would not have had any chance of success.

Unfortunately, there is once again no hard and fast rule for this sort of timing. With many families and couples, simply working on interactional problems in the present is effective, but the therapist should be able to determine when hidden agendas from the past deserve priority.

Timing is important in terms of the therapy as a whole, as well as *within each session*. What, for example, is the right moment at which to give an assignment? Again, it is impossible to give general rules, but we would suggest that it is bad timing always to wait until the end of a session before giving an assignment (Van Dijck and Van der Velden, 1977), since the client will tend to regard it as an afterthought. It is far better to give an assignment while discussing the problem and to make the client write it down immediately.

Many more cases could be cited of situations in which timing is of crucial importance. The examples we have selected simply emphasize the fact that the treatment model and the techniques which go with it cannot be applied indiscriminately. The imaginative resources needed to choose the right moment for the right intervention cannot be replaced by a set of rules or written instructions. There is no substitute for training, experience, supervision, and intervision (cf. Chapter 9).

5.18 WHERE SHOULD THE SESSIONS TAKE PLACE?

For the first appointment a decision has to be made about where the sessions are to take place—at the therapist's office or in the family's home. The choice depends on the nature of the family and how much room both they and the therapist have. Either will have advantages and disadvantages.

The advantages of therapy at the clients' home are the following:

1) The therapist has the opportunity of assessing the family in their own environment. Take the example of the Mayor family: The youngest son was the identified patient and during the first session problems emerged between him and his elder brother, aged 15. A look at the bedroom revealed that the two boys were sleeping in bunk beds, with the older boy on top. He always woke his brother when he went to bed, and this caused arguments. The middle son had his own room and refused to take sides. The therapist suggested that the eldest and the middle son should change rooms, as the eldest son went to bed last and would appreciate the privilege of having his own room. Another reason for the move was to strengthen the relationship between the middle and the youngest son.

   Firsthand knowledge of how the clients' home is arranged and information about the wider social environment, such as the influence of friends and family, are particularly important during the assessment phase of therapy. The therapist's primary concern will be to observe how the members of the family cope with the environment in which they live.

2) It is useful to see how the family responds to playing the role of host and this may accelerate the process of getting to know each other. The family will be more at ease and will probably be more open as a result.

3) If therapy takes place at the therapist's office and there are very young children who cannot be included, a babysitter is necessary. This is a serious drawback for families who are not well off. Minuchin (1974) says that the center where he works has a special fund to help in such cases.

4) If the sessions are held at the clients' home, it is possible to be more flexible about who takes part. Should the therapist wish to talk to the parents alone for a short time, the rest of the family can go into another room. Small children do not have to sit through whole sessions—they can play or do whatever they normally do at home. When a therapist treats families with children under the age of 10 at his office, he must make

sure that toys are available, so that the situation is as natural as possible.

5) Some therapists simply do not have suitable space available —social workers, for example, often work in extremely cramped conditions. In such cases there is little choice but to hold the sessions at the clients' home.

Disadvantages of sessions at the client's home:

1) A visit to the therapist requires an effort on the part of the family—which is a good thing in itself. Once clients have made this basic effort, they are usually better motivated to work hard on the therapy. This follows on from social-psychological theories on cognitive consistency and the reduction of dissonance (cf. Festinger, 1957).

2) Having the family play host can also prove a distraction. Serving coffee, etc., takes up a great deal of time and may interrupt the flow of a conversation. The experienced therapist, however, will not be put off by this and he may even gather valuable information from it.

3) The advantage of being able to see how the family responds to disturbances disappears after several sessions. The therapist then has enough information on that point and the interruptions are no more than that.

4) When a therapist goes to a family, the latter is "playing a home game" and the former is "playing away." This can complicate matters should a power struggle take place between the therapist and a member of the family. This ties in with point 1 on the basic effort required of the family.

5) It is very difficult to tape sessions held at the family's home, especially on video. Of course, this disadvantage only holds for therapists who use these kinds of instrumental aids. The same applies for not being able to use one-way screens.

6) Getting to and from the family takes more of the therapist's time.

Weighing up the advantages and disadvantages, we come to the following conclusion, to which there will inevitably be exceptions. The disadvantages in 1, 4 and 5 are fairly serious and therefore we usually try to have the family come to us. The advantages in 1 and 2 are important and to exploit them we like to hold several sessions at the family's home, especially at the outset of therapy.

5.19 CO-THERAPY VERSUS SOLO THERAPY

Co-therapy—that is, two therapists operating together—has become popular as family therapy has gained ground. We are not referring to the situation where someone who is still in training is attending sessions run by an experienced therapist as an observer. Along with Minuchin (1973, 1974) we would describe such a person as a "junior therapist." In an excellent article, Van der Pas (1973) sums up the pros and cons of co-therapy, the most important advantages being as follows:

1) Two therapists see more than one.
2) The therapists feel "safer" working together.
3) They can take on different roles alternately—when the one confronts, the other can be supportive.
4) It is easier for two therapists to "model" in exercises (cf. Section 5.8.1).
5) They can serve as a model for the clients by discussing their relationship with one another.

We would agree, however, with Van der Pas that the drawbacks to this method outweigh the above advantages, only the first of which is of real value. Anything that escapes the notice of one therapist is bound to be picked up by the other, but is this advantage sufficient to justify co-therapy? Therapists can also work in a team, with one or more therapists observing the session from behind a one-way screen (cf. Papp, 1977, 1980). This allows for an even greater degree of objectivity.

The other alleged advantages are of dubious value. Working together to give each other confidence is a dangerous practice. Instead of being confronted by one therapist who is unsure of himself, the family faces two, each of whom keeps waiting for the other to take the initiative. The method is not beneficial to a therapist either, because it obviates the necessity for him to work on his own blind spots.

This last point also applies to the third "advantage." If one therapist naturally tends to be more supportive and the other more confronting, they will rapidly become established in their roles and neither will feel the need to do anything about his own shortcomings. Their repertoire will be less extensive than if each has the benefit of feedback from someone observing behind a one-way screen or someone who listens to recordings of the sessions (cf. Section 9.3).

Two therapists working together with clearly divided roles is not constructive for the therapists or the family. When one therapist is supportive and the other confronts, there is the danger that they will cancel one another out or that the members of the family will play them off against one another. Pitfalls such as this are also present if, for example, one therapist is supportive towards the wife and the other supports the husband, thereby producing coalition patterns which make further progress extremely difficult.

Point 4 (modeling) is more valid, but, as we saw in Section 5.8.1, an experienced therapist on his own can also model for different members of a family.

In theory, the model provided by the relationship between the two therapists should have an important function as far as the family is concerned. In practice, this does not always work out quite so well and the clients' interests are certainly not served by therapists' arguing with one another or becoming locked in their own power struggle.

So far we have seen that the "advantages" of co-therapy are minimal. A further drawback is that shared responsibility makes therapists hesitant about giving assignments. A directive therapist who tends to intervene a lot will sometimes let things go when working with a "slower" colleague for fear of being seen as the one who always issues directives.

A further disadvantage which is difficult to ignore is that co-therapy involves the time of two therapists as opposed to one. Not only do they conduct sessions together but between sessions they spend time deciding on strategy, ironing out differences of opinion, etc. An interesting description of the time and energy needed for co-therapy, albeit one with a different emphasis, is provided by Tilmans-Ostyn and Tijsma (1973).

In conclusion, we feel that less experienced therapists, in particular, would do well to restrict themselves to solo therapy. When they need support, advice, or feedback, they should work with members of a team behind a one-way screen or invite a colleague to sit in on a particular session. Even experienced therapists may need feedback from time to time to help them overcome their blind spots.

In certain cases, however, co-therapy can be beneficial. In Section 5.9.2 we saw how a therapist can invite co-therapists to certain sessions to act as models.

Some people consider co-therapy essential for sexual problems (cf. Masters and Johnson, 1970). A male therapist may find it difficult to gain the confidence of a female client or to act as a model for her. In such cases, co-therapy with a woman therapist is called for. The reverse also applies when a man is attempting to discuss his sexual problems with a woman therapist. However, opinions on this are divided. Some authors feel that sexual problems can be treated by a solo therapist. Prochaska and Marzilli (1973) have this to say: "While Masters and Johnson believe dual sex therapist teams are essential, we did not have the staff available for such teams. Nevertheless, we have found that individual therapists can be very effective, especially when the therapy is done with the couple together and when the couple's communicaton is encouraged towards their partner rather than towards the therapist." On the basis of our experience we would support this opinion.

5.20 THE THERAPIST'S STYLE

It is extremely difficult to write about something as elusive and subtle as a therapist's manner and the way he speaks to clients. It is further complicated by the fact that there is no such thing as a right and wrong style for family therapy.

In a sense the above typifies our own style. We try to be explicit about our doubts and uncertainties instead of searching desperately for solutions or trying to think up "good" questions to ask. This means that on a metalevel the therapist does *not* come across as hesitant and unsure of himself. It takes self-confidence to admit that you do not know something.

Despite the difficulties and unavoidable pitfalls, we would like to attempt to discuss some points of style which we consider important, by means of several postulates which overlap to a certain extent.

1) *The therapist should show clearly his concern and involvement in points which come up.* He should listen attentively, nod, and ask questions when something is not clear (cf. Cleghorn and Levin, 1973; Ivey and Moreland, 1974). The reverse happens if the therapist is over-friendly, answers before he could possibly have heard what the problem is, accepts vague chatter without comment and then changes the subject.

2) *The therapist should not be afraid of interrupting clients in order to examine what they are saying in greater depth.* This applies to both supportive and confronting interventions. At the start of therapy the

therapist should "disguise" the confrontations (cf. Section 5.10) so that he is not seen as a threat by the person concerned.

3) *The therapist should emphasize his expertise in firm but friendly terms.* This ties in with what Haley (1963) describes as the "upmanship of the therapist" and what Minuchin (1974) calls the "leader of the orchestra."

In our culture, the view that exercising authority and using it to manipulate other people is not permissible is all too prevalent. A relationship with a therapist inevitably contains authoritarian elements because one party is asking another for help. At the start of therapy, in particular, the likelihood of effecting change increases considerably if the family sees the therapist as an expert. This does not mean, however, that he should be excessively authoritarian, refuse to admit his own mistakes and ignore the opinions of members of the family. By conceding his own errors and asking for clients' views, he can make clear in a subtle way that he is sure of himself, while at the same time increasing the clients' self-esteem.

The therapist can underline his confidence in his own skill and ability by the way he gives feedback and assignments, asks the members of the family to talk to each other, presents behavior rehearsal, etc. He should exude self-confidence when making requests and suggestions. He should not ask hesitantly and apologetically: "Could you perhaps say that to each other?"; neither, of course, should he say: "Right, now you will say to each other. . .," but rather: "I would like you to say this to your husband." It is vital for the therapist to show his clients that he takes it for granted that his directives will be carried out. If clients do not want to do as he asks (for example talk to one another), he should not give in too easily. If he has made up his mind that something should be done and he has explained it, then that is what must happen, preferably without much further discussion. He can implicitly refer to his own professional expertise by saying something like: "Try it again; it is important, believe me."

Minuchin (1974) strongly believes in the therapist emphasizing his professional expertise. He will sometimes quite explicitly say that he has a great deal of experience with the very problem which is being discussed, so that his clients will trust him completely.

4) *The therapist should not be afraid to accept responsibility* (a point linked to the previous one). The fact that he sometimes knows better

than the family what is constructive and what is not means that he has to have the courage to accept responsibility for the course of events.

Gerald and Hannah Hill both had a number of extramarital relationships and were reluctant to give them up, as their relationship with one another was fairly shaky. The therapist realized that they were, in fact, very jealous of one another and they were using the extramarital partners both as an escape and as a way of hurting one another. He gave them the following option: They could carry on seeing their lovers, but only when they had resolved their differences with one another. They were, therefore, to see the other relationships as an extra rather than as a replacement. If they failed to stick to this agreement, therapy would serve no purpose and would, therefore, be discontinued. The therapist used all his powers to effect a dramatic change. He was convinced that Gerald and Hannah would never get closer if they could run away from one another at the least sign of trouble. When such possibilities exist, therapy is doomed (cf. Belz, 1969).

5) *The therapist may lay down conditions.* In the above example the conditions governed the therapist's willingness to continue treating the couple. The view that the "customer is always right as long as he is paying" is far too prevalent in many areas of mental health. As a result, therapy which is certainly doomed to failure is embarked on and is unnecessarily prolonged without any real hope of success. This situation is described in the following examples:

  (a) During the first assessment session with Mr. and Mrs. Whitehorn, it emerges that Mrs. Whitehorn has been in psychoanalysis five days a week for the past five years. Mr. Whitehorn is not happy with this state of affairs. "She discusses everything with her analyst and doesn't tell me anything," he comments tersely. Both partners want couple therapy to help them cope with serious communication problems, but the therapist refuses to help them for the time being—and rightly so, in our opinion. He is prepared to work with the couple once Mrs. Whitehorn has stopped seeing her analyst and is not prepared to discuss the matter any further until that time. He considers it his moral duty not to embark on a course of treatment which is by definition doomed to failure (cf. Section 4.3.1.11).

  (b) Mandy wants individual therapy. Her problems apparently are connected to her relationship with her husband, who is already having individual therapy. After consulting with a colleague, the therapist tells her that he will only work with husband and wife together. He wants no part of an arrangement in which each of them is "coached" by separate "trainers" for the "match" with one another.

(c) Mrs. Fox has been married for 30 years. She now has a lover, about whom her husband knows. The triangular relationship is proving difficult for her, and she wants to talk about it. Over the telephone, the therapist tells her that he wants to see her together with her husband. Mrs. Fox protests so the therapist more or less tells her to "take it or leave it." It is vital for him to see both of them—anything else would be a waste of his time. Mrs. Fox does as he asks.

(d) In the second session, the same Mrs. Fox said that she could not talk about certain matters because she had promised her friend not to. The therapist said that he had every respect for her feelings, as he was also a man of his word. In his opinion, what she was refusing to discuss was, however, absolutely crucial. He stopped the session and suggested that Mrs. Fox tell her friend that she had to be able to talk freely. If she did not do so, further sessions would be futile. In the end they agreed that the friend would come along too.

All of these examples show that the therapist can attach conditions to starting or carrying on with a therapy if he feels that a situation would otherwise develop which would prevent him from doing his job properly.

6) *The therapist should adapt his use of language to that of his clients.* This applies especially to his use of professional jargon. He should use simpler language with people who are less well-educated and can also modify the way he speaks to conform with the usage of certain subcultures. With a couple of his own age and background, he can use an informal form of address and an informal way of expressing himself, while this may be threatening to older couples. Minuchin (1974) calls this adapting "mimicry" (cf. Section 5.1.1).

7) *If the therapist finds himself in a difficult position, he should not be afraid to say so.* The following example illustrates this: After their first session, Monica telephones the therapist with all kinds of information about her husband, which she feels—probably rightly so—should be talked about. The therapist says that he himself will not raise these

points at the session. If Monica thinks that they should be discussed, she should broach the subject herself. During the first five minutes of the subsequent session, the therapist feels increasingly uncomfortable because she does not do so. He keeps thinking about the fact that Monica should be saying something and her silence on this point makes him feel powerless to proceed any further. He therefore says, "Monica, you phoned me and told me certain things. I feel uncomfortable because I don't know what to do with the information. I think you should talk to Tim about it." Everything then comes out, and a weight is lifted from the therapist's shoulders.

8) *The therapist may make value judgments but he should not impose them on his clients.* We should point out that there is a difference between value judgments and knowledge of constructive or destructive patterns of interaction. Therapists often judge things as good or strange on the basis of their own experience (cf. Minuchin, 1974). This is a dangerous practice. The therapist should always be aware of his own "hidden agenda," about which he may be open. In Section 6.3 we cite the example of the therapist who says to a husband: "I find your demand rather odd, but it is probably very important to you, and that's why you (*addressing the wife*) should take it seriously." By being frank about the fact that this is a value judgment, he in fact frees himself from it.

9) *The therapist should be able to move around.* This relates to the points we make in Section 5.12 about topographical interventions. In our view the therapist should not be too rigid about where he sits or how he is sitting. One moment he may be on the edge of his seat listening attentively, the next he may lean back in a relaxed manner. We would also point out that it may be important to touch clients; it heightens contact and bridges the gap between people. For example, we tend to touch someone's arm when we want him to stop talking for a moment.

In summary, we are clearly advocating a directive approach to family therapy. This means, on the one hand, that the therapist has to spend a great deal of time and use all the means at his disposal for structuring, intervening, and giving feedback. On the other hand, there should always be time for a certain type of behavior, such as using the informal means of address, joking, and touching, which will bring the therapist and the clients closer together. The clients' respect for the therapist should derive from the therapist's confidence in his own methods, not from formality and an authoritarian attitude.

We would like to conclude this chapter by reiterating the problems of discussing style. We have outlined our own style in general terms without by any means suggesting that it should be adopted by everyone. We simply wish to describe the principles which have led us to work as we do. What we are trying to convey was perhaps best expressed by Erickson (cf. Haley, 1967b, p. 535) when he observed: ". . .in dealing with the crucial situations of therapy, you must express yourself adequately, not as an imitation."

CHAPTER 6

Contracts and

Assignments

6.1 INTRODUCTION

Liz and Paul consulted a therapist because their marriage was threatened by escalating arguments which were marked by long periods of silence, as well as verbal and physical aggression. In the first assessment session, the therapist listed the various subjects they fought over, including bringing up the children, sex, and money.

At the end of the session, he told his clients that he thought their conflicts were caused and maintained by two mechanisms. The first was constant confusion about the content aspect and the relationship aspect of what they said to one another (cf. Section 1.5.1.1). When they disagreed about anything, they argued on the content level, overlooking the fact that the main stumbling block was which one of them should make the decisions. As a result, neither of them really paid any attention to what the other was saying because they both felt threatened with regard to both their position in the marriage and their own self-esteem. Both of them thought that, in behaving as they did, they would achieve temporary recognition from and control of the other.

The direct result of this constant power struggle was that hardly any positive remarks passed between them. On the rare occasions when this did happen, the person who made the positive remark was usually immediately squashed by the other and therefore came to occupy a weaker position in the power struggle. This also meant that positive behavior was punished rather than rewarded. In such circumstances it was not surprising that they hardly ever did or said anything that the other person found pleasant.

The therapist came to this conclusion partly on the basis of what they told him about their recent past, but more particularly from the way they responded to one another during the first session. At one point, Paul admitted that Liz had been right about something they had been quarreling about and that what he had done was wrong. Liz only responded to Paul's admission of guilt, ignoring the rest, and started laying down the law. The fact that he had made himself vulnerable by acknowledging that she was right was not rewarded—in fact, it was punished.

The second mechanism, which is present in many families, was formed by punctuation problems (cf. Section 1.5.1.2). For example, after Liz had had an unsuccessful telephone conversation with someone who was important to both of them, an escalating quarrel developed. According to Liz, Paul attacked her for handling it so badly and became angry → she became angry → Paul then became angrier, and so on. According to Paul, however, she started it. He made an extremely scathing remark about the telephone conversation → she overreacted → he became cross → she more so, and so on. This kind of vicious circle usually occurs where there are differences of opinion. It is often impossible to say where it starts and quite irrelevant to attempt to do so. The problem with Liz and Paul was that their escalating quarrels happened very frequently. Neither of them was able or willing to do anything to resolve this situation by examining the effect of his or her behavior on the other person. This was also connected with the power struggle aspect referred to earlier, which tended to dominate everything else.

In Section 1.3 we saw that problem families are usually characterized by tension between parents, often not unlike that exhibited by Liz and Paul. The parents—and sometimes the other members of the family—have become embroiled in a subtle struggle for power and have forgotten how to reward one another. They have become experts in finding ways of punishing one another. Apparently trivial problems can develop into gigantic conflicts. The family does not have the ability to solve its own problems satisfactorily.

In Section 2.2.1 we outline a number of the stages distinguished by D'Zurilla and Goldfried (1971) in which problem-solving ought to take place. Among other things, the emphasis is on brainstorming and on trying out new ideas. In problem families, the opportunities to do this are simply not present because of the defensive attitude of the members of the family and the virtual absence of channels of communication.

Any suggestion or idea from another person is regarded as a threat—to agree would be to undermine one's own position. It is at this point that negotiating *behavior contracts* becomes an important issue in which the therapist can provide a helping hand. Instead of unstructured, implicit and destructive clashes, the clients learn to make mutual expectations and wishes explicit and to honor them. In the following section, we outline a number of principles which should be taken into account by both the therapist and the members of the client family when learning how to negotiate contracts.

6.2 FROM DESTRUCTIVE INTERACTION TO BEHAVIOR CONTRACTS

Behavior contracts may be regarded as agreements reached between two or more people in which each party indicates in clear and precise terms the activities he or she plans to carry out within a given period of time (cf. Rose, 1972). The crux of this type of contract is the "quid pro quo" principle introduced by Lederer and Jackson (1968). This is based on the idea that all interactions in all relationships are characterized by the expectation, usually unconscious, that for everything you do you will get something in return.

In problem families, however, interactions are characterized by the fear of getting nothing in return. The reverse is, in fact, true: People are often punished for making sacrifices. As we saw with Liz and Paul, it becomes more and more difficult to reward one another and therefore so much easier to disregard one another's positive traits and even to respond to them in a punishing way. It is possible to arrest this vicious circle only by initiating a process of interaction which consists of mutual rewards. Rather than focusing attention on the *cause* of the destructive interactions, it is often more important to concentrate on the *effect* and to make every effort together to change the interaction processes.

At the end of the first session with Liz and Paul, the therapist had charted the various areas in which they waged their particular conflicts. Both of them expected that he would want to track down the underlying causes of all their problems. Partly for this reason, they both tried to point to the past behavior of the other as being responsible for the present situation. The therapist made it quite clear that he was not interested in the past; he told them he could help them solve their problems by focusing attention on learning a different kind of behavior and other ways of dealing with one another. After they had agreed to the suggested approach, the therapist proposed making an immediate start. He asked them to name any activity which they would like to see the other person doing in the course of the next week. Paul said that when he left for work in the morning, it annoyed him that no one waved him goodbye. It made him feel he was living in a hotel. The therapist helped him to translate this negative feeling into a positive statement of what he would like Liz to do—see him off to work in the morning. Liz said she was prepared to do so. Then it was her turn to tell him what she wanted him to do. Again it was something extremely trivial. A year before she had bought two lampshades and Paul had still not put them up. She would like him to do so during the next week. Paul said he would and so the following was agreed: During the coming week Liz would wave to Paul as he left for work on three mornings and Paul would undertake to put up the lampshades. The therapist checked to make sure that they both regarded the contract as reasonable, that is, neither felt pressured to do more than the other. Once this had been done, the agreement was sealed by writing it down.

This and other examples from the therapy involving Liz and Paul illustrate a number of principles and practical suggestions which we describe in the following sections. They are important for any therapist wishing to work with behavior contracts.

6.3 IMPORTANT POINTS ON DRAWING UP A CONTRACT

1) Wishes relating to the behavior of the other person should be expressed in *positive* terms: *Not* "she's always so annoying when I leave; I want her to be less irritating," but "her behavior in the morning annoys me; I wish she would do such and such." The critical party must come up with alternatives (cf. Section 2.2.3.1). Experience shows that many clients find it difficult to express their irritation in this way. Particularly at the beginning of therapy, therefore, the therapist will have to be very much aware of this and guide his clients in their new behavior.

2) Promises the clients make one another, particularly at the beginning, must be *concrete* and *specific*. It is not enough for the wife to ask the husband to be nicer to her. For one thing, he will never know when he has satisfactorily complied with her wishes. He may, for instance,

think he has been extremely nice, when she does not think he has. It would be more appropriate if she said something like "I would like you to kiss me when you come home from work" and/or "tell me about your day for 15 minutes when you come home." Put in such terms it sounds horribly formal and contrived, but it should be remembered that if an agreement is not sufficiently specific there are likely to be problems about whether it has been adhered to or not. This is to be avoided, especially in relationships characterized by extreme mistrust.

3) Learning to negotiate and carry out contracts is subject to certain general principles, one of the most important being the principle of "shaping" (cf. Craighead et al., 1976; Liberman, 1970). This means that the parties should work on *small attainable steps*. In order to ensure the maximum chance of success, the first contracts should not make difficult demands on the clients. This is why, in the example we gave, Liz only agreed to wave to Paul on three mornings—which seemed fair to everyone. The success of a satisfactorily completed contract is two-fold. The partners reward one another and find satisfaction in noting that different and more pleasant behavior is possible. The therapist is also likely to praise them for having done what they said they would do. As he is an important figure to both of them, they will attach a great deal of importance to his praise. The level of difficulty of their mutual demands should be gradually increased. With Liz and Paul, initially simple contracts were followed by agreements about more and more difficult and sensitive topics, such as the amount of time spent with the children, relationships with friends, and money.

The description of the contract agreement by Liz and Paul in Section 6.2 shows that in the first instance negotiations took place via the therapist ("I would like her to do such and such. . ."). He then passed on the wishes to the other partner. Although this might appear to contradict the view, which rightly prevails in therapy circles, that the clients should learn to talk to one another (cf. Section 5.6), we feel that shaping can be used successfully here too. In the first few sessions it may still be too difficult for direct negotiations to succeed. In such circumstances it makes sense for the therapist to choose to occupy a central position because it increases the chances of success. In addition, he provides an example of how such negotiations ought to be conducted. Once several successful contracts have been carried out, it is time for the therapist to withdraw gradually from the negotiating process.

Another principle which links up with shaping is that of ensuring that initially agreement focuses as much as possible on behavior which occurs every day or at least several times a week. The first contract between Liz and Paul was not ideal in this respect—Paul only needed to carry out his assignment once. The danger in such cases is that the reward effect will be minimal. If one person has to do something pleasant for the other every day, it means that the partner will have a pleasant experience every day. This increases the likelihood of breaking down the old destructive pattern. At the outset of therapy, however, it is often difficult to include a form of behavior that occurs frequently without contradicting the principle of "a small step at a time." The danger is that the contract will become too difficult.

4) We recommend—again especially at the beginning—that *contracts be put down in writing*. This reduces the chance of misunderstandings and at the same time shows how much importance the therapist attaches to them. It also increases the couple's involvement in the contract. We also recommend having the couple copy out the contract at home on a large sheet of paper and having it displayed in a place where it can easily be seen. The therapist can also underline the importance he attaches to the contract by writing down what has been agreed or by saying that he will do so when he plays back the tapes of the session. He should also touch on the agreements again during the next session. Even if serious new complications have developed during the intervening period, *he must check what has happened as regards the contract*—even if only very briefly—and what consequences this has for the continued progress of therapy.

5) Theoretically, arrangements accepted by everyone during a session should be observed. There can be two reasons for this not happening. The contract may have been too difficult, in which case the therapist will have been at fault for not keeping to the twin principles of being specific and taking small steps at a time. This can be discussed and a better contract can then be drawn up. It is also possible that the contract has not been fulfilled because one or more of the parties has not been sufficiently committed to making it work and has suddenly decided that he or she does not want to work in this manner. One way of obtaining information about this is to agree with the clients that they will *telephone* the therapist before the next session if they feel that they are failing to observe the contract or part of it. If they do not call,

but the terms of the contract are not fulfilled, the therapist can be fairly certain that there is resistance to the contract or lack of commitment; otherwise he would have heard from them.

Liz and Paul illustrate precisely the opposite of this. The day before the second session, Paul rang the therapist and told him that he had not been able to carry out part of the contract—a clip for one of the lampshades was missing and he could not buy one anywhere. The therapist thanked him for his call and felt convinced from that point that the therapy stood a good chance of success. The fact that Paul managed to communicate such a trivial piece of information merely because he had been requested to do so was indicative of the importance he attached to therapy and how much energy he was putting into it.

6) Another device the therapist working with behavior contracts can use is the *inventory* or questionnaire (cf. Knox, 1972; Stuart, 1972a,b; Appendix 1). It should be in the style of the treatment, that is, concrete and specific, and it should contain questions about areas of conflict and the wishes of the partners with regard to one another. It may also incorporate questions on the positive aspects of the relationship, such as things one partner does which the other enjoys. The questionnaire can be filled in by each member of the family separately before the first session and serve as an aid to the therapist for assessment in general, as well as in looking for problems on which he will have to work with the clients in particular.

7) *Monitoring* (cf. Section 5.3)—the systematic charting of problem behavior—is an important technique related to assignments, contracts, and questionnaires, though it is by no means essential to them.

Before attempting to change the problem behavior of one or more members of the family, it is useful to find out how often it occurs. For instance, Liz thought Paul paid too little attention to the children and Paul was prepared to work on changing this. The therapist then suggested that the first thing to do in this situation was for Liz to note systematically for a week how much time he devoted to the children. Paul gave his permission for her to do so. Once monitored, this would constitute the baseline for further arrangements. Moreover, constantly repeating these observations during the therapy could serve as accessible evaluation material for all of the parties concerned.

8) Sometimes it is difficult for the therapist *to avoid making value*

judgments. Peter was highly irritated by the way Ann tidied up "her" kitchen. She washed up everything in sight, creating as far as he was concerned an excessively clinical impression. Despite the fact that they had a dishwasher, he insisted that she should leave out a few dirty cups and saucers to create a more relaxed atmosphere. The therapist said he found it difficult to relate to Peter's desire but at the same time he made it quite clear that this did not make it less legitimate. He advised Ann to take it seriously because, whatever the reason, it was important to Peter. In fact, the couple did manage to find a satisfactory solution to this point in a short period of time.

In general, therefore, we would say that the therapist can express his own opinion or make value judgments but that he must be very careful not to force them on the clients. Only then will he serve as a good model to family members who try to force values and ideas on to one another.

9) In point 3, we described the central position which the therapist occupies in drawing up a behavior contract—especially at the beginning. He should help both partners specify their wishes with regard to one another. While he is doing this he should also make it clear that he regards the contract as very important, that he has *confidence* in the family's ability to carry it out, and that it will lead to change of a positive nature. This is often a question of style, but the therapist should not be reluctant to make use of his authority as an expert (cf. Section 5.20). If he is hesitant or unsure of himself, he is not likely to have much success with his assignments (cf. Erickson, 1971). This applies equally to assignments in contract form.

10) In order to avoid any misunderstanding, it is useful to explain the "quid pro quo" principle which underlies behavior contracts. Many people in fact interpret it in terms of "if you keep your part of the bargain, then so will I." In so doing, they place responsibility for their own assignment with the other person. It is therefore important that clients understand that, in practice, quid pro quo boils down to "I do one thing *and* you do another." If one person fails to discharge his or her responsibilities, that is no reason for the other to default.

11) Again, to avoid complications of the kind described in point 10, it is best, particularly in the early stages of therapy, to include two tasks which have *nothing to do with one another* in a behavior contract. Then

there can be no question of *mutual dependence*. That was unfortunately the case with John and Nel. At her request they had agreed to go out to dinner and Nel was to provide special wine. However, John did not keep his part of the bargain, which meant that Nel was unable to undertake hers.

12) If it seems as if one of the partners is undertaking a more difficult assignment than the other, the therapist should point this out and ask the person concerned if he or she still wishes to do it. This eliminates the danger that the person will privately feel discriminated against and therefore become less motivated. If the discrepancy between the two assignments is considered too great, then the contract can still be revised.

13) An important principle is contained in the expression *transfer of change*, which refers to applying what has been achieved during therapy sessions in general terms in everyday life. In the early stage of therapy, clients will only be able to make contracts with one another and do as they have agreed under the supervision of the therapist. Gradually, however, they will have to learn to work out attainable and satisfactory solutions to conflicts without the therapist's help. Once they learn to do this, we can speak of transfer of change and the end of the therapy is in sight.

In Section 5.16 we described in broad outline how the therapist can encourage this process of generalization. As far as contracts are concerned, this means applying a number of principles described above in reverse. For instance, the steps can be made bigger and bigger (point 3), or the contracts can gradually become less and less specific as long as they are still precise enough to prevent misunderstandings (point 2). Towards the end of therapy, it is a good idea to discontinue writing down what has been agreed (point 4). This gives the partners a greater sense of their own responsibility. Telephoning when someone fails to carry out an agreement should also be scrapped (point 5). During the sessions, the clients can be given the opportunity to resolve existing problems *themselves* and in so doing to work out contracts. In time it will also be possible for the therapist to cut down his interventions to a minimum (point 7). We regard this as one of the most important ways of bringing about transfer of change.

During one of the last sessions with Liz and Paul—they had been cut back from once a week to once a month—an acute problem emerged.

Paul had become intensely irritated with Liz's drinking and this had led to a serious fight. Liz denied that she drank too much. The therapist did not go into the problem in detail, but simply asked whether they had talked to one another after the quarrel. Apparently they had not. The therapist then asked them to tackle the problem there and then. Paul reformulated the problem and asked Liz if she wanted to work on it. His main problem was that he had actually no idea of precisely how much she drank. Liz suggested she should make a note of the quantity and Paul responded by agreeing not to broach the subject in the presence of the children. He also agreed that when he did talk about it, he would not do so in an aggressive way. The therapist asked them to leave it at that and to work out the precise details themselves at home. If this had emerged in one of the earlier sessions, the therapist would have helped them to be specific about it and would have asked them to write things down. Now he deliberately chose to give them the responsibility both for drawing up the contract and for carrying it out.

6.4 POSSIBLE APPLICATIONS

The fact that we have referred repeatedly to Liz and Paul might suggest that the behavior contract is primarily suited to couple therapy. We would, however, emphasize that all of the techniques and principles we have described apply equally to the treatment of families and other natural groups (cf. Lange and Van der Hart, 1973). Being specific about mutual expectations and carrying out the wishes of another person are assignments which are in no way restricted to partner relationships.

We can illustrate this with an example of a behavior contract between a child and his parents. Simon, age eight, was referred by his parents to a child guidance center because he was very introverted and would not talk about what he did at school or with his friends. With the help of the therapist, he managed to put into words during the first session, which everyone attended, how annoying it was for him that his parents asked him every day when he came home what he had done at school. He would prefer no questions then. He had no objections to their asking about school while they were eating dinner. He would then be prepared to say a lot more on his own initiative. But there was more to it than this. The problems with Simon were related to problems in the relationship between the parents and these too were tackled in the way described above.

6.5 TREATMENT CONTRACTS

In any type of relationship, being specific about wishes and arrangements reduces uncertainty. People know where they stand with one another, at least on certain points. We have already described the importance we attach to this for the relationships between members of a family, but we should not lose sight of the fact that it also makes things clearer between the therapist and his clients. This is something which must be brought about as early as possible in the treatment—particularly in the interests of the family members. They are in a strange situation, having not the slightest idea of how the therapist is going to label the problems, how he intends to tackle them, and what he expects from them. The therapist is in a much stronger position. He knows how he is going to try to obtain insight into the precise nature of the problems and the amount of effort the members of the family will have to put into solving them. He knows his own methods and how he will try and communicate his ideas. In our view it is vital that the family's uncertainties about the therapist should be removed as soon as possible. It is, therefore, up to him from the very first session to make clear what they can expect from him. In order to do so, he will first have to make an inventory of the current problems in concrete terms without going into any one of them in detail. It is wise for the therapist to structure the listing of the problems (cf. Section 4.3.2).

During an assessment session, it is also advisable for the therapist to make his own style and principles as clear as possible. If he usually tends to interrupt quickly when irrelevant remarks are made, he should not avoid doing so. If he is used to dealing with problems in concrete behavioral terms, he should not be satisfied with vague descriptions which cannot be observed. He can show from the very first session whether he is less interested in the *causes* of individual problem behavior (which usually means placing the blame on someone else) than the *effect* that behavior has on others.

The following incident which occurred during the ninth session with Liz and Paul illustrates the importance of being frank and open with clients as soon as possible. At one point Paul wanted to recount a lengthy anecdote; when the therapist interrupted him, Paul looked at him in dismay. Suddenly the expression on his face changed and he said, "You're quite right and you warned me at the beginning that you would interrupt me when you wanted to." By interrupting, the therapist had not reneged on an implicit contract; he had, in fact, done the reverse—what he was doing was part of an explicit arrangement with the client.

In addition to the short summaries in rounds, as we described in Section 4.3.2, it is important at the end of the first session for the therapist to give his overall impression of the composition of the family and the problems with which it is faced. He can at the same time indicate how he proposes working with them and what his strategy will be. He can then check with the various members of the family that they agree to work in the suggested manner, even if this requires considerable effort on their part. If they agree, they can in turn be assured of maximum commitment on the part of the therapist.

By making his position clear, the therapist is complying with a fundamental principle of human relationships—that people have the right to know where they stand with one another. There must be no uncertainty on the part of the clients and at the same time they must make their position clear to the therapist. They are presented with a choice of accepting his methods, by means of which the treatment contract is drawn up (possibly in writing), or of rejecting them. Presenting them with alternatives can be particularly important when the therapist's interpretation of the situation does not wholly correspond to that of one or more of the clients.

During the first therapy session with a couple, of which the husband was the identified patient, the therapist devoted considerable attention to the way husband and wife behaved towards one another. At the end of the session he told them that in order to treat the man's symptoms, it would be necessary to work on interactions between the two of them. The idea that the husband was not simply the patient, but that their relationship as a whole would be the focal point of attention surprised them, but nonetheless they accepted it. This brings us to another advantage of this approach. Once clients have explicitly promised to cooperate on a particular strategy or approach, their effort increases. Finally, as part of the treatment contract it is often useful during the first session to create a frame of reference with the clients concerning the length of treatment. Naturally this will vary considerably from case to case, but the therapist can always refer to his experience and mention how long he has needed to treat similar problems in the past. At the same time, a decision can be made to evaluate progress after four sessions. On the basis of this both parties can decide whether they wish to carry on.

6.6 CHANGING TREATMENT CONTRACTS

On several occasions we have referred to the need for the therapist to be explicit at an early stage about his method and the strategy of treatment. We would, however, also like to emphasize the fact that it will not always be possible or desirable during the first few sessions for the therapist to tell the clients everything about the course therapy is likely to take.

In this connection Rose (1972) refers to "successive structuring" as a way in which the therapist can gradually explain his approach to clients. The demands on them can be modified to suit the stage of treatment which has been reached. Such an approach is recommended in families where one or more people have serious individual complaints.

Aponte and Hoffman (1973) describe how Minuchin structures gradually, using the example of a family in which the daughter, age 12, is suffering from anorexia nervosa. Despite being convinced that the girl's symptoms are closely bound up with the structure of the family, and in particular with the relationship between the mother and the father, Minuchin begins by focusing attention on the girl's symptoms. This is ostensibly dangerous since it means going along with the family's idea of the girl as the "patient," but Minuchin justifies his approach as follows. It would be unacceptable to the parents if the therapist, confronted with such an obvious and acute problem, did not devote considerable attention to it during the first session. The parents first have to be won over by the therapist, which would not happen if he turned his attention to them from the outset. This does not mean, however, that he should concentrate exclusively on the child. By examining the relationship between the child and parents at a relatively early stage, he at least makes it clear to them that the problem cannot simply be solved by focusing on the child. It does mean, however, that an essential part of his strategy—trying to change the relationship between the parents—can only be implemented at a later stage. The contract on that is negotiated later.

Successive structuring is also appropriate with problem families from lower socioeconomic groups with relatively little education. There is not much point in the therapist's explaining his expectations and all the details of his strategy at the outset—to do so would probably confuse them and reduce their motivation. In such cases it is best to operate on the principle of small steps at a time (point 3). The therapist can gradually make his requirements more demanding and adapt them to the stage of treatment which has been reached. To begin with it will be sufficient to require all the members of the family involved in the therapy to be present and to accept the suggested procedures. Once the first few sessions have increased motivation, the therapist can widen the first treatment contract, for example by means of homework assignments. In this way he can make explicit at each stage of treatment what his demands are in relation to the effort required from the clients and their motivation.

In summary, we have described three approaches to treatment contracts which are by no means mutually exclusive. We recommend, generally speaking, that as soon as possible, clients should be offered a provisional treatment contract which incorporates as clearly as possible the therapist's ideas, principles, and style. This means that fewer things will come as a surprise at a later stage. The approach suggested by Zuk (1972) can be put into effect in combination with this by announcing after the drawing up of the first provisional contract (usually a vague one) that a final version will be concluded after the fourth session. In cases such as those described by Rose (1972) and Minuchin (1974), in which the therapist has to maneuver with extreme caution, it may be best to begin by making relatively simple demands and then gradually increasing their scope and difficulty.

6.7 REFLECTION

In this chapter we have concerned ourselves with the practical aspects of behavior and treatment contracts. Particularly as regards behavior contracts, we can understand that many people may wonder if problems can really be solved using this method. Is it not very contrived to extort agreements this way? Is it justified to teach people the quid pro quo idea? Does not that lead to a considerable loss of spontaneity and freedom? We do not think so. Thibaut and Kelley (1959), in their enlightening book about social interaction, emphasize the "reward and cost" idea which corresponds more or less to our quid pro quo. Their numerous experimental studies have all shown that social actions are always preceded by a sort of profit/loss analysis (cf. Donnenwerth & Foa, 1974). Behavior which produces loss eventually rather than profit (both in the widest possible sense) will disappear at a certain moment. It is, therefore, realistic for members of a family to calculate explicitly what they are going to get out of their relations with one another and what it is going to cost them in return.

It is precisely on this point that many problem families are deficient. They seem to exist only thanks to all kinds of suppressed or wrongly worded desires or recriminations. It is therefore important for the therapist to help the family members express their distorted and suppressed wishes as clearly, explicitly, and constructively as possible, so that all of them are aware of what is expected of them and the kind of effort they will have to make. By entering into contracts, they learn this once more in a nonthreatening atmosphere that increases the chance of mutual rewards. It is much easier to invest energy in meeting the wishes of someone else if that other person is prepared to do the same. Certainly, to begin with, this appears to be anything but spontaneous, but it does result in breaking down a destructive circular process. In due course, the new behavior starts to lead a life of its own and this raises the level of spontaneity.

Even though the quid pro quo principle lies at the root of behavior contracts, it is not necessary for both partners to have a part in behavior contracts at every stage of treatment. In later stages in particular, one of the parties often responds positively to the other's wishes without feeling the need to demand something immediately in return. One-sided contracts are therefore important, too. After all, the idea is not for people to spend the rest of their lives negotiating. Sometimes it is important to do something for somebody else without being rewarded (cf. Section 2.2.4.2 about self-perception theory). Lepper, Greene, and Nisbett (1973) argue in favor of this on the basis of an experiment which has become something of a classic and has been repeated subsequently with many variations (cf. Anderson et al., 1976; Deci, 1975; Lepper and Greene, 1975; Zeegers, 1977a). Lepper et al. asked two groups of children to carry out a painting task, knowing in advance that this was something the children enjoyed doing. One group was promised a substantial reward, the other was not. For the next two weeks they observed how much effort the children put into their painting activities. As expected, the children who had not been promised a reward exploited the material at their disposal much better than the others. The authors concluded that the reward was a kind of "overjustification." The children had enjoyed painting beforehand but the large reward that was promised led to the new self-perception: "I use this material because I am rewarded and not because I like it."

The experiments conducted by Lepper and others are important in connection with behavior contracts. Receiving a reward every time one does something for one's partner can result in viewing oneself and the relationship with one's partner in a less positive light than if no reward were offered. The experiments suggest, however, that this reasoning only applies when there is intrinsic motivation. This implies that a one-sided contract works only if people enjoy doing things for one another. In the early stages of therapy this is not often the case, which is why contracts involving both parties are then extremely important.

Objections to reciprocal behavior contracts are often formulated in terms of ideas of freedom, according to which people should be taught to be themselves ("free," in other words) in all circumstances and to stand up for themselves. The reward/cost idea, the object of which is a constant search by both parties for an optimal state of equilibrium in the relationship, conflicts with this. However, the type of freedom suggested above is, in our view, completely fictitious. When people enter into a lasting relationship with one or more other people, they do indeed lose a measure of their freedom in the sense that they constantly have to consult one another in order to maintain a fair balance within the relationship. This leads to a situation in which people are explicit about their wishes in relation to one another and can also lay down explicit limits governing the extent to which they are able to meet the wishes of others. Only when this has been done would we speak of freedom.

CHAPTER 7

The Present,

the Past, and Rituals

7.1 INTRODUCTION

In Section 5.17 we cited the example of a couple, Mr. and Mrs. Wells, where the wife was the identified patient because of sexual problems. It soon emerged during therapy that the difficulties sprang from the resentment she felt towards her husband because of his adultery with her sister. The interactions between husband and wife were colored by thoughts and feelings bound up with this past event.

The majority of examples we give in this book concern topics which center on the present and the future. We usually work on communication problems which play a role during the current life stage of the clients, adhering to the principle of concentrating on the here and now. The therapist will often be justified in applying the rule of "not discussing the past," especially when the past is simply being used by one partner to make accusations against the other (cf. Section 2.2.3.5). However, if application of this principle means that the therapist pays no attention whatsoever to his clients' past experiences, it can have dangerous consequences.

Often something like the adultery referred to above, although it supposedly belongs to the past, is by no means over and done with. It is still so much alive for one or more members of the family that in cognitive and emotional terms it is a real feature of the present.

Lange (1977c) describes a particular couple therapy which was in danger of failing because the therapist spent too long dealing only with the interactions between the partners in the present. To begin with, there was no discussion of the feelings of aggression which the wife had for her father as a result of what had happened in the distant past. Only after she had managed to overcome her resentment by talking things out with her father (cf. Framo, 1976) was it possible to proceed with the rational problem-solving method described here.

The past can play a role in two ways in family therapy. Sometimes there is resentment between two or more members of a family (as with the Wells couple), and sometimes there are unresolved problems with someone outside the nuclear family, for example a (deceased) parent, grandparent, sibling, former partner, or employer. In this chapter we describe various ways of making the past alive and real again and of settling unresolved issues. Symbolic actions and rituals play an important part in this process.

7.2 WRITING A LETTER TO THE PERSON IN QUESTION

Mr. and Mrs. White had begun couple therapy. Time and again they kept coming back to the same problems: Mr. White felt that his wife did not give him enough support and failed to show affection when he most needed it. Mrs. White claimed that he was exaggerating and, while she did love him, she could not show affection on command. In other words, her husband's behavior was causing her to be unaffectionate. However, their problems had other aspects in addition to the vicious circle of their interaction with one another. Mr. White was preoccupied with what other people thought of him. He looked for support and understanding everywhere and was bitterly disappointed and became very emotional when he did not get it. The therapist decided to devote attention to this individual aspect within the framework of couple therapy. When he asked Mr. White about his parents and his relationship with them, Mr. White broke down and tearfully described the resentment he felt towards his father, who had never taken him seriously and had always made fun of his (sexual) problems. His father still made him feel he knew best, and that he, Mr. White, was a fool.

Once all this had been explained, the therapist told Mr. White to write his father a letter in the coming week. The letter was to be written in stages—half an hour every evening. Mr. White was not to disguise his aggression in any way—he was to be perfectly frank—but he was not to mail the letter.

Mr. White did as instructed and at the next session reported a tremendous feeling of relief. The first few days he had written a great deal and had been very angry, but now his anger was gradually subsiding and he was beginning to understand his own contribution to the interactions with his father. The problem, however, was not yet completely cleared up. The therapist, therefore, asked him to write a second letter telling his father what was worrying him, but in a more subtle way, without sounding accusing. In the letter he was also to emphasize that they still had a chance to improve their relationship.

Mr. White agreed, even though he was afraid that his father would be shocked and hurt. The letter was written and mailed the following week. Mr. White senior was very pleased with his son's letter. He had felt for some time that there was something wrong, but had not known how to broach the subject. As a result of the letter the relationship between father and son deepened and intensified.

To the best of our knowledge Bowen (cf. Anonymous, 1972) was the first person to advocate writing letters to other members of the family in order to clear up problems. Bowen thinks that these letters, often different letters to various members of the family at the same time, should always be mailed. In our view this is not always necessary. Sometimes the mere act of writing can be so cathartic that it enables the past to be buried and forgotten. Thus, even writing letters to deceased relatives (or other relevant people), who will naturally never receive them, can in itself be extremely beneficial.

Writing to someone outside the family may be approached in several ways. It is sometimes useful to ask the client to write different letters—an aggressive one, a pleasant one, and a neutral one, for example—and then to choose which should be sent. It may, however, be better, as in Mr. White's case, to start with one type of letter, on which the client must work every day (Rubinstein, 1977). The exact instructions, which differ from case to case, should be drawn up with the client (cf. Section 7.4.2.1).

7.3 CONVERSATIONS WITH THE PERSON
    IN QUESTION

Writing letters as described above is often the first step towards resolving matters from the past which are taking up a lot of energy. If, however, this is not sufficient to clear up the problems completely, it is often advisable to arrange a talk between the client and the person in question. We should now like to describe three ways in which this can be done.

7.3.1 Meetings with the therapist present

Framo (1976) describes how he draws up a treatment contract with the clients during the first session which stipulates that, if the therapist considers it necessary, the clients' parents or grandparents will attend at least one session. This clause in the contract ensures that Framo can be present at talks between adult clients and one or more parents.

Even if this type of provision has not been included in the treatment contract, the therapist is free to suggest inviting a parent to a number of sessions. He can then help client and parent to express their feelings about the past in a positive way without reverting to recriminations.

7.3.2 Meetings at which the therapist is not present

Clients usually do not want to involve their relatives, but this is not necessarily a reason for deciding against it. If the therapist is convinced of the importance of involving a sibling or parent, he can usually persuade his clients to bring the person in question to a session. This, however, is not always necessary. A good alternative is for the client to talk to the parent alone. The therapist's job then is to "coach" the client by discussing in advance how he or she should go about it, starting with instructions on the best way of broaching the subject. For example, it is better to telephone the parent in question to make an appointment rather than waiting until a suitable opportunity presents itself. The dramatic emphasis of a special appointment increases the chances of success. The therapist will also instruct the client on how to conduct the talk itself. The client must ensure that both he and the parent feel free to talk about what is bothering them without becoming involved in futile debates and accusations. In short, the client should attempt to put the newly acquired principles of communication (cf. Section 2.2.3) into practice.

When instructions alone are not enough, role-playing in which the therapist plays the part of the parent or relative is a useful aid. Most clients are apprehensive about talking to a parent. Our experience, however, is that such talks not only work out better than expected on the whole, but that they almost always produce a great sense of liberation and relief for both parties and often prove to be the beginning of a better relationship.

7.3.3 Imaginary conversations

Sometimes resentment and other unresolved emotions relate to someone who is no longer alive. Writing letters can then provide a solution and disposing of them in some way can be used as a leave-taking ritual (cf. Section 7.4). In such cases imaginary conversations can also be conducted.

The client pretends that the deceased person (for example, his father) is sitting with him. He starts talking to him. The therapist may decide to play the role of the father and answer the client from time to time, giving him the opportunity of going on. The client can also play the part of the father and change seats according to the role he is playing. This Gestalt-like approach (cf. Passons, 1975; Kempler, 1974) is difficult for some clients, but when it works it is highly effective.

7.4 RITUALS

7.4.1 Introduction

We discussed above a number of ways in which clients can express unresolved feelings from the past in relation to other people or events. The objective is for the client to come to terms with these feelings and rid himself of the oppressive elements involved. We now go on to give a more detailed account of one of the most effective means of liberating oneself from the burden of people or events from the past, the ritual. Rituals are not only effective in leave-taking. There are a number of other areas where devising and prescribing a ritual are indicated.

First we need to define the term itself. Selvini Palazzoli (1974) who uses "rituals for the whole family" describes it thus: "A family ritual is an action or a series of actions, accompanied by verbal formulae and involving the entire family. Like every ritual it must consist of a regular sequence of steps taken at the right time and in the right place" (p. 238). In our view this definition omits the essential character of the ritual, which consists of symbolic actions. We therefore prefer Van der

Hart's (1983) definition, which is that rituals are prescribed symbolic acts which must be performed in a certain manner and a specified order, and may or may not be accompanied by verbal formulae. Apart from the formal aspects, the ritual contains an element of emotional experience. The ritual is performed with great involvement; where this is not so, we are dealing with an "empty ritual."

We consider rituals to be symbolic actions which serve to define social relationships, roles, and status, and which can also alter these definitions.

7.4.2 One-time rituals: rites of passage

Generally speaking, there are two types of rituals in therapy—those which are performed once, and those which are *repeated* (cf. Section 7.4.3).

The aim of a one-time ritual is often to enable a family or individual to make the transition from one phase of the life cycle to the next (cf. Section 1.6). Sometimes they serve to correct previously unsuccessful transitions. A leave-taking ritual, for example, often has the function of enabling an interrupted process of mourning for a member of the family to be resumed and concluded (cf. Ramsay, 1977; Raapis Ding-man, 1975).

The function of one-time rituals in therapy can be compared with that of the traditional *rites of passage* in certain cultures. Our own culture does not have many traditional rituals apart from those at marriage and death. Where therapeutic rituals are intended to correct previously unsuccessful transitions, we may compare them with the healing rituals prevalent in many cultures (cf. Kiev, 1964).

Van Gennep (1909; cf. Van der Hart, 1983) established that most transition rituals are characterized by the following order: separation → transition → reconciliation. Each phase is accompanied by different rites. At a burial, separation dominates, at a marriage ritual, reunion is the most important factor, and at initiation rites the element of transition is essential.

7.4.2.1 Leave-taking rituals

Leave-taking rituals, in particular, are very useful in therapy (cf. Van der Hart and Ebbers, 1981) and enable the separation to be effected in a prescribed symbolic manner. This can be approached in two ways.

The first is based on carrying out certain actions with an object which symbolizes the relationship with the person or situation involved—for example, a wedding ring, a piece of furniture, or a photograph. The unique situation and characteristics of the client are always considered when working out the details. The method can perhaps best be illustrated by the two following examples.

(a) Selvini Palazzoli et al. (1974) describe a leave-taking ritual in which a *burial* was the central symbolic event. A family with a small daughter, Marella, age two and a half, had a second child, a boy, who was born with an incurable illness. The parents decided not to tell Marella about his arrival. She responded by eating less and less and this became even more pronounced when the baby died and the parents stopped visiting the hospital.

The therapists treating the family advised the parents to tell Marella the truth and to perform a related ritual. The father was to explain in a simple way that her little brother had died and been buried, and that they would have to bury his clothes too. The ritual was performed as follows: The family went into the garden and the father dug a hole in which the mother slowly laid the baby clothes one by one. Marella carefully placed a pair of shoes on top. The experience was as moving for the parents as the real funeral. The father filled in the hole and concluded the ritual by planting a tree. Marella started eating again the same day. The following day she talked a great deal about her baby brother. Some time after Marella's symptoms had disappeared the parents sought help in their relationship with the father's family.

(b) Van der Hart (1983) describes the leave-taking ritual of José, 34, a divorced mother of three children. The departure of her husband three years previously had left a big gap in the family (cf. Peck, 1974) and José was neglecting her parental role as a result. The children had started playing the role of parents and she was behaving like a child who needed to be cared for. The therapist suggested performing a leave-taking ritual to help José come to terms with the loss of her husband. The ritual was to consist of two parts: The first involved José's tearing up a particular letter from her former husband and solemnly burning the pieces. The letter, which had been written shortly after the couple's divorce, suggested that the husband might eventually return, which had only given José false hope. The second part of the proposed ritual was to consist of José's melting down her wedding ring into an attractive piece of jewelry that would at the same time have a symbolic meaning for José's future.

The second part of the ritual was modified because José realized at the jeweler's that melting the ring down was not the best solution. She knew that she had to get rid of it. She exchanged the ring for two tiny gold shoes, which symbolized the long and arduous road ahead and the difficulties she was determined to overcome. Her life was in fact very difficult for some time, but the ritual helped her cope with a major impasse.

The second way of performing a leave-taking ritual is by creating a ritual framework within which the writing of one or more *farewell letters* occupies a central position and is followed by some sort of *closing ceremony*. Rubinstein (1977) has ritualized the assignment as follows: The client has to sit down at the same time and in the same place every day and write for at least an hour. He must have a photograph of the person to whom he is writing in front of him. If he runs out of ideas or does not dare to write something down, he has to remain seated. He does not have to force himself to write but he may not get up. He starts each session by reading through what he has already written. He is allowed to repeat himself to emphasize an important point. After a while, the client will realize that he has written down everything which is important, and he can then finish and sign off. Ritualizing the letter-writing assignment means creating a fixed framework in which it takes place. Within the framework, symbols are used which accentuate the special nature of the assignment—for example, the table with the photograph or the part of the room which is used only for writing the letter. A closing ceremony can be added if necessary.

Van der Hart and Van Dijck (1977) cite the example of Martin, a young man who was writing farewell letters to his deceased parents as part of grief therapy. When he had almost completed the letters, he was instructed to burn them and bury the ash by his parents' graves. He was then to undergo a "cleansing ritual," whereby he would shower his whole body thoroughly, go to town and buy new clothes, and then take his girlfriend out for dinner—as a ritual of reunion. The therapist gave him only general instructions. Although Martin had been skeptical about the value of the suggested procedure before he started writing the letters, he subsequently found the whole ritual meaningful and necessary to bring his mourning to an end.

7.4.2.2 A cleansing ritual

Although a transition ritual always has something to do with disengaging oneself from the past, the emphasis need not necessarily be placed exclusively on that aspect. Below are two examples.

The first concerns a young couple, Jan and Anneke (cf. Van der Hart, 1983). Although they were married, they had not managed to build up an adult marital relationship. They both seemed to have stronger relationships with their parents than with each other. They were somewhat hesitant in their sexual relations—for example, neither dared to take the initiative in making love, which meant that in spite of their both wanting to, they seldom had intercourse.

The presenting symptom was Jan's compulsive cleanliness. He spent hours every day washing himself and cleaning objects in the home. He performed these activities alone, when Anneke was in another room watching television or reading.

In the first place, only the presenting problem was tackled, but this behavioral approach failed, as it had done on a previous occasion. Jan said that he was unable to monitor, exaggerate, or decrease his symptomatic behavior, and he failed to carry out his assignments.

The therapist decided, therefore, to place the symptoms within a ritual context. He told Jan and Anneke that in certain cultures important transitions in the life of a family or individual are often accompanied by a cleansing ritual. He explained that they were going through the transition from childhood to being a young married couple and that Jan was trying to complete the transition with his ritual washing. The therapist told them that the ritual was not quite right yet or it would not keep coming back to bother them and prevent them completing the transition. This was probably because Jan was performing the ritual alone, when it was something they should be doing together. He proposed that during the coming week Jan and Anneke should think deeply about the transition to an adult relationship and should try and become aware of their feelings for one another. They would then automatically know the right moment for their cleansing ritual. They were to soap each other carefully and thoroughly under the shower, after which they would rinse and dry one another. Then they were to leave the shower and "be together" in a way that gave them both pleasure.

Two weeks later they reported that they had performed the ritual. They had not done everything they had been instructed, because they had started late in the evening, after they had been out for dinner together (a new development). "That's why what you meant—that we should have sex after the shower—did not happen, but it did a couple of times afterwards," they said. Subsequent discussions revealed that Jan and Anneke had indeed made the transition. They went out together more often, saw their friends more and their parents less. Their sexual relationship improved and, although Jan's compulsive washing had not disappeared, it could now easily be treated with behavior therapy. He was capable of assuming the responsibility for changing his own behavior.

7.4.2.3 A ritual for spoiled children

In the previous example, the therapist used an action with which both partners were familiar—namely showering. For the purpose of the ritual both the context and the nature of the action were changed. Jan and Anneke showered together, instead of alone as they would usually have done. In the example cited by Van der Velden (1978), use is also made of an existing habit.

The family in question had ill-behaved children who lit fires in the bathroom and were unable to amuse themselves. They ate badly with the result that the evening meal had become a particular ordeal for the parents (cf. Section 7.4.3). The children's poor appetites were apparently the result of eating too many sweets. The therapist had the impression that the parents also enjoyed sweet foods. After a great deal of thought, he came up with the following advice: "Tonight, Mrs. Field, you will cook roast beef, potatoes, and string beans, but only for yourself and your husband. The children will be given a completely different meal—chocolates, potato chips, licorice and toffees, and instead of milk, coke. You will then say to them, 'Children, your father and I feel that the eating habits in this house leave much to be desired. You eat nothing but chocolate cake and cookies and your father and I eat too many potato chips and peanuts. This is not doing any of us any good, and that's why we've given you this strange meal. Enjoy it, because after this we're going to eat properly.' "

The mother, as the more articulate of the two, was to say this, but the father was to add that he agreed with her entirely.

The parents felt highly motivated to perform the ritual. Three weeks later they returned, elated, "I feel as though I've been born again," Mrs. Field said. They had done as agreed, but the elder son, age 10, wanted meat, beans, and potatoes instead of sweets. The younger boy, age eight, had eaten about five potato chips, looked around in bewilderment, thrown away the sweets, and asked for ordinary food.

The problems cleared up immediately and supper became the most pleasant part of the day. The parents stopped eating junk food. Cookies and chocolate cake were banned and their place was taken by bread, milk and fruit, with only occasional sweets. Mr. Field had even prepared an elaborate and delicious meal for his wife. The transition also had more positive effects: The parents managed to solve the other problems with the children on their own, and further guidance proved unnecessary.

7.4.2.4 Indications

So far we have described one-time rituals. The writing of the farewell letter is possibly the easiest to prescribe because the clients can decide on the content themselves. The indications for a farewell letter have been dealt with in Sections 7.1 and 7.2. Ritualizing the assignment only serves to increase its effectiveness.

Generally speaking, a one-time ritual is indicated where the problems can be regarded as transition problems. The ritual is an effective aid in helping the client make the transition to the new phase. There are, of course, problems which do not fit so neatly into that category. It is then a question of whether the therapist has the imagination to relabel the complaints to transition problems and to think up an appropriate ritual.

A ritual is not, however, necessary in all such cases. Sometimes a minimum of guidance is needed to help a family with transition problems through a crisis if they have sufficient problem-solving ability which can be evoked during therapy. Paul and Martine, for example, sought help when the tension of Martine's pregnancy became too much for Paul. Martine had badly wanted a child, and Paul had let her have her way, even though he did not consider himself ready to be a father. This resistance to fatherhood came out during the pregnancy. He touched her less and less, and as the arrival of the child drew nearer, he said that he did not want to be present at the birth, even though Martine felt she needed him.

During couple therapy the therapist placed the emphasis on direct conversations between Paul and Martine. This enabled both of them to express their feelings, wishes, and ideas about pregnancy, the approaching birth, and their changing situation. At home such a discussion would have ended quickly because of the frustration it evoked. In therapy, they were encouraged to go on. One of the consequences was that Paul was able to give Martine the support she needed during childbirth. After the birth he sent the therapist a card which read, "All three of us worked very hard!" A while later Paul and Martine made an appointment for several sessions to discuss the part each of them was to play in caring for their child. As soon as they indicated that they could organize this themselves, therapy was terminated.

In our view families with an enmeshed structure (cf. Minuchin, 1974; Hoffman, 1975) qualify particularly for a therapeutic ritual. A transition requires a change of "rules," a new definition of relationships, and a change of roles—in short, a complete transformation of the structure of the family (Minuchin, 1974). This type of family is hardly (if ever) capable of tackling all of these aspects and a family ritual can then prove exactly the right way of making everything fall into place. The therapist does not talk about changing the "rules" but gives the family an assignment which involves adhering to a new set of rules. The aim of the ritual is to maintain cohesion and eliminate confusion, and it is therefore generally seen as nonthreatening compared with other interventions. Rituals instigate and accompany a transition in the life cycle of the family, but at the same time they stabilize family life.

7.4.3 Repeated rituals

Transitions *between* the stages of the life cycle can be ritualized, as we have seen, but rituals also take place within one particular stage (cf. Bossard and Boll, 1950). There are, for example, set ways of putting children to bed, coming home from work, spending Saturday evening, or celebrating Christmas. A family meal can be a formalized occasion in which every gesture and sequence of events has symbolic value, so that we can then speak of a "family ritual." The ritualizing of such events serves to preserve the homeostasis *within* a stage of development of a family. It means that the continual conflict about the "rules" (who decides what on this occasion) is avoided and that the members of a family enjoy being together.

Family rituals can also be experienced as the constraints of convention—especially when they represent the feelings and opinions of only a minority in the family. This can be seen in family rituals which are connected to religion. The Stavast family, consisting of parents and three children, always went to church on Sunday morning, after which they had breakfast together. This was the parents' way of putting their faith across to their children. It was a communal activity which united the family and was continued even when the children no longer saw the point of it and wanted to spend Sunday mornings in a different way. When they communicated this to their parents, the atmosphere in the family became strained and conflicts arose.

7.4.3.1 Changing an existing ritual

In some problem families it can be useful to alter certain daily rituals or to ritualize family responsibilities. An example of the first is provided by the Holdans, a family with children of school age. Mr. Holdan's position in the family is solely that of breadwinner—he does hardly anything else. His wife and children form a coalition against him. The therapist directs the mother and father to put the children to bed together. The details of a ceremony are carefully worked out. Although the father wants no part of it, on the grounds that "the children will not cooperate anyway," he soon begins to enjoy it and his wife and children appreciate his participation more and more.

7.4.3.2 Ritualizing family tasks

Some families have difficulty agreeing on a fair division of household duties and how they are to be carried out. Every time a particular task comes up there is an argument. In families with small children a frequent complaint is that there is stress when the father arrives home from work. He wants time to himself to read the newspaper, while the mother wants him to occupy the children so that she can get on with the cooking.

Early morning is the worst time for the Taylors (cf. Van der Hart, 1976). The family consists of Sally, 28, Patrick, 29, and their daughter, Jennifer, three and a half. Sally is the "identified patient," owing to compulsive cleanliness. The more tense she is, the more her symptoms bother her. The causes of tension are discovered by using a monitoring assignment (cf. Section 5.3). One source of daily annoyance is Patrick's laziness in getting up in the mornings. Sally gets up first and spends a great deal of time washing herself. She then gets Jennifer up and feeds her. In between she tries to rouse Patrick. She does not have the time to have breakfast herself, which in turn irritates Patrick, who would like all three of them to sit down together at the breakfast table. His getting up late, however, makes this impossible.

In four sessions they work on ritualizing this part of the day. They agree that during the week Sally will wake Patrick once at 7:30. Patrick is to get up between a quarter and five to eight, and at a quarter past eight they are to sit down to breakfast together. Sally gets up earlier because she needs so long to wash and dress. She is able to cut down this time gradually with the help of specific instructions. At a later stage the breakfast itself is also ritualized. There is disagreement as to who is to help Jennifer at the table and what they are to eat. For health reasons Sally buys only cheese and meats for breakfast, while Patrick wants sweet rolls and jam. The therapist helps them make clear arrangements on this point and agree on what the consequences will be if they do not keep to them.

The Taylors succeed in ritualizing breakfast time to everyone's satisfaction. They come to see breakfast as a ritual emphasizing their relationship as members of a family and something enjoyable for all concerned. The peaceful atmosphere this creates is one of the factors which eventually help Sally to reduce her obsessive thoughts and compulsive behavior.

7.5 DISCUSSION

1) Much of this chapter is devoted to *apparently individual interventions*, such as letter writing, talking to a parent, and rituals designed to help one member of a family come to terms with unresolved emotions. If anyone wonders what this has to do with family therapy, we would once again emphasize (cf. Section 1.3 also) that family therapy does not mean dealing only with interactions between members of a family. Individual problems can and often must be treated as well. The difference between family therapy and individual therapy is that in family therapy the person concerned does not go through the changes alone and does not become alienated from the rest of the family. The other members are closely involved, for example in the preparations for a talk with a parent or for a leave-taking ritual, or they are present at imaginary discussions. The effect of individual change on the structure of the family and the interactions within it can be constantly examined, which in turn helps the rest of the family change.

2) How does the ritualizing of communal activities in a family differ from behavior contracts (cf. Chapter 6) and mastering learning theory techniques?

In Section 7.4.3 we described what we mean by ritualizing interactions. The importance of this lies not only in creating an exact form and order for action and interaction, but also in the symbolic value for those involved. There is more to it than merely establishing a smooth routine (cf. point 3). According to the degree of formalizing and symbolizing involved, behavior contracts and learning theory techniques often lead to the ritualization of actions and interactions. In Section 7.4.3.2 we saw how the Taylors negotiated on each step of their waking and breakfast rituals. This is an example of intense ritualization. When a husband and wife make a behavior contract establishing that they will go to a film together during the course of the coming week, this is a far less intense process.

3) Performing rituals enables the members of a family to express feelings of group cohesion, which increases (cf. Bossard and Boll, 1950) when the ritual is performed daily in a harmonious atmosphere and gives everyone involved pleasure. In families which are not sufficiently well-knit, so-called "disengaged" families (Minuchin, 1974), better integration can be achieved by introducing communal tasks and rituals.

Inducing group cohesion (as well as eliminating confusion) is important in transition rituals. Some families seek help when they have to make a transition in their lives but are afraid of disintegration of the group. As rituals accentuate belonging together, they are less threatening than other interventions for families like this. They bring about and accompany a transition in the life cycle of a family and at the same time stabilize family life.

4) This book presents a treatment model with the help of which members of a family can gradually learn methods and techniques to identify and solve problems on their own (cf. Section 2.2.1). Ritualizing family duties *step by step*—for example by drawing up behavior contracts—fits into this framework. This is not so with a transition ritual whereby either the individual or the family is helped to make a "leap" instead of a cautious step.

We would suggest that a therapist should prescribe a *transition ritual* when the method of taking small steps—which people can apply themselves to other problems—has little or no chance of success. In Section 7.4.2.4 we mentioned the type of family to which this would apply. In the case of Jan, who sought help for his compulsive washing (cf. Section 7.4.2.2) the therapist concluded that a ritual rather than the step by step approach was indicated only when behavior therapy had failed twice. The ritual brought about a change in the relationship between husband and wife which motivated them to follow the behavior therapy instructions.

5) Altering an existing "family ritual" or ritualizing a particular family task can be done in two ways. The first corresponds with our basic aim of increasing the problem-solving ability of the family: The members of the family identify the problem areas; the therapist then translates the problem into terms of interaction and helps them say which problem areas they wish to see changed. He lets them negotiate the points and helps them make arrangements to solve their difficulties. Drawing up (ritualized) behavior contracts is one method of doing this. For the therapist to be able to follow this course of action, the family has to be capable of negotiating on their wishes and requirements. In certain families, for example those in which messages are usually inconsistent or the making of mutual accusations has escalated to a great degree (cf. Section 6.1; Van Dijck, 1977), this is not possible. The members of the family are incapable of changing their destructive patterns of interaction through negotiation. If the therapist nevertheless decides to attempt to change the patterns of interaction by means of a ritualization in such cases, he will be wise to formulate the proposals himself.

6) Prescribing rituals and ritualizing actions or interactions are *effective therapeutic techniques* (cf. Selvini Palazzoli, 1974). The question is, why is the effect of these techniques so powerful? A possible explanation is provided by the theory of self-perception, the essence of which is that new behavior leads to a different perception of self, different attitudes, and different emotions (cf. Bem, 1972; Lange, 1977d).

In Sally and Patrick's case the interactions connected with getting up and eating breakfast were ritualized. They agreed, for example, that Sally would wake Patrick only once, and at a set time. Patrick's getting out of bed would then be because of his own sense of responsibility and no longer because Sally was pressuring him. This implies a change in self-perception: "I am no longer someone who can't get up in the morning. I am someone with a sense of responsibility, who can get up on time." This attitude makes itself felt in a wider context and means that he will assume greater responsibility in other areas of family life too.

Not just the practical aspects of the actions are important in performing a ritual. Often the actions are dramatized in some way. This has a very strong influence on the self-image. Dramatization is also involved in transition rituals in which one intervention is supposed to achieve a radical change in one's self-image. Rituals which are performed repeatedly have a more cumulative effect on the self-image.

Ritualizing interactions within the family is closely connected with ending a power struggle. With Sally and Patrick, the struggle started with getting up in the morning. Sally wanted Patrick up, and Patrick resisted more and more. A pattern of interaction like this can lead to a situation in which people become less and less willing to take on the responsibility duties, as was the case with Mr. Holdan (cf. Section 7.4.3.1) whose only role in the family was that of breadwinner. Especially when the ritual has playful qualities, and performing it is an enjoyable experience for all concerned, it may well put an end to a power struggle.

CHAPTER 8

Separation and

Trial Separation

8.1 INTRODUCTION

The greater part of this book is devoted to the strategies and techniques a family therapist can employ to help the members of a family relate to one another in a constructive way. This may lead to a resolution of problems. Complaints may disappear—but not necessarily. In Section 4.3.1.10 we describe a number of situations in which there is little affection left in the relationship or in which love is one-sided. Sometimes, even if a couple is still emotionally involved with one another, a pattern of recurring conflict is present and extremely difficult to break down.

The Carsons provide a good example of this. In the first session, the husband proved to be extremely tense, suspicious, and volatile as regards his wife. Their relationship was characterized by a far-reaching power struggle. Initially family therapy achieved a degree of success, with the result that Mr. Carson became more self-confident. As there was no change, however, in the number of escalating conflicts which were taking up so much energy, the question of whether it was responsible to continue the marriage was raised. However, separation was not an easy step to take either. They were concerned about the children whom they both loved deeply, and, in spite of all the hate, they did have moments of deep affection.

In this chapter, we examine the demands made on a therapist by a situation such as that described above. Questions which arise are, for example: Should a couple separate or not? Is a trial separation possible? If separation does take place, how can the therapist best provide guidance for his clients?

8.2 TRIAL SEPARATION

8.2.1 A case study

Once the word "separation" had been used regularly by Mr. and Mrs. Carson, the therapist advised a trial separation. He suggested that one of them should go and live somewhere else for several months. The aim was for each of them to gain more insight into his or her individual potential while at the same time experiencing clearly what the other person meant to him/her. During the trial separation they were only to have contact about practical matters such as the children's visits.

After a week's reflection, Mr. and Mrs. Carson decided to go ahead with a trial separation lasting three months. The details were worked out with the therapist. Mr. Carson would stay with his parents for several weeks and start looking for a furnished apartment. During this period the couple would not meet with the therapist and they would make no final decisions about anything. An appointment was made for the first therapy session after the trial separation. It was also agreed that they would be free to contact the therapist if the situation threatened to become too difficult for either of them.

Three months later the Carsons went back to the therapist. They had both telephoned him once, but it had not proved necessary to meet. Mr. Carson had realized how attached he was to his wife and that he would have to control his bad temper and suspicious nature in the future. Mrs. Carson had discovered that she loved her husband and was prepared to try to react less vehemently to his fits of temper. Mr. Carson returned home and, although there was still tension, the power struggle had been reduced to such a degree that it was possible for them to live together as a family again.

8.2.2 Some considerations regarding trial separation

1) In the above example, the *indication* for the trial separation lay in the couple's inability to reduce the frequency of escalating conflicts.

According to Hoogduin and Van Dijck (1976), this is one of the most important reasons for suggesting a trial separation, especially when the clients themselves have begun describing the situation as "hopeless" and frequently talk about separation. Often they ask the therapist's advice on whether or not they should separate. As Hoogduin and Van Dijck point out, the therapist does not have to accept the responsibility of making this decision. Clients must decide themselves on the course their lives are to take. Because the decision is so difficult, a trial separation is meaningful. It provides the information and insight which are necessary when making a final decision.

A lack of emotional involvement which seems to be leading to separation is another indication for a trial separation. Separation makes a couple aware of what they mean to each other, whether they can live without one another, and what being alone feels like. It may lead to a couple staying together or result in the final separation taking place in a more satisfactory way than it would have otherwise done.

2) The *length* of the trial separation may vary. Hoogduin and Van Dijck suggest two weeks to two months, and Toomim (1972) thinks that three months is the ideal period. Generally speaking, two weeks is too short.

Lange (1977e) mentions a number of factors to be taken into consideration when deciding on the length of the trial separation. A short period will usually be best for clients who "live on top of each other," are always together, and never do anything independently of one another, while clients who are often apart because of business trips or hobbies, for example, will derive greater benefit from a longer period.

In the example cited by Lange, the clients themselves had arranged short trial separations in the past. The husband had stayed with friends for several weeks on each occasion. This can also be a reason for prescribing a relatively long trial separation which takes place under the guidance of a therapist (within the framework of therapy) and which is to be different from those that have taken place in the past.

3) It is interesting to note that, even if in the past clients have been through trial separations which did not result in definite decisions, this need not necessarily be the case again. A well-presented and well-managed trial separation can still be effective. The situation is analogous to clients with hyperventilation problems who have tried unsuccessfully to use the plastic bag technique. Hoogduin (1977b) describes how precise and dramatic instructions can lead to success in such cases.

Haley (1976) implies the same in his analysis of the present-day "Little Hans." In the case he describes, the family's previous attempts to keep a dog had been unsuccessful, but by following the therapist's instructions they managed it.

4) It is important to discuss the *details* of a trial separation thoroughly and to make definite arrangements. The first question is: *Who is to move out?* Often, for practical reasons, it is the husband, although, of course, the wife may leave home for several months, while the husband looks after the children. A change of roles sometimes leads to new self-awareness and insights into the relationship with one's partner. Taking turns moving out is also possible and may provide couples who cannot decide who should go with a solution. A further advantage of taking turns is that it provides maximum information for the final decision on separation, especially about who is to stay with the children.

The second detail which has to be discussed is *where the person who leaves home is going to live during the trial separation.* This can cause problems. Ideally, whoever it is should move into rented or borrowed accommodation alone. This provides the opportunity for reflection and the experience of living alone. However, it is usually difficult to find suitable accommodations on short notice. Another important consideration is that the setting should not contrast too sharply with the situation at home or what could reasonably be expected after a final separation. If someone moves from a comfortable house to a barren little room, his or her decision will be influenced by the wrong factors. If, on the other hand, the trial separation is too pleasant—for example, because it is spent with kind, understanding friends or family—the harsh reality of living alone will not be experienced. We are not saying that we have solutions to the above problems. Most people simply do not have enough money to rent extra accommodations for several months and so they have no choice but to move in with friends or family. It is vitally important that they should nevertheless fend for themselves as far as possible.

A third point is *how often the partners are to see each other (if at all) during the trial separation.* Some people like to have a meal together once a week or go out with the children. Toomim suggests that this is possible only when both partners have the right of veto. As soon as one person does not want to carry on the arrangement, he/she should be able to withdraw without protest from the other. We agree with Toomim, but would add that too much contact during this period should be avoided, since it is likely to make the trial separation less clearly defined and thereby destroy its most important function.

The fourth point concerns *arrangements with the children.* How frequently and for how long is the person who has left home to see the children? Where will the meetings take place? Much depends on the housing available for the spouse moving out.

The therapist should also discuss with the parents *how they are to explain the trial separation to the children.* Gardner (1972) has a number of valuable suggestions regarding this. In his view it is essential that the differences between the parents are not disguised in any way. The situation should be explained clearly to the children, and they must be made to understand that it is not their fault.

5) Toomim (1972) considers regular *therapy sessions with both partners* necessary during the trial separation. We are less categorical about this. Often these sessions only create problems, as the partners are not experiencing anything together. The sessions can even be disturbing and inhibiting, especially if the partners have decided not to see each other at all during the trial separation. A session together can be useful *from time to time* in order to adjust arrangements which are not working or to evaluate the situation. It is also wise to keep open the possibility of an *individual session with one of the partners,* as happened with the Carsons. A trial separation can precipitate crises which make this necessary. In Toomim's view, most clients are subject to great emotional swings during a trial separation and can go through a wide range of moods, ranging from deep depression to euphoria, not necessarily in the same order of course. Unlike grief therapy (cf. Ramsay, 1977; Raapis Dingman, 1975), it is not clear what a therapist can do for his clients at this stage. Toomim does not give conclusive answers either. In order to be capable of making a well-founded and responsible decision at a later stage, it is important that all emotions are consciously experienced. Depression should not be suppressed too hastily, even when accompanied by symptoms such as insomnia and physical symptoms such as headaches.

6) We agree with Toomim that final decisions should not be taken during a trial separation. The sudden freedom may cause a tendency to form new relationships or accept other commitments. The way clients deal with their freedom is different in every case and depends largely on their reasons for a trial separation. Whatever happens, one

should guard against taking on new commitments of a final nature before the end of the agreed period. This could easily happen in a burst of enthusiasm but would be premature. It would, moreover, go against the "spirit" of the trial separation, which is to create a short period of reflection, only *after* which decisions are made.

7) In cases where this period ends in a definite decision to separate, the couple will usually need guidance during the separation process. We shall deal with this in the following section. Even if the clients decide to stay together, there is still a job for the therapist to do. He can help them express their motives and find ways of getting along better. As a fair amount of preparatory work has already been done, this need not take up many more sessions. The trial separation described by Lange (1977e), for example, was followed by three sessions, after which a "dramatic behavior contract" was drawn up, carried out, and evaluated.

8) Hoogduin and Van Dijck (1976) warn against the theoretical danger that some couples may decide on a permanent separation at the mere suggestion of a trial separation. However, this does not seem to apply to any of the 15 cases they cite. Nevertheless, because the possibility of premature divorce cannot be disregarded completely, trial separation should be advised only where all attempts to improve the relationship have proved completely fruitless. It is difficult to specify the precise criteria and a decision will depend largely on the therapist's judgment based on his experience and insight. A good basic rule is to recommend trial separation if one partner (or both) regularly threatens divorce or is obviously not emotionally involved with the other. In extreme cases the advice for a trial separation comes after one or two therapy sessions, but usually this occurs only at a later stage. In either case, there are practically no arguments against a trial separation, since it is not an intervention which leads clients to a point of no return. At most it prevents a regrettable decision being taken unnecessarily or being postponed so long that one or more of the people concerned suffers serious psychological damage.

9) The mere suggestion of a trial separation can have an effect. Mr. and Mrs. Frost, a middle-aged couple with four children, provide a good example of this.
Although both of them still felt a great deal of affection for one another, they were locked in an "impossible" escalating spiral. Many

years ago Mrs. Frost had had an affair, which she had confessed to her husband a year prior to therapy. Since then he had been obsessively jealous. He interpreted all types of behavior on his wife's part as evidence that she was again having affairs. He refused to believe her in spite of her protests. Eventually it became impossible for her to relate to her husband in a positive manner. She felt deeply resentful because she thought he was constantly spying on her. They had tried therapy previously, both together and separately, but without success.

After several sessions the therapist saw that a step-by-step problem-solving approach would have no effect on this irrational pattern. He wanted to suggest a prescription of the symptom, but before he had had a chance to explain what this entailed, the husband interrupted him. His anger and suspicion were such that he found every assignment and strategy nonsensical. The therapist expressed his respect for the husband's feelings and said that as matters stood it would be impossible to go on. Divorce was perhaps the only solution, as the couple would otherwise destroy one another. It was a pity, as there were clearly still many positive aspects to their relationship. The therapist went on to suggest that during the coming week they should consider two options: (a) a trial separation, and (b) exaggerating the husband's suspicion and the wife's feeling of being spied on.

A week later they came in laughing and chatting, something which had not happened before. The idea of a trial separation had given them such a shock (cf. Van der Hart, 1977; Lange, 1977e) that they were able to put the past behind them. The husband had stopped spying and nagging and had been "rewarded" with an unusual amount of loving behavior from his wife. This made him feel more secure and reduced his feelings of jealousy. Several more sessions were devoted to discussing how they could best express their irritations and unspoken desires even in this euphoric situation in order to prevent a "relapse" at a later stage.

10) The "threat" of a trial separation does not always result in a breakthrough. Usually the trial separation does indeed take place. Not much is known about its long-term effects.

Hoogduin and Van Dijck (1976) report that all 15 couples they describe came to a decision within two months. They provide no information, however, on what the decision was or its effects.

Toomim (1972) is more explicit on this point. Of the 18 couples she mentions, 12 separated and six established a new and more satisfactory relationship. At the time of the follow-up, 18 months later, 11 of the couples who had separated were still on good terms with one another, as were all six of those who had stayed together.

8.3 FINAL SEPARATION

In recent decades, the number of marriages in the Western world which end in divorce has increased dramatically. Divorce is now as much a feature of our complex society as marriage itself. Everyone comes into contact with it in one way or another (cf. Hoefnagels, 1975; Norton & Glick, 1976).

Many people who feel that divorce is imminent seek help to prevent it in family or couple therapy. Sometimes this has the desired effect —the partners learn to understand one another better, become more honest and open, and come to mean more to each other. Their affection increases and the power struggle ends. As we mentioned in Section 4.3.1.10, couple therapy does not have these results with all clients. Where there is little or no emotional involvement, couple therapy will not save a marriage; indeed, it would be pointless to attempt to do so. It may be better in the long run for the couple to separate instead of grimly holding on to a loveless relationship. The same applies where the emotional involvement is one-sided—love or affection from one partner and indifference or rejection on the part of the other. Sometimes, even when there is sufficient emotional involvement, it seems that the escalating spiral of negative patterns of interaction cannot be ended. The Carsons (Section 8.2.1) provided an example of this. In their case, however, the trial separation led to a positive breakthrough. This is by no means always the case. Some people experience such peace and discover so many opportunities for developing individual potential during a trial separation that they do not want to go back to their partners, even if they do still love them. In such cases the trial separation becomes a definite separation.

Divorce does not mean the end of the family therapist's work. On the contrary, he has to prepare himself for the difficult job of guiding his clients through this stage. The main difficulty is that he has to deal with subsystems from the previous family which are suddenly faced with entirely new problems. For example, the parent who has to carry on without the children might be experiencing loneliness and difficulty restructuring his or her life. This may also apply to the parent who is left to care for the children, and who has to deal with questions such as how to fill the emptiness in the family, how to bring up the children alone, and how to restructure family life in such a way that his or her life is not completely taken over by the children and their needs.

It almost goes without saying that the children will miss the parent who has left. This is usually further complicated by the fact that they do not know exactly what has happened. Wallerstein and Kelly (1977) consider this to be the main problem of divorce. In most of the cases they have analyzed, one or more of the children suffers guilt feelings. Some parents reinforce these feelings by constantly telling the children that they are a nuisance. Even if they do not, many children feel that it is their fault that their parents have divorced. These feelings, together with the tense reactions of the parents, can cause various forms of symptomatic behavior, such as problems with school work, aggression, and social anxiety. Auster (1977) recommends therefore that, during the process of divorce, the parents make the following points very clear to the children: (a) The divorce is the result of problems between the two of them and has absolutely nothing to do with the children, whatever they may think; (b) there is nothing at all that the children can do to change the situation or bring the parents together again; (c) even though the divorce will probably mean spending less time with one of the parents in the future, this does not mean that that parent loves the children any less.

Auster also points out that divorce often means practical changes in a child's life—for example, moving, changing schools, and having more limited financial resources. This naturally applies to the parents too. Preparing the family for this type of problem and guiding it through this stage may be one of the therapist's tasks.

It is not our intention to deal in detail with the situations which arise during and after a divorce. This subject is handled in depth by Gardner (1972) and Weiss (1975), both of whom discuss a number of important aspects and problems connected with divorce in a systematic way. Weiss, for example, devotes an entire chapter of his book to the most common emotional reactions to divorce and the ways in which they can be dealt with. Other chapters discuss problems such as how to break the news to friends and family and how to handle relationships with outsiders which will inevitably change.

Although in one chapter Weiss talks about the most common reactions of children of divorced parents and how to respond to them, he lays the emphasis on the parents' problems. Gardner's book complements Weiss in a useful way in that it is written *for* the children of divorced parents instead of about them. He tells his readers (aged seven and above) in a moving way why people get divorced, the kind of problems they can expect as children, and what they can do about them. Like Auster, he stresses that children should not think that their parents divorced because they were a nuisance.

> If you're one of the children who think like this, ask your parents whether they got divorced because you were bad. I'm sure they'll tell you that badness had nothing to do with it. However, once in a while, a parent will tell a child that he did get divorced because the child was bad. If one of your parents says such a thing to you, do not believe it. If he says this, it usually means he has problems or troubles of his own that make it hard for him to see things the way they really are (Gardner, 1972, p. 9).

By taking the blame, children keep on believing that it is also in their power to get their parents to marry again.

> It's best for children who think like this to stop trying to find ways to get their parents together again, to accept the fact that they will not get married again, and to realize that there's nothing they can do about it. It's something the children cannot control. There are many things in life which we cannot control, and a parent's divorce is one of them. Children must learn to accept this. Once they accept this fact, they must then try to make up for their loneliness by doing things with their friends, their classmates, and other people (Gardner, 1972, p. 10).

Gardner gives his readers important tips for testing whether their parents love them or not, thus dispelling the myth that parents always love their children.

> Another way to decide how much a parent loves you is to see how much he goes out of his way to help you when you're in trouble or how much concern and sympathy he shows when you're sick, hurt, or in trouble. The loving parent will make a great effort to help you when you need it, and he will be upset and sympathetic when you're having difficulty.
> One more way to tell whether you're loved is to see how pleased your parents are with the things you learn to do. Do they smile with pleasure when you show them some new thing you've learned or done? (1972, p. 27).

If a parent does not come to visit a child at all, the child can assume that the parent possibly does not care much about him any more. These children receive comforting advice and support from Gardner.

> First of all—and this is very important—it does not mean that you are no good or that *no one* can ever love you. If a parent doesn't love you, that is sad for him because he loses out on the fun of loving, and loving someone is fun. . . .
>
> It is, in such cases, best to accept the fact that you cannot get their love and to start trying to get love and friendship from other people (1972, pp. 30-31).

Although Gardner's book is directed towards the children of divorced parents, as far as tone and style are concerned, it is revealing for parents too. It will help parents put themselves in their children's place, anticipate their feelings, and react to them adequately.

PART III

Training

CHAPTER 9

Training for

Family Therapy

9.1 INTRODUCTION

In the previous chapters we discussed the principles and techniques of therapy which may be used to treat families. We should now like to consider some of the ways in which therapists can be trained for this work. We begin by outlining the objectives of training before examining the various forms it can take and the types of people for whom it is suitable. In our analysis we devote special attention to the short course.

9.2 OBJECTIVES OF FAMILY THERAPY
TRAINING

9.2.1 Assessment of objectives

We have already indicated the importance we attach to treatment contracts in which objectives accepted by both the clients and the therapist are set out in explicit terms (cf. Section 6.5). The same type of procedure should be used in the training situation with regard to the relationship between trainer and trainees. The objectives of training are likely to vary from one group to the next—for example, experienced therapists taking a course in specific techniques will have quite different objectives from beginners who are less familiar with the subject as a whole. The objectives will, therefore, partly be defined by the trainees, but the trainer's limitations play a role here too. He will not be able or willing to work on everything.

In Section 9.4.2 we describe how several assessment sessions took place with the staff of a psychiatric clinic prior to a course organized on their behalf. These provided the basis for a kind of "training contract." They gave the trainers the opportunity to discover what the participants knew about family therapy. The participants also formulated their objectives and the trainers indicated the areas in which they were or were not prepared to work and the kind of commitment they expected from the trainees. The advantage of a "course contract" is that it makes the situation absolutely clear and people know where they stand. From the outset, the supervisor or trainer acts as a model for the trainees by demonstrating the importance of contracts in terms of his own behavior.

9.2.2 General objectives

In addition to the objectives which the trainer or supervisor and the trainees define in consultation with one another, there are a number of general objectives affecting the training of family therapists which can be highlighted to a greater or lesser extent at various stages of training. Cleghorn and Levin (1973) suggest that the therapist should be trained in three distinct types of skills: perceptual skills, conceptual skills, and executive skills. *Perceptual skills* refers to the therapist's ability to observe patterns of interaction and understand their effect on individual family members and the family as a whole. *Conceptual skills* means the ability to formulate observations in terms which apply to the family as a whole rather than to a particular individual. The therapist must be capable of noting how the family functions as a system and of translating the identified problem into interactional terms. *Executive skills* relates to the ability to influence family members in such a way that they learn how they function together as a family. It also means that the therapist has a behavior repertoire which he can use to influence interaction sequences and thereby change the way in which the family behaves.

Obviously these three types of skills overlap to a certain extent. The perceptual skill of observation also has a conceptual aspect in that it involves formulating one's own ideas about what is observed. This overlapping in no way detracts from the usefulness of dividing skills into three categories, which Cleghorn and Levin also employ to categorize a number of more specific objectives. In so doing they make a distinction between what experienced and inexperienced therapists should be taught.

Table 9.1 can be used as a kind of checklist by means of which both trainers and trainees can decide the points on which they wish to work. However, it is arbitrary in many respects—for example, the differences between the objectives for beginners and advanced trainees is not immediately apparent. Cleghorn and Levin base the distinction on the idea that less experienced therapists can only help families or couples which already have a number of ways of effecting change open to them—for instance normal families in crisis after a death. It would not be right, they argue, for them to work with families with chronic pathological patterns of interaction. On paper the distinction makes sense but in practice it just does not work, since it is usually impossible to match families with a particular therapist in this way. Cleghorn and Levin, moreover, use the word "beginners" to describe people who have been working for some time as therapists but who do not yet deserve to be called experienced. A therapist can only be called experienced once he or she has fully mastered the skills prescribed for beginners. However, it is extremely difficult to apply this distinction in the absence of any objective criteria against which it can be measured. In our view, it would be better to restrict the use of the word "beginners" to people for whom the training course represents their first contact with family therapy. The difference between a beginner and an experienced therapist will then primarily center on the beginner's lack of practical experience, which means that he cannot hope to acquire and develop certain skills, primarily executive ones, at once. After a certain time, a beginner should be capable of assessing and analyzing interaction patterns, but unlike his more experienced counterpart he will often respond to the content of what is said rather than giving immediate feedback on what he has observed during the session (cf. Section 5.7). In the first stage of training with beginners, perfecting perceptual and conceptual skills should be emphasized and not too much should be expected in terms of executive skills.

Cleghorn and Levin refer to executive skills in somewhat abstract terms. What, for example, do they mean by "work out new adaptive behaviors and rewards for them"? As in therapy itself, we feel that it is important in training to be precise and specific, partly in order to act as a model for trainees. In Chapters 4, 5, and 6 we refer to a number

TABLE 9.1
Checklist of Basic and Advanced Objectives
Devised by Cleghorn and Levin (1973)
for Training in Family Therapy

Perceptual and conceptual skills	*Executive skills*

a. *Basic*

1. recognize and describe interactions and transactions	1. develop collaborative working relationship with family
2. describe a family systematically; include assessment of current problem	2. establish therapeutic contract
	3. stimulate transactions
	4. clarify communications
3. recognize effect of family group on oneself	5. help family members label effects of interactions
4. recognize and describe the experience of being taken into the family system	6. extricate oneself from the family system
	7. focus on a problem
5. recognize one's idiosyncratic reactions to family members	

b. *Advanced*

1. conceive of symptomatic behaviors as a function of the family system	1. redefine the therapeutic contract periodically
2. assess family's capacity to change	2. demonstrate relationship between transactions and the symptomatic problem
3. recognize that change in a family is more threatening than recognizing a problem	3. be a facilitator of change, not a member of the group
4. define key concepts operationally	4. develop a style of intervening consistent with one's personality
5. deal with feelings about being a change agent, not just a helper	5. take control of maladaptive transactions by:
6. become aware of how one's own personal characteristics influence one's becoming a family therapist	(a) stopping a sequence and labeling the process (b) making confrontations in the context of support
7. assess the effectiveness of one's own interventions and explore alternatives	6. work out new adaptive behaviors and rewards for them
8. articulate rewards to be gained by family members making specific changes	7. relinquish control of the family when adaptive patterns occur

of techniques for the stages of therapy described by Cleghorn and Levin: behavior contracts, monitoring, behavior rehearsal, etc. It is important for beginners and experienced therapists to practice these techniques, although, as we have already noted, not too much should be expected from beginners in terms of executive skills. The same applies to a number of questions of style which we recommend in our approach to family therapy (cf. Section 5.20). While agreeing with Cleghorn and Levin that every therapist must find his own style as far as this is concerned, we nonetheless feel that a certain degree of authority and self-confidence is necessary to ensure success.

In Section 2.2.3 we describe a number of "communication rules" which the therapist should teach his clients—talking in specific terms, passing constructive criticism, speaking for oneself and not for others, not asking "why?", avoiding debating tricks, etc. In our view, mastery of these rules should also be one of the objectives of the training of therapists—both beginners and, where necessary, more experienced practitioners.

Cleghorn and Levin refer in various places to the need for reflection on the part of the therapist—he must be able to see the effect the family is having on him and vice versa. We would add that the therapist must be capable of integrating the techniques and methods of family therapy into his own life and applying them in his own relationships. In Section 9.4.2 we describe how we attempt to achieve this in a training course with the staff of a psychiatric clinic. It is particularly important for therapists who are just beginning—it increases motivation and allows them to try out various techniques without exposing clients to any dangers.

In summary, Cleghorn and Levin list a number of possible objectives for training in family and couple therapy. Various elements can be used depending on the style of the trainer and the level of the trainees. They make a distinction between beginners and experienced therapists. For present purposes, beginners will be taken to mean trainee therapists with no practical experience. Even in training beginners, a range of executive techniques should be dealt with (cf. Chapter 5), though this might consist of no more than familiarizing them with techniques which increase conceptual and perceptual skills and which can be put into practice at a subsequent stage. We should now like to consider the various types of training and the stages at which they are appropriate.

9.3 TYPES OF TRAINING

9.3.1 The course

In this context, a course is taken to mean a training situation in which one or more trainers and between 10 and 20 trainees spend a limited period of time together. The course may assume a variety of forms, depending on the kind of participants and trainers available.

9.3.1.1 Various types

The workshop is an intensive training course for a limited period, e.g., five days, often on a residential basis. While it is quite understandable that therapists sometimes have to offer their courses in a short period of several consecutive days, there are a number of disadvantages to the workshop. For instance, it is not possible to experiment during the training period with the acquired experiences; and, connected with the above, a workshop may be an "experience" but it offers little opportunity for transfer of change (cf. Section 5.16).

Bearing this in mind, we prefer a course to be more spread out over time. It might consist of sessions ranging from two hours minimum to four hours once a week or once every two weeks, with homework assignments (also carried out in sub-groups) in between (cf. Lange & Zeegers, 1978). A course of this type may vary in length from three months to about two years, according to the goals of the training program.

9.3.1.2 Individual participants as opposed to existing groups

Courses are usually made up of individuals who do not know one another. The only thing they have in common is the desire to find out more about family therapy. In our view, the success rate with this type of group is fairly low. Epstein (1972) conducted follow-up research in relation to a number of training courses with groups of individuals (cf. Epstein and Levin, 1973), from which it emerged that hardly any of the participants had managed to integrate what they had learned during the course into their work. In many instances the people in charge resisted change and other members of staff felt threatened by the "new experts." As a result, there were few opportunities for course participants to develop, so some of them left to find jobs elsewhere. When this happened, other members of staff of the same organization had gone to training courses, with the same results.

The alternative to a group consisting of individuals is a course aimed at people belonging to the same organization. As this is not always feasible, we feel that participants who did not previously know each other should take steps to develop their newly acquired skills together after the course has ended.

Now that more organizations and institutions are interested in family therapy, the opportunities for in-service training are much greater than they used to be. Examples of this are provided by the Community Mental Health Center in Rotterdam, which organized four workshops for its own staff in 1973, and by our own experiences, for instance with a social work agency, in which the entire staff were trained by us during 10- and 15-week courses. The question of how participants can integrate their newly acquired skills into their own work is dealt with in great detail during such courses. We would recommend that trainers should make themselves available to the organization to supervise developments and provide guidance, after the course, for example by helping in the consultations between trainees and management on the consequences of new insights, or by supervising groups (see the sections below), or in advising individual members of staff with regard to current problems in their family therapies. It is vital here too that clear agreements are made before the training begins so that management, trainees, and trainers all know where they stand.

9.3.1.3 Inexperienced as opposed to experienced therapists

In Section 9.2.2 we saw how Cleghorn and Levin (1973) formulate specific objectives for experienced and inexperienced therapists. We should now like to consider this approach in the light of our interpretation of it and with a view to determining the consequences it has for a course of training.

In our opinion, all courses should consist of a theoretical framework based on the literature. For beginners, however, the literature will have to be more wide-ranging and more general than for experienced therapists. In the following section we describe in detail courses for experienced therapists and show that a large amount of literature on the systems approach of dealing with symptoms is not necessary, since this is a subject with which the participants are likely to be familiar. The literature should, therefore, be confined to a number of specific aspects such as techniques for bringing about behavioral change.

The selection of particular subjects for a course with experienced therapists is also important with regard to executive skills. For example, in a recently held course, it was not necessary to devote much attention to conceptual and perceptual aspects during a role-playing exercise because what was happening was seen and understood by everyone. The participants wanted to know what to do and how to do it to implement change; therefore, the emphasis from the outset was on executive skills.

In conclusion, especially in courses with experienced therapists, it is important to specify in advance the topics which will be dealt with and the subjects which will receive less attention. It is easier for the trainer to present a standard program with beginners.

9.3.2 Study and training groups

In order to ensure that what has been learned during the course is not immediately forgotten, it is useful to split up the participants into semi-permanent groups consisting of from three to five people. The groups can meet after the course has finished and, building on what they have learned, study literature together and develop executive skills by means of role-playing. For beginners this is a necessary transition between the course and actual practice. At this stage, an extra aid for beginners is to follow therapy conducted by an experienced therapist from behind a one-way screen or by means of audio or video recordings. This has an important modeling function. Discussion—both before and after the session observed—will increase the effect.

9.3.3 Supervision

Usually one or more courses will constitute the first step, certainly for beginners. Supervision in the initial stages is an important part of the learning process, just as it is for training in individual therapy. During supervision of individual therapy, it is usual for the supervisor and the trainee to have a discussion based on the former's comments on a session which has taken place. In family and couple therapy, the supervisor is usually more directly involved in the treatment. If he does not follow the sessions or listen to the tapes, it is extremely difficult to work on executive skills. There are two basic ways in which this kind of supervision takes place:

(a) The trainee makes an audio or videotape of the session, which is later played back to the supervisor. They then discuss what the trainee felt the problem was, what he set out to achieve, and what his further strategy will consist of. The supervisor can, moreover, give feedback on the therapist's style and method.

In some cases it is important to discuss the personal characteristics of the trainee himself. However, definite agreements should be made in advance as far as this is concerned. The working points of the supervision should be clear from the start. A variation on this type of supervision consists of several trainees bringing and discussing their own tapes. In this way, they learn about one another's problems and solutions (modeling). Moreover, opportunities will arise during the supervision to practice executive skills by means of role-playing.

(b) A disadvantage of the type of supervision described in (a) is that comment can be passed only once the session has finished. An unsuccessful session cannot be rescued. The most the therapist can hope is that he will be more successful the next time. An alternative consists of "live" supervision using a one-way screen enabling the supervisor (and perhaps other trainees) to follow a number of sessions from an observation room. Before the session starts, the trainee therapist should explain the problems he is having with the family he is treating, set out his objectives and strategies, and say what, if anything, he expects from his supervisor. They can agree on whether the supervisor will come in if he thinks things are going wrong. This means that the supervisor may take over the session and attempt to redirect it. If this approach is agreed on, it must also be decided how the supervisor is to withdraw. Sometimes it will be desirable for him to remain until the end of the session. At other times, he can leave once the stumbling block has been removed. The point at which he leaves will be largely dependent on the extent to which he judges that the trainee will be able to continue in the direction he has suggested.

Irrespective of the length of time the supervisor is involved in the session, he is responsible for resolving the topic for which he was called in and for showing the trainee how to proceed. The worst thing he could possibly do would be to enter the room, make a few brief comments, and then leave the trainee to sort out the mess. Montalvo (1973) describes a number of effective ways in which trainees and supervisors can arrange the supervisor's intervention. The supervisor can, for instance, stay behind the one-way screen and keep in touch with the trainee by means of a telephone or intercom. Another variation is when the supervisor or a group of colleagues calls the trainee out of the session in order to discuss strategy with him, rather than discussing it with him by telephone (cf. Papp, 1977, 1980).

In conclusion, we would suggest that working with "real" clients under supervision is a necessary part of any course after initial theoretical grounding. Supervision can take many forms varying in degree and intensity. The supervisor is more closely involved in the therapy if he is present while it takes place than if he only discusses it later. The degree of intensity will vary according to how much time is spent on supervision of the therapy as a whole.

In our view, the transfer of change principles (cf. Section 5.16) should also be borne in mind during supervision. This means that the supervision will have to be much more intensive during the early stages. For this reason, the type of supervision referred to in (b) should be used to begin with, and the techniques described in (a) as the frequency of supervision decreases.

9.3.4 Intervision

Intervision is a form of training which closely resembles supervision but without the formal distinction between supervisor and trainee. It involves several therapists with roughly the same degree of experience working together, for example by viewing or listening to each other's tapes or by observing one another from behind the one-way screen. This approach may be usefully complemented by selecting, reading, and discussing literature together. We strongly advise therapists working in the same organization who have started practicing family therapy to form an intervision group. For experienced therapists, too, this is a useful method of exchanging experience and developing expertise.

9.3.5 Summary and diagram of a family therapy training program

In the above section, we describe four types of learning experience which can be useful to the trainee therapist. It will be clear that they do have a definite order. It would, for example, be pointless to begin with intervision. As far as this is concerned, we agree with a number of the principles formulated by Brinkman (1974) on the training of behavior therapists. Figure 9.1 crystalizes our ideas in diagram form.

As with many schematic approaches, the diagram probably looks

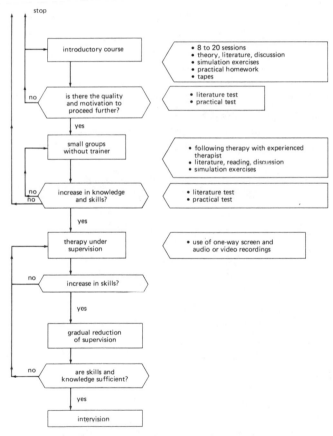

Figure 9.1. Diagram of a family therapy training course.

neater than the process actually is. It leaves unresolved the question of how to judge when to proceed from one stage to the next, which is particularly difficult as far as executive skills are concerned. At the moment we are considering devising a number of standard problem situations in which people playing roles take part in a session conducted by trainee therapists. This could be recorded on videotape and scored by observers in terms of specific skills. A further problem with the diagram is that the stages are likely to overlap to some extent. For example, a trainee could very well be taking part in supervision and intervision groups at the same time. Indeed, this can even prove highly productive.

In the diagram we mentioned only one course, conducted at the beginning of training. However, it is quite possible to divide this, with an introductory course in the beginning followed by a course on a higher level after a period of supervision and intervision.

The diagram has no definite end, but in our view it does not necessarily need one. As we said in Section 9.3.4, intervision is useful, even for experienced therapists, though it is not always absolutely necessary for them. The point at which it ceases to be a necessity and becomes simply useful will, however, always be arbitrary.

9.4 DESCRIPTION OF A SHORT COURSE

In this section, we describe a workshop-like short course, the elements of which might provide a model for a longer course. The course was organized for the staff of a psychiatric clinic who wished to improve their skills regarding specific aspects of family therapy. The majority of them were experienced therapists. First we describe a number of elements usually found in a training course and then we illustrate a number of specific principles and techniques which might be used in such circumstances, by following the progress of the course. Finally we describe how the course is evaluated.

9.4.1 The general principles

Courses for both beginners and experienced therapists, as suggested in Section 9.3.1.3, are based on the three following components:

(a) *Theory and attitude formation* based on lectures and talk by trainers, reading assignments and discussion. This relates primarily to perceptual and conceptual skills.

(b) *Modeling* by the trainers to improve executive skills. This takes place in an explicit way when the trainer acts as a therapist during the simulation exercises. Sometimes a real family will be brought in for a session. Explicit modeling also takes place when a trainer's tapes are viewed or listened to and commented on by a group of therapists. Implicit modeling takes place in discussions between trainees and trainers. For instance, by means of his response and the immediate feedback he gives, the trainer can serve as a model to the trainees for directness of approach and for sticking to certain communication principles (cf. Section 2.2.3). Finally, covert modeling occurs when the trainer describes cases in which he has employed a certain approach. When more experienced trainees are involved, the trainees themselves may quote from their own experience and discuss the problems they are having with certain families. Trainees may also serve as models for other trainees—in both a positive and a negative sense. Often it can be useful to see how *not* to do things.

(c) *Exercising*—particularly executive skills—can take place in several ways which complement one another. The most obvious one is for the trainee to act as the therapist during simulation exercises. It can also be useful to practice at home with one's partner. In the following sections we give several examples of how this can be done.

9.4.2 The course

Sixteen members of a psychiatric institution had formed a family therapy working group. They came from different intramural and outpatient departments and represented such disciplines as nursing, psychology, psychiatry, and social work. The majority had been working with families for some time and had taken a number of family therapy courses. Some of them, on the other hand, had had relatively little experience doing family therapy. All of them, however, were involved in the practical side of mental health care and had taken part in in-service training on how to conduct therapy sessions. The course consisted of the following stages.

1) The preliminary stage

The above information came to light in the course of two interviews with the organizer of the work group. The objectives of the group with regard to the proposed course were also specified. The members of the group wanted to examine the use of the systems approach (cf. Chapter 1), to learn how to assess family problems in operational terms (cf. Chapter 4), to translate individual problems (the "psychiatric patient") into relationship problems, and to use the principles of behavior change in family therapy.

The organizer also thought that the group structure would benefit from training in how to work together, but we felt that, in view of the short time at our disposal, it would be impossible to work at this explicitly in conjunction with the highly technical objectives outlined above. For practical reasons it was agreed that we would organize a course lasting three full days for one day a week spread over a period of three weeks. It was also agreed that the course would be evaluated in the following way: Each member of the group would be asked to formulate specific objectives at the outset and then at the end of the course we would check to ascertain how far those objectives had been achieved. The evaluation was to be coordinated by a student at the institution using a structured interview with each of the participants based on Contract Fulfillment Analysis (CFA, cf. Stelmachers et al., 1972), a variation of Goal Attainment Scaling (cf. Kiresuk and Sherman, 1968). The trainers were told in advance of the participants' individual objectives in order to enable them to discuss with the group at the start of the course which of these objectives they felt they could relate to. From the preliminary interviews, 53 specific objectives came to light, which could be grouped under five separate headings: therapeutic expertise, understanding one's own functioning, working with a co-therapist, extending one's field of work and increasing the motivation of the nursing staff.

2) The contract (first day)

After all the participants had briefly introduced themselves, the first day started with one of the trainers commenting on the objectives formulated by the trainees. At the same time, he pointed out that the trainers did not feel that "increasing the motivation of nursing staff" and "attempting to find a co-therapist" really qualified as objectives. This did not present any problems as only two participants had suggested them and agreed that they should be withdrawn.

The structure of the course was then described, together with the kind of commitment expected from the participants. The group accepted the proposed approach, which is described below. The contract which came into being in this way therefore contained the first elements of implicit modeling. In our view, working towards a contract is precisely how therapy with clients should also start (cf. Chapter 6).

3) The theoretical framework (first day)

After the contract had been drawn up, one of the trainers described the systems approach (cf. Chapter 1) for approximately half an hour. The other trainer then used a previously constructed sheet to explain the main techniques and principles of behavior change (cf. Chapters 2, 4, 5, and 6) which we employ. This part of the course was deliberately kept brief since we feel that it is sufficient during the first phase simply to create a theoretical frame of reference. This can be elaborated during the remainder of the course using literature, practical homework assignments, and simulation exercises.

4) Demonstration of trainers' methods (first day)

In Section 9.4.2 we emphasize the importance of modeling in training courses in general, whereby the trainers demonstrate their own techniques before the trainees start practicing them. To this end, a number of people in the group played the role of a family visiting a family therapist for the first time. Both trainers worked in turn with the family, demonstrating assessment techniques and the drawing up of a treatment contract. This was then discussed with the whole group. Apart from the modeling aspects referred to above, a demonstration by trainers has other advantages. Later the participants can act as therapists and lay themselves open to criticism. However, it seems to us only fair that the trainers should first set the example and show that they are not afraid of criticism of their methods.

5) Participants as therapists (first day)

After the lunch break, the session resumed with the same group acting as the family. At their own request, two trainees acted together as co-therapists and began assessing the problems and making an inventory. This was constantly interrupted at short intervals by the trainers for immediate feedback (cf. Section 5.7), so that strategy could be discussed both for the present and the future. The central questions were: "How do you see the family as a system?" "What do you wish to achieve?" and "How do you intend to go about it?"

Many of the trainers' comments at this stage focused on the style of the therapists. They were too hesitant, responded too late, or failed to respond at all to destructive interactions. For a detailed description of the important elements of style see Section 5.20.

6) Homework assignments (first day)

The participants were asked to carry out one of the following assignments with a partner, friend, or member of their family. The first concerned a behavior contract. The trainers explained in detail how mutual wishes ought to be formulated in concrete and positive terms and the pitfalls to be avoided (cf. Section 6.3). For the second assignment, the trainees were to write down mutual sources of irritation with their respective partners and then discuss them at a pre-arranged time (cf. Section 5.3.4). There were two main reasons for these assignments: First, we have found that if people experiment with these techniques in their own relationships, they have valuable firsthand experience which increases their understanding of the principles of self-regulation using the techniques of behavior change. Second, they can put across the assignment to clients much more convincingly if they have carried it out themselves. Explaining the purpose of the assignment to one's partner and persuading him or her of its value is also a useful exercise in this respect.

The first day ended with suggested reading (articles and chapters selected from books) on the systems approach, assessment, behavior contracts, and several specific subjects such as co-therapy. This was based on what the participants had said they wanted at this stage of the course. As a homework assignment, each of them was asked to prepare at least one question or observation about the reading material for the next session, the object being both to involve everyone and to avoid endless discussion on the second day of the course.

With some courses, for example those involving university students or students at a school of social work, it is a good idea to have a short multiple choice test geared to the reading assignment. This need not take very long to complete—no more than five minutes—so that it does not really seem like an examination, but will nevertheless allow the trainers to check that the participants have read the articles in question. If this procedure is to be adopted, it should be announced in advance so that it can form part of the "contract" with the trainees.

7) Discussion of homework assignments (second day)

The first hour of the second day was reserved for discussing the homework assignments. Each participant had prepared questions and comments on the literature. The practical part of the homework had been carried out by almost all of the participants and their partners with a great deal of enthusiasm. This had provided them with firsthand experience of how such techniques work and the problems which may accompany them, with the added bonus that in some cases the exercise had actually had a positive effect on the relationship in question. The participants also confirmed that motivating their partners was useful practice for the kind of skills they would need to use with future clients. Discussing homework assignments in this way contains an element of indirect modeling. In a therapy session which follows homework assignments, the therapist should always ask explicit questions about how clients have experienced them (cf. Chapter 6). This link between course and therapy was made explicit here by the trainers.

8) Simulation exercise (second day)

The morning and part of the afternoon were devoted to giving the trainees the opportunity to act as therapists. Once again, several of them played the role of a family with whom a session was to be held, with a view to concluding behavior contracts and giving the family "learning assignments" (cf. Lange, 1972; Van Dijck, 1977). The "family members" were asked to incorporate certain features into their responses, such as expressing their wishes in relation to one another in vague or negative terms. During the exercises the participants took turns acting as the therapist. After each turn a discussion concentrating on technique and style took place. In total five different trainees acted as therapist.

Taking turns in the group is one way of making sure that everyone in the course has an opportunity to play the role of the therapist. Another approach which is particularly effective for certain specific skills, such as arranging, carrying out, and discussing behavior rehearsal or drawing up a behavior contract, consists of working in *groups of three*.

For instance, if the subject to be dealt with is negotiating behavior contracts, two members of the group agree to be a couple with a certain problem. The third person, the "therapist," then has the assignment of trying to help the couple to conclude a behavior contract. In the process, many common problems will come up, such as being specific about one's wishes, expressing oneself in positive terms (cf. Chapter 6), and questions of style. At the end of his part, the "therapist" receives feedback from "the couple" on the basis of criteria supplied in advance by the trainers. Then it is someone else's turn to be the "therapist." In this way, within approximately one hour each member of the group can have a turn. If all the participants are divided up into groups of three, the trainers can walk around the room, sitting in on all the groups in turn. They can either give immediate feedback or note down points to be brought up in the subsequent discussion with the whole class. Working in groups of three can be followed by simulation exercises within the whole group which are not focused exclusively on one theme.

9) Watching a videotape (second day)

We ended the second day by watching a videotape of an assessment session one of the trainers had held a few weeks earlier with a family consisting of parents and two children. The object of this was to demonstrate our method "live" once again (modeling). It also enabled us to refer to techniques and aspects of style which had come up during the exercises and the ensuing discussion. There were several reasons for using an assessment session. The most important one is that the skills required to conduct a concrete and structured assessment session are essential for therapy as a whole. In a relatively short course as the one we are describing, it is therefore important to devote a proportionately large amount of time to this stage. The specific skills required in subsequent stages of therapy can be discussed in detail later, for instance in supervision and intervision. A practical advantage of using a videotape of an assessment session is that it saves time because no previous knowledge of the case is required.

10) Homework and evaluation (second day)

The participants were asked to read several articles related to specific topics in which interest had been expressed, either in the course itself or in the preceding consultations. The same approach was to be followed as for the first reading assignment—each participant was to prepare one question or comment for the following session. There were also practical homework assignments: "Writing down irritation" was again set for those participants who had not managed to complete it the first time. Specific monitoring was also included: After conferring with one another, the partners were to score on paper certain types of behavior which they found annoying. The trainers explained how they were to do this and the pitfalls to avoid (cf. Section 5.3.3). To round off the day, everyone in turn was asked what he or she thought of the course so far. By and large, all the participants were quite happy to continue along the lines already indicated. It was agreed that, on the third day, we would continue with simulation exercises and devote attention to showing how trainees could consolidate the skills they had learned in the course once it finished.

11) Discussion of homework assignment (third day)

The literature and the practical assignments were discussed in the same way as on the previous occasion. Further suggestions for reading were also made.

12) Simulation exercise (third day)

A large part of the day was spent practicing behavior rehearsal techniques (cf. Section 5.8). A "couple" described an incident which they had not been able to talk about at home. The task of the "therapist" was to get them to repeat what had happened, which would then serve as input for immediate feedback and modeling by the "therapist." Several of the trainees and one of the trainers played the role of the therapist. The proceedings were broken off every five or ten minutes for comment.

13) Planning for the future (third day)

Approximately an hour and a half was spent deciding how the group would continue working in the future. The participants who were already working with families and couples were clearly motivated to use the strategies, techniques and interventions they had learned during the course. The people whose experience had been confined to individual therapy had gained greater insight into the relational context within which psychiatric problems occur. They too wished to apply what they had learned. As a result of the course, the interest in co-therapy had declined but, on the other hand, supervision was considered to be highly desirable. The group decided to set up three supervision groups, each led by one of them with considerable experience of family therapy. One of the group leaders was already a member of an intervision group which he felt gave him the experience necessary to enable him to supervise his own group. The other two group leaders agreed that the trainers would provide them with supervision and consultation in a form to be worked out later together.

Finally, it was agreed that a follow-up session involving all of the participants would be arranged approximately 12 months later. This type of arrangement can be regarded as putting into practice the transfer of change principle (cf. Section 5.16), in which questions such as "how can you continue on your own?" and "what further assistance can we provide?" are central (cf. Lange and Van der Hart, 1973).

14) Completing an evaluation questionnaire (third day)

The last 15 minutes were spent recording the participants' views of the course on the basis of a number of satisfaction items. This is dealt with in detail in the following section.

9.4.3 Evaluation of the course

9.4.3.1 Results of the satisfaction items

Table 9.2 gives the scores in relation to a number of satisfaction items on a scale from 1 to 10 (the higher the score, the greater the degree of satisfaction). In general, it may be concluded from the table that the participants were highly satisfied with the course. They were particularly pleased with role playing and the consideration given to planning for the future.

The table only lists the averages of the total scores of the whole group, although total scores were also worked out for two subgroups, one consisting of psychiatrists and psychologists and the other consisting of social workers and nursing staff. The respective average scores were 7.9 and 8.6. The difference was significant on a .05 level.

TABLE 9.2
Average Scores in Relation to Satisfaction Items

Items	Average Score
a. enjoyable/not enjoyable	8.1
b. not useful/useful to me personally	8.6
c. practical/impractical	7.8
d. not very instructive/highly instructive	8.3
e. role-playing: not important/very important	8.8
f. theory: not very important/very important	7.8
g. arrangement for the future: not very important/very important	8.9
With reference to the trainers	
h. clear/unclear	8.6
i. ability to demonstrate: poor/very good	8.5
j. not useful for other people/useful for other people	8.1
Average total	8.34

9.4.3.2 Results of the Contract Fulfillment Analysis (CFA)*

Three months after the course, the student who had helped the participants specify their objectives had a follow-up discussion with each of them individually. They had agreed not to take part in other training courses in the intervening period. The object of the follow-up discussion was to establish the level each of the trainees had reached in relation to his or her objectives.

Kiresuk and Sherman (1968), Bensing and Dekker (1973), and Van der Veer (1974a, b) describe how these levels can be quantified and how a total score can be calculated for each participant. A training course can be said to have succeeded if the total score is 50 or more; this figure corresponds to the level at which the trainees are aiming—in other words, the level they expected to reach as a result of taking the course. The average final score for the whole group was 54.1. Only three participants scored less than 50.

---

* A variation on Goal Attainment Scaling (GAS) as described by Kiresuk and Sherman (1968). The most important difference between the two is that in Contract Fulfillment Analysis (CFA) the participants may specify their own objectives and indicate afterwards the level they have attained, while with GAS this is done by the trainer/therapist.

The effect of the course can be calculated in another way by recording progress scores in relation to five dimensions incorporated into the participants' objectives. This means establishing, for each dimension, the number of chosen targets and determining three months after the course whether they had made progress, stagnated, or actually gone backwards in relation to these goals. The results are shown in Table 9.3. The table shows that no one actually scored less than before the course in relation to a particular target. It also shows that the most progress was made in increasing therapeutic expertise.

9.4.3.3 Correlation between satisfaction and CFA scores

The correlation was calculated between satisfaction at the end of the course on the one hand and the two CFA scores on the other. The Spearman rank correlation coefficient was weakly negative in both cases: $-.179$ and $.-233$ respectively ($p<.40$). The data show that there is no relation between the scores using the two evaluation instruments, which is surprising in that it would be reasonable to assume that a high degree of satisfaction with a course at its conclusion would be connected with the idea of having made progress. Moreover, it would be

TABLE 9.3
Progress in Relation to Five Dimensions

	Number of Targets	Progress	No Change	Deteriorated	Average Improvement*
Therapeutic expertise	21	20	1	—	1.8
Understanding of own functioning	15	9	6	—	1.4
Cooperation with co-therapists	14	10	4	—	1.4
Extension of field of work	2	2	—	—	1.0
Raising motivation of nursing staff	1	1	—	—	1.0

* The maximum possible improvement is 4, if the participant was on level -2 before the course and on level $+2$ during the follow-up discussion.

reasonable to assume that satisfied participants would be more motivated to work in the direction of objectives specified on the course than participants whose attitude to the course as a whole was less positive. Obviously, these factors are not as crucial as they might appear to be and enthusiasm and satisfaction after a course has finished are not effective ways of assessing its real long-term effects. Another important consideration is that CFA is only useful in establishing the effect of the course in relation to the participants' own specified objectives. It makes no allowance for unexpected consequences which are, however, expressed in the satisfaction scores.

9.5 OTHER TECHNIQUES AND EXERCISES

We should now like to deal with some techniques and exercises which were not used during the three-day course we have just described.

9.5.1 The "stop" tape

Lange and Brinckmann (1976) made a videotape of an assessment session into which the word "stop" was spliced at ten crucial points. Before describing how the tape can be used, we should like to describe how it came into being.

The original tape was made for an evaluation study. Every time the word "stop" appeared, trainees had four minutes in which to think what they would have done at that moment had they been the therapist and to write down their answers on a special form. For each of the ten pauses, criteria had been drawn up to assess the participants' interventions, which were scored by two independent observers as follows: 2 points for a correct intervention, 0 for a reaction clearly at odds with the model dealt with on the course, and 1 for a reaction somewhere between the two. This procedure proved to be fairly reliable—the correlation coefficient between the observers was .80. In a later study (Lange and Zeegers, 1978), the correlation even increased (r = .86) after the criteria had been slightly modified.

The "stop" tape was designed in order to investigate whether a short course on directive family therapy has any effect on the extent to which trainees understand what should be done in therapy sessions. The scores of participants who had just taken a course were compared with those of trainees about to take part in a course. The differences were considerable and highly significant statistically (p<.001).

The experience of Lange and Zeegers (1978) with the "stop" tape was interesting. They compared each participant's score at the first five pauses in the tape with his or her score at the last five. In the group which had taken the course, there were no appreciable differences, but in the control group there was clear evidence of a learning effect. Scores for the last five pauses were considerably higher than for the first five. Evidently, after comparing their own interventions with those of the therapist, the participants had come to realize what kind of intervention was appropriate. It was this discovery which led to the decision to use the tape at the start of training courses.

The tape can be employed in a variety of ways. One of them is described above: Each participant watches it on an individual basis and writes down his or her reactions. Another approach is to watch the tape in a small group. The pauses are then longer so that more time can be spent discussing the most suitable form of intervention.

9.5.2 Demonstration tape

Actually watching therapy take place is usually limited to a few sessions from the first stages of therapy and takes place by means of a one-way screen, videotapes, or by using role-playing exercises. It is rarely possible to let trainees see the whole process from start to finish. In order to get round this problem, Lange and Zeegers (cf. Zeegers, 1977b) devised a demonstration tape showing a complete course of therapy in three hours. Fifteen sessions in all were recorded on tape, from which a series of episodes was selected and edited together in sequence. This material proved very useful for teaching purposes. Many institutions in the Netherlands requested a copy, which had to be refused in order to protect the privacy of the clients. At a later stage, however, a video reconstruction was made in which the therapy fragments are acted out by professional Dutch actors and the original therapist (subtitles in English). The fragments alternate with spoken English commentary which links up the various parts and explains the therapy techniques. The complete program consists of five tapes: The first tape deals primarily with the principles of assessment; the second and third tapes show the techniques the therapist uses in order to bring about change in the pattern of communication within the family—particularly immediate feedback, behavior rehearsal, modeling, behavior contracts, and behavior exercise. The fourth tape (fragments of the sixth to ninth sessions) focuses on increasing problem-solving behavior and how "a problem from the past" is approached by means of a ritualization. In the fifth and last tape (fragments of the tenth to twelfth sessions) a "farewell ritual" with a deceased father is demonstrated. The tape then shows how the therapy gradually becomes less directive (transfer of change) and is finally brought to a close. In this way, a program of edited highlights demonstrating and explaining the principles of family interaction and the accompanying basic strategies and interventions emerged.

9.5.3 Describing one's family of origin

The basic skills which have to be learned on a family therapy training course fall into the conceptual and perceptual categories (cf. Section 9.2). In order to be able to carry out interventions, the therapist must be capable of diagnosing what is happening. For this he has to perceive and be able to label the transactions and the divisions of roles in the family. An exercise to increase his ability to do this can be set as a homework assignment during a course. It involves asking the trainees to think back to the last year of their lives they spent living at home with their parents. They must try to concentrate on the situation as it then was in as much specific detail as possible and then go on to describe their own family in terms of systems. In this way, they can describe the power relations within the family using concrete examples, the coalitions which existed, and the extent to which there was inconsistent communication or confusion concerning content and relationship. These are just a few of the concepts which are available to participants and which are described in detail in Chapter 1.

A similar assignment could be given by asking trainees to think about their present families. However, we have a number of serious objections to this, not least the fact that the degree of involvement is sometimes so great that emotions are aroused which cannot be dealt with satisfactorily during the course. This can have unpleasant consequences both for the trainee and for his or her relations with a partner or family member. Another objection is that the degree of involvement hampers observation so that the instructive value of the exercises is reduced. Choosing the family of origin is, therefore, a compromise. Most participants can distance themselves more easily and have less difficulty in describing phenomena in objective terms than if they were asked to describe their current families. At the same time, there is greater emotional involvement in this approach than in simply "observing" a family of strangers. By examining one's family of origin, one experiences what system concepts actually mean, rather than just studying them.

In principle, the above assignment is carried out on an individual basis at home. However, there must be some possibility of guidance with it. Some people become highly emotional so that at the very least they need to talk about it with someone. This can take place in subgroups, in a session with all the other trainees or in an individual interview with the course leader. In our view, the first of these three approaches is the best. The fact that there is some discussion about the assignment does not necessarily mean that what the participant in question has written down should be made public. It is enough to talk about the ways in which certain things have been experienced and what their effect has been. This also applies to other practical homework assignments, such as the ones described in Sections 9.5.4 to 9.5.6.

From our description of this exercise and the underlying philosophy, it will probably be clear that it is best to use this assignment near the beginning of a course. This ties in with Cleghorn and Levin's (cf. Section 9.2) recommendation that conceptual and perceptual skills be practiced first. Moreover, it is useful at an early stage to remove obstacles which could prevent the participants from deriving maximum benefit from a course.

Bowen (cf. Anonymous, 1972) places the emphasis in his courses for trainees on becoming aware of one's relationship with one's family of origin. His trainees are given the assignment of writing a letter to each of their relatives separately—father, mother, brothers and sisters (cf. Section 7.2)—and describing how they see the relationship with the person concerned and the changes they would like to make. This sometimes leads to existing contacts becoming more intense or conversely to the conscious reduction of contacts which are unsatisfactory.

Bowen's philosophy is that family therapists often have "hidden agendas" based on their own circumstances, which prevent them from approaching certain types of families or individuals impartially. One way of resolving this problem may be to change one's relations with the other members of the family. As far as this is concerned Bowen goes considerably further than the present authors; the exercise we have described is primarily intended to allow the trainee therapist to practice mapping out the situation in a family in a way that motivates him. At the same time, we have ourselves experienced the kind of situation to which Bowen is referring. For instance a trainee once remarked after carrying out a certain exercise that he had always played the role of a go-between at home and had never been a party to a conflict. He found that this was also happening in the groups with which he was working as a therapist. Another trainee had rebelled violently against her authoritarian father and now found herself doing much the same thing in her therapy with families where the father was authoritarian. She entered into coalitions with the mother and children against the father and was regularly "sucked into" family systems.

In both the above cases there were clear indications that the trainees had not fully come to terms with experiences from their families of origin. When this happens we think it wise to suggest that they should work on the problem, for instance by writing letters as suggested by Bowen or by using the three letters or continuous letter technique described in Section 7.2

9.5.4 Scoring contraventions of communication rules

In Section 2.2.3 we introduced a number of communication rules, which when used properly can help people get along with one another better and stand up for their own interests in a more constructive fashion. A family therapist frequently sees that his clients are not observing the rules, that they are asking questions instead of giving their own opinions, speaking on behalf of someone else instead of for themselves, and using vague ways of referring to someone rather than being explicit. If a therapist is to help his clients effect changes to rid themselves of bad habits, he must be capable of *observing* what is happening. He cannot afford to allow himself to be overwhelmed by the sheer quantity of information he receives from his clients. He must constantly pay attention to the way in which this information is communicated, both to him and to the other persons present, and he must be able to identify its destructive aspects. That is not to say, however, that he must constantly give feedback.

The selective nature of human observation, including that of therapists, is confirmed by a large amount of research (cf. Krech, Crutchfield, and Ballachey, 1962). People most often observe things they recognize or things which interest them. They identify such things quickly from the stream of information which they constantly receive. The assignment described below is aimed at influencing the selective perception of trainee therapists in relation to destructive communication habits and to make sure that contraventions of communication rules are spotted quickly and often. The trainees are requested to select a social situation, preferably one with emotionally charged interactions, in which they can observe interactions—for example a board meeting or a serious discussion among a few friends. Some television programs could also be used for this assignment. Observation then takes place in a systematic way, using a list of all the communication rules. Every time someone contravenes one of these rules, this is noted by the trainee. Variations are of course possible. Instead of simply recording scores, it is also possible to describe the context and the way in which the communication takes place. The degree to which the observer himself is involved in the situation is also variable. Participant observation does not have to be excluded. It may, in fact, help the trainee to learn more about himself.

9.5.5 Expressing appreciation and receiving compliments

In the majority of problem families it is rare for people to express their appreciation of one another. Compliments are few and far between. On the other hand, family members have no hesitation in expressing their dissatisfaction when one of them does something wrong. In families characterized by intense power struggles this contributes to a vicious circle whereby an increasingly negative climate develops and the family members do less and less for one another. If there is no positive reaction, one feels less inclined to do anything for one's partner/father/mother/brother/sister a second time. In short, it is important to stimulate clients to recognize when this is happening and to help them to express their appreciation for the positive behavior of other members of the family in a direct and unconcealed way.

A necessary corollary to paying compliments is being able to accept them. People often react defensively or with obvious irritation when they receive a compliment. For instance, if someone says, "I like your new dress," it would be much better to say, "Thank you very much, I like it too," rather than, "It's only a cheap thing." Another example: If a partner says, "You've done a good job on that," it would be much better to say, "Thanks, it was quite difficult really," rather than, "It was broken so I had to fix it." These examples may sound rather cryptic but their meaning is obvious—it is useful to help family members to show their appreciation for one another where possible and to help them to accept compliments more readily.

The habit of seldom being complimentary to members of one's family is by no means the exclusive preserve of problem families. Many trainee therapists are in the habit of showing how keen and alert they are in reacting to problematic and negative behavior and of ignoring the positive aspects of their clients' and other people's behavior. If the therapist wishes to change the behavior of clients on this point, then he himself will need to have a good deal of experience of expressing his appreciation of other people and of responding positively to compliments. For this reason we have trainees in our courses practice this skill in a variety of ways, for example at home with one's partner or with someone they have invited specially to carry out the exercise. The parties begin by paying as much attention as possible to the positive aspects of the other's behavior. At a previously agreed time, one of them begins by referring to one positive aspect of the other person's behavior and expresses his appreciation of it in explicit terms. The other person listens and thanks the speaker without in any way making excuses for himself or talking about himself in a defensive way. The exercise is then repeated with the roles reversed.

The emphasis we place on being able to express appreciation in positive terms in no way contradicts our view on constructive assertiveness (cf. Section 2.2.2); it is, on the contrary, part and parcel of the same thing. Standing up for oneself if the other person is at fault is one aspect of assertiveness; the ability to express appreciation for the other person in his or her presence is another, no less important aspect.

9.5.6 Practicing positive labeling

In Section 2.2.4 we describe how important positive labeling of symptomatic behavior can be in the psychotherapeuticprocess. We also indicated that there is a difference between positive labeling and providing support or expressing appreciation. Positive labeling entails putting certain aspects of the problem behavior in a different and more positive light, whereas support is usually based on understanding of or appreciation for behavior other than that which is problematic.

In many psychotherapy training courses, the trainees are taught how to identify problem situations and possibly provide feedback on them. In the model we have described here, it is often necessary to give immediate feedback on destructive interactions. However, despite the undeniable importance of providing training in this aspect, it is also very important that trainees should be taught how to use relabeling and positive labeling (cf. Section 2.2.4).

Van der Velden et al.(1980) describe an interesting exercise which can be used during a course. Each trainee in turn presents a problem situation which may center on individual or interactional difficulties. It may be invented or based on personal experience. His neighbor must then try and put a positive label on the problem as it has been presented, attempt to discover positive aspects of the problem behavior, and describe it in such terms. If he is unable to do so, then it is the next person's turn and the next—until the person who has presented the problem is satisfied. Then it is someone else's turn to describe a problem. The exercise has many possible variations. If the group is very large, a selection of problems will suffice; otherwise the exercise would take up far too much time. All of the participants can then write down their relabeling and report their findings in turn. Another way of doing it is to set the exercise for homework groups, each consisting of approximately five people.

Another variation consists of putting the emphasis on brainstorming. One person describes a problem and the rest of the group comes up with as much positive labeling as possible. The quality of the labeling and whether it is practicable are not at issue at this stage; indeed, even the most unlikely suggestions are acceptable. This relieves the pressure on the trainees to come up with viable and carefully constructed relabeling, with the result that they feel less inhibited and can make better use of their creative impulses. This exercise is particularly important when the trainee is just beginning to perceive the value of positive labeling. Naturally, at a later stage, all the ideas which have emerged during brainstorming are discussed and analyzed in terms of applicability.

Positive labeling can also be practiced at home with one's partner. Sometimes, for example, we ask trainees to select a feature of their partner's behavior which annoys them and then try to describe it in a new and more positive light. They are not to say anything to the partner, but are free of course to discuss the exercise in their homework group. One trainee, for example, said he was irritated by his wife's insistence that the evening meal should be served at exactly the same time every evening. He interpreted this as an excessive desire on her part to control other people. As a result of the positive labeling assignment he came to realize that his wife spent a lot of time preparing an attractive meal, that she made sure that eating together with their three children was an important period of calm in the family's day, and that it was therefore important, particularly for the children, that meals be served at regular times. The wife's complaints were relabeled as justified concern for an important family ritual.

It is also possible to use one's own behavior to practice positive labeling, and in so doing to discover new and more positive aspects to it. If the relabeling takes place "live" as described above, it is important for the trainees to make sure that the new labels really are acceptable. The trainer should warn them that they should not label their own behavior or that of their partner as positive if in so doing they have the slightest suspicion that they are doing themselves or their partner an injustice. The following example will serve to illustrate this point. A trainee is constantly annoyed with her husband's lack of involvement with bringing up the children. A positive new label is available—he works hard for the family. However, one needs to consider very carefully whether this new label will really be acceptable to the wife. If she is really dissatisfied with her husband's role in the family, there is no sense in glossing over the situation by means of positive labeling. It would be much better in such circumstances to examine the consequences of the conflict and to be explicit about it. The wife would not really accept a positive label, even if she formulated it herself.

9.6 DISCUSSION

This chapter has looked at the different forms training courses in family therapy may take. We have followed the progress of a three-day course (Section 9.4) describing in the process a number of general course components. In Section 9.5 we examined additional techniques and exercises which were not included in the course itself. We should now like to make a few critical observations with regard to the foregoing.

1) We do not wish to suggest that we have been in any sense exhaustive in describing the techniques and exercises which can be used in training courses. The elements we have mentioned tie in with the treatment model presented throughout this book. Every course will have a different emphasis and therefore most course organizers will need to adapt their exercises to fit in with the specific features of what they wish to convey to their students. This may mean that some of the techniques we described here will be used, while others will not or

that new variations of some course components will be devised which better meet the needs of the students. We have described these techniques and exercises merely to stimulate fellow trainers. We do not intend them to be taken over indiscriminately.

2) Practical reasons—traveling, etc.—made us decide to confine the course described in Section 9.4 to three full days. Generally speaking, however, we are in favor of more sessions of shorter duration. Shorter sessions provide better opportunities to pursue a gradual approach in integrating literature and practical homework. This is especially important in training with beginners (although this was not the case here) who must learn to take one step at a time. The trainer must ensure that the students receive comment, literature, and practical exercises in an order which closely corresponds to the therapy process itself, that is, focusing to begin with on general knowledge (conceptual skills) and from there proceeding to assessment, behavior contracts, behavior rehearsal, and learning assignments. Each separate subject must be preceded by literature, a brief introduction, and modeling by the trainer. The last stages are more holistic in that they involve practicing with overall therapy rather than one single technique or intervention. In the short course we have described, the steps taken were relatively large. Students were asked to read a great deal of literature and do practical homework assignments at one and the same time. A gradual increase in assignments is probably preferable, particularly as far as the practical aspect is concerned. For a description of such a longer course, see Lange and Zeegers (1978).

3) Practicing at home forms an important part of the training course we have described in this chapter. Many of the exercises necessitate involving one's partner, for example scoring irritation or concluding a behavior contract. Giving assignments of this kind is based on our philosophy that family therapists must integrate the principles which they wish to teach their clients into their own lives. In order to promote this kind of integration, Lange and Zeegers (1978) have developed a *course for couples* in which the partners of ten trainee therapists play a full and direct part. The course is divided into nine weekly sessions with the whole group, during which the participants discuss their homework, watch videotapes and take part in various role-playing exercises. Between the sessions, two meetings are organized of the homework groups, each of which consists of two or three couples. The groups discuss both the practical homework and the reading assignments. The

trainees watch the videotapes together as a group and make their comments on them. The course is basically organized in the same way as that for individuals, but with a number of differences. One considerable advantage of involving couples is that it makes the practical homework easier because the partner is fully aware of what is going on and is in fact participating in the course as an equal. A second advantage is that practicing and demonstrating techniques need not be confined to role playing—the actual interactional problems of the participating couples provide the necessary material to demonstrate interventions and communication principles. This considerably helps the integration of principles of therapy in their own daily lives. From the research by Lange and Zeegers, it appears that couples who have taken part in a relatively short course of this kind undergo considerable change in the way they relate to one another and solve their own problems.

4) We used two different *evaluation procedures* to assess the course described in Section 9.4 The first—measuring satisfaction—is the more usual method and the least laborious. It is completely based on simple "self-reporting." However, it has not proved to be a satisfactory method for assessing actual change. Poelstra and Lange (1975) have therefore been developing attitude scales and semantic differentials, by means of which they hope to be able to show clear differences in attitude and knowledge between trainees and a control group. The new method will not, however, reveal any information about students' competence in executive skills. As far as this latter aspect is concerned, we should be thinking along the lines of observation and scoring during therapy sessions, although in practice this is usually not viable.

A solution which lies somewhere between the two is provided by the "stop" tape described in Section 9.5 This is a reliable and valid way of finding out and assessing what the student would do in a family therapy session if he or she were the therapist. However, it is not a measure of *executive* skills in the sense that people do not always do exactly what they say they are going to do; in addition, the way in which interventions are carried out (tone, posture, choice of word) is vitally important. Of course, the tape as described can only be used in training in family therapy which is based on a model as described in this book, since the interventions are evaluated according to criteria based on that model. That is not to say that tapes cannot be made for other courses in a similar way.

Another form between simple self-report and measuring executive skills can be found by using the CFA (or GAS) as described in Section

9.4.3.2. Preceding the course each participant is shown how to formulate his goals in specific and observable levels of behavior. These can refer to executive skills. Later on he—or others who work with him—may indicate at which level he functions.

5) In Section 9.3.5 we set out the successive stages of a family therapy course in diagram form. In fact, the diagram can only be really effective once the problem of the criteria for deciding whether to proceed from one stage or learning situation to another has been resolved. A solution to this problem now seems in sight as far as the earlier stages are concerned. After the students have taken part in the introductory part of the course and have worked in small groups, without doing therapy themselves, they can be tested to see whether they have learned anything. The "stop" tape can be used to determine whether their understanding has increased. However, evaluating any development of executive skills still remains a difficult problem in view of the virtually complete absence of objective criteria. Research and experiment on this subject therefore deserve the highest priority.

Appendices

APPENDIX 1

Questionnaire

for Couple Therapy

The purpose of this questionnaire is to provide a general picture of the background and nature of your problems. Please answer the questions as fully and as accurately as possible, without discussing them with your partner.

Naturally your answers are confidential.

Date: Telephone number:
Name: Occupation:
Address: Referred by:

A. Please underline the applicable
 1. Sex: male   female
 2. Date of birth:
 3. Marital status: living together   married
                                 remarried   widow   widower
 4. Nationality: American   other:
 5. Education: primary school   secondary school
                                 technical school   university
                                 technical college   other
 6. Presently living at: home   clinic   friends or family
                                 boarding house   rented room   other
                                 (please specify):
 7. Presently living with: husband or wife   child(ren)
                                 boyfriend or girlfriend   other (please
                                 specify):
 8. Number of children: 0   1   2   3   4   5   more than 5

 9. Number of boys: 0   1   2   3   4   5   more than 5

10. Number of girls: 0   1   2   3   4   5   more than 5

11. Number of children of
    above ages:

0-3	4-7	8-11	12-16	17-20	over 21
0	0	0	0	0	0
1	1	1	1	1	1
2	2	2	2	2	2
3	3	3	3	3	3

12. How long have you
    been living together: 0-5   6-10   11-15   16-20   more than 20 years

B. Underline the points you feel apply to yourself:
 1. headaches
 2. stomach complaints
 3. suicidal thoughts
 4. suicide attempt(s)
 5. use of drugs
 6. tension
 7. feeling loved
 8. inability to relax
 9. dizzy spells
10. feelings of panic
11. trembling
12. indecisiveness
13. dread of weekends and holidays
14. heart palpitations
15. sexual complaints
16. in love
17. depressed
18. alcoholic
19. too ambitious
20. insomnia
21. happy
22. tired
23. fainting spells
24. nightmares
25. accommodation problems
26. cannot find/keep a job
27. shy
28. inability to enjoy life
29. concentration problems
30. use medicine
31. inability to stand up for myself
32. inability to make friends
33. forgetful
34. gastric complaints
35. financial problems
36. poor appetite

C. Please underline the points you feel present or have presented problems in your relationship.

We have used number 6 as an example of how the questions should be answered:

6. Friends: (a) separate friends
            (b) amount of time spent with friends
            (c) discussing personal matters with friends
            (d) too few friends/too many friends
            (e) other:
If you have separate friends but this does not lead to problems, do not underline (a). If this does cause problems between you, you should underline (a).

Please answer all the questions in this way.

1. Communica-
   tion:

   (a) we don't talk to each other enough
   (b) we have nothing to talk about
   (c) the way we talk (impatiently, angrily, etc.)
   (d) calling names
   (e) different intellectual levels
   (f) different interests (e.g., work, acquaintances)
   (g) other:

2. Money:

   (a) too much money spent (by whom? on what?)
   (b) shortage of money
   (c) children's money
   (d) household budget
   (e) other:

3. Sex:

   (a) when (morning, evening, etc.)
   (b) how (partner insensitive, not enough foreplay, etc.)
   (c) how often
   (d) premature ejaculation
   (e) difficulty in reaching orgasm
   (f) impotence
   (g) contraceptives
   (h) infidelity
   (i) lack of information about sex
   (j) other:

4. Religion:

   (a) different religions
   (b) religion and the children
   (c) donations to the church
   (d) celebration of religious festivals
   (e) other:

5. Recreation:

   (a) amount of time spent on certain activities
   (b) disagreement as to how leisure time is to be spent
       (e.g., fishing, in bars, etc.)
   (c) as a family or alone
   (d) when
   (e) where to go on holiday
   (f) competitiveness (e.g., in sport) between partners
   (g) other:

6. Friends:

   (a) separate friends
   (b) amount of time spent with friends
   (c) discussing personal matters with friends
   (d) too few friends/too many friends
   (e) other:

7. Children: (a) number of children (too many/too few)
               (b) age differences
               (c) potty training
               (d) amount of time spent with children
               (e) activities
               (f) sex education
               (g) child-rearing problems
               (h) handicapped child
               (i) unwanted child
               (j) stepchildren
               (k) adoption
               (l) other:

8. Responsibili-
   ties at home: (a) partner does too much/too little around the house
               (b) partner too involved/not involved enough
               (c) other:

9. Parents/
   in-laws: (a) who to visit
               (b) how often
               (c) interference in the marriage
               (d) dislike of in-laws
               (e) dislike of one or both parents
               (f) financial support to in-laws
               (g) financial support to parents
               (h) parents and in-laws dislike each other
               (i) one or both own parents dislike me
               (j) other:

10. Alcohol: (a) excessive use (by whom)
               (b) disagreement as to how much is acceptable
               (c) when and where
               (d) money spent on alcohol
               (e) unpleasant results of drinking (e.g., flirting, uncon-
                     trollable anger, physical violence)
               (f) other:

11. Other problems:

12. Which of the above problems do you want to deal with first?

13. Order of importance of the problems as you see them:
     (1)
     (2)
     (3)
     (4)
     (5)

D.
1. What are your interests, hobbies and other activities at present?

2. What do you enjoy doing alone (e.g., going for walks, visiting friends, shopping)?

3. What do you enjoy doing with your partner (e.g., eating out, movies, discussing work or the children)?

4. Is there anything you do which particularly pleases your partner?

5. Is there anything your partner does which particularly pleases you?

6. What sort of behavior in yourself would you like to see more often?

7. What sort of behavior in your partner would you like to see more often?

8. What do you expect from therapy? What do you hope to gain?

9. Is there any information which you think may be important and which has not come out in answering the above questions?

APPENDIX 2

Assignment: Writing Down

Points of Irritation

This assignment is intended to assess what behavior on the part of your partner irritates you.

We do this as follows: Buy a small notebook and pencil which you should have on you at all times. Every time something annoying happens or every time you are annoyed because something isn't happening, make a note of it.

For example: You are having dinner, and your partner is slurping his soup. Do not say anything but make a note: "Slurping, dinner, 7 p.m." Then go on eating.

It is very important you make a note *immediately* if something irritates you, even if your partner is present. Do *not* discuss it.

Sometimes you will have to add something by way of explanation, for example the situation in which the behavior occurred.

Discussion of everything that has annoyed you takes place at a previously arranged time. If so agreed, you are to conduct the discussion in a certain way, as described in the instructions for the "Discussion in Rounds" assignment.

Agreements
Time of day:
Discussion:
Assignment for:

Assignment:

Discussion in Rounds

This assignment is intended to teach people to talk about matters which are very important to them without getting entangled in a yes-you-did-no-I-didn't discussion. It allows both partners equal opportunity to speak and to listen to each other properly. This reduces the danger of one person dominating the discussion.

We do this in the following way: Every subject to be talked about is treated *separately,* that is, *one subject at a time.* The whole discussion, therefore, consists of a number of little "talks," each conducted in the same manner, namely, in three "rounds." A "talk" takes place as follows: The partner who wishes to discuss a particular point begins by expressing his/her opinion, thoughts, or feelings on the matter. The other partner listens attentively, without interrupting. When his/her time is up, the other person may respond, and when time is up again, the first "speaker" has the last word. Thus:

Round one: A talks; B listens without interrupting.
Round two: B responds to A; A listens without interrupting.
Round three: A responds to B; B listens without interrupting.

After the third round, the "talk" is over and *nothing further is to be said about it.* The subject is closed and you now go on to the next subject, which you treat in the same way. B now begins by talking and A by listening.

Once again—each talk consists of *three rounds* and is about *one subject.* Do *not* spend *longer* on it than agreed. If you have trouble keeping to the time limit, use a kitchen timer. It does not matter if you finish before the time limit is up, but on no account should you exceed it.

Agreements
The talk is to take place in:
The time limit for each round is:
The time limit for the whole discussion is:

APPENDIX 4

Assignment:

Monitoring

This assignment is intended to provide certain information on behavior which is causing problems. The most important point here is *how frequently* certain behavior occurs.

We go about this as follows: Buy yourself a small notebook and pencil which you are to have on you at all times.

You have made an agreement with the therapist as to *when* and *which behavior* you are to take particular note of this week. Every time it occurs, make a mark in your book, even if your partner is present. Do *not* discuss it. It is important to mark the behavior as soon as it occurs. What you are doing, in fact, is *counting* how often a certain type of behavior occurs.

For example, you have agreed to note *how often* your partner interrupts you between 8 p.m. and midnight. The results could be something like this:

Monday: 11
Tuesday: 111
Wednesday: 1
etc.

Once again—note it immediately and do not discuss it.

Agreements
Behavior of:
To be noted by:
Time:

Behavior of:
To be noted by:
Time:

Discussion:

Assignment: The Mood Meter

and the "Interview"

The purpose of this assignment is to allow one's partner to share in one's feelings and moods and the events which have contributed to them. The assignment consists of two parts: roughly indicating one's mood on the *mood meter* and the explanation of it in the ensuing *interview*.

The mood meter

Take a large sheet of paper and draw two axes. The horizontal axis represents the days of the week, marked at equal intervals. The vertical axis is marked from 1 to 10.

Hang the sheet in a prominent place on the wall. Each of you is to indicate your mood *every day* by marking a number above the relevant day. If you are in a good mood, you will mark one of the higher numbers. The worse your mood, the lower the number. Each person is to use a different colored pen.

It is very important to fill in the graph *at the same time every day*.

What you are to register is your mood *at that very moment* and not an *average* of the whole day or the last few hours.

Do not allow yourself to be influenced by what your partner has filled in. It is important that your own moods are reflected as accurately as possible.

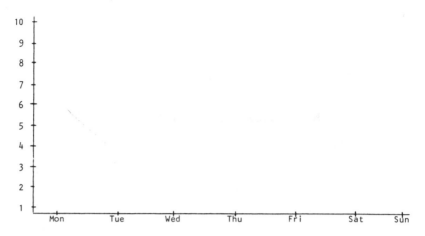

Examples

You have agreed to fill in the graph at 7:30 p.m. At that time on Monday evening your mood is good, but it could be slightly better. You indicate it thus:

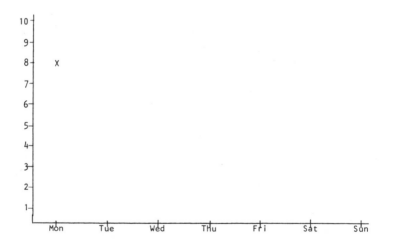

At the same time the following day, you feel rotten. Your cross is much lower than that of the previous day. (For clarity's sake, your partner's moods have not been filled in.)

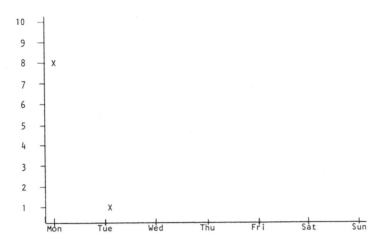

The interview

Once the graph has been filled in, you have to find out why the other person filled it in as he/she did. We go about this by means of the *interview*. Assume that partner A has filled in a 4. A now has to explain to B what the 4 means. B helps A by interviewing him/her about the score. Interviewing here means B asking questions which stimulate A to reveal exactly what is going on in his/her mind. B is supposed to make his own feelings and mood as neutral as possible in order to allow A's feelings to come out as clearly as possible.

As soon as A's score has become clear, the roles are switched and the same things happen with B now explaining what his/her score means to him/her and A doing the interviewing. Once you know about each other's moods at that moment, the subject is closed and *you are not to discuss it further.* Once again, you are only supposed to find out *what is going on in your partner's mind* and not to discuss whether or not these feelings are justified.

Agreements

Time at which your moods are to be filled in and discussed:
Who is to be responsible for the discussion?:

APPENDIX 6

Assignment:

Formulating Wishes

This assignment is designed to teach you to reformulate mutual *accusations* as mutual *desires* or *requests*. During the coming week, make a list of things you want your partner to do or things you think he/she should change. There are several very important rules. The *desires* or *requests* must be expressed in terms of *concrete behavior* in *concrete situations*.

Do *not* say, for example: "I wish you would pay more attention to me," but *rather*, "I wish you would sit down with me for a while when you get home from work and tell me about your day."

The desires must be formulated in positive terms. The emphasis should *not* be on disapproval, but rather on what you *do* want to see happen.

Do *not* say, for example: "I wish you wouldn't hang your coat over the chair," but *rather*, "I would like you to hang your coat in the hall."

It is important to start with the small (often seemingly irrelevant) points you would like to see changed and not with major matters.

Number of wishes:
Do/do not* tell each other about them.
Do/do not* discuss them with each other.

*Underline the applicable.

APPENDIX 7

Assignment:

Fulfilling Desires

This assignment is designed to make you aware of the often small everyday things you do to please your partner.

Take a large sheet of paper which is to be hung in a prominent place. Draw a horizontal line dividing the paper into two. Then divide the page into seven equal columns, each representing a day of the week. On both the top and bottom half of the page write the word "For..." followed by the name of one of the partners.

The page should look like this.

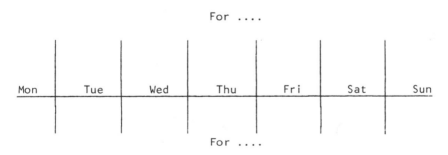

For ....

| Mon | Tue | Wed | Thu | Fri | Sat | Sun |

For ....

This is the scoreboard for a daily competition. Every day each person is to think of *as many things as possible* which *he/she is certain will please his/her partner*. When you have thought of something and actually have done it, write it down on the scoreboard.

For example, on Monday A did the dishes, put his slippers away, and talked about his day (all of which please B). A writes this down in the Monday column on the half of the paper marked "For B." B writes things down on the half marked "For A."

Thus, the person who has written down *more* in the column for the other person is the winner at the end of the day. The deciding factor is *how many* things one person has done for the other, and not whether they are important or not. The next day this is repeated and once again there is a winner.

There is to be no discussion about it whatsoever—not even about whether something has really pleased the other person or not.

You must of course *play fair*. Do not write down anything which you know does not really please your partner.

REFERENCES

Abramson, E.E. (1973), A review of behavioral approaches to weight control. *Behavioral Research and Therapy*, 11(4), 547-556.

Ackerman, N.W., F. Beatman & S. Sherman (eds.) (1961), *Exploring the base for family therapy*. Family Service Association, New York.

Anderson, R., S.T. Manoogin & J.S. Resnick (1976), The undermining of intrinsic motivation in preschool children. *J. Pers. and Soc. Psych.*, 34(5), 915-922.

Andolfi, M. (1979), *Family therapy: an interactional approach*. Plenum Press, New York & London.

Anonymous (1972), Toward the differentiation of the self in one's own family. In: J.L. Framo (ed.), *Family interactions*, Springer, New York.

Antons, K. (1973), *Praxis der Gruppendynamik; Uebungen und Techniken*. Verlag für Psychologie Dr. Hogrefe, Göttingen.

Aponte, H. (1976), The family-school interview: an eco-structural approach. *Family Process*, 15(3), 303-312.

Aponte, H. & L. Hoffman (1973), The open door: a structural approach to a family with an anorectic child. *Family Process*, 12(1), 1-44.

Auerswald, E.H. (1968), Interdisciplinary vs. ecological approach. *Family Process*, 7, 202-215.

Auerswald, E.H. (1972), Families, change and the ecological perspective. In: A. Ferber, M. Mendelsohn & A. Napier (eds.): *The book of family therapy*. Jason Aronson, New York.

Auster, S.L. (1977), Divorce counseling. *Am. J. of Orthopsychiatry*, 47(3), 536.

Bach, G.R. & P. Wyden (1968), *The intimate enemy: how to fight fair in love and marriage*. Avon Books, New York.

Bandler, R. & J. Grinder (1975), *The structure of magic*. Vol. 1. Science and Behavior Books, Palo Alto, Calif.

Bandura, A. (1969), *Principles of behavior modification*. Holt, Rinehart & Winston, New York.

Bandura, A. & R.H. Walters (1963), *Social learning and personality development*. Holt, Rinehart & Winston, New York.

Bateson, G. (1951), Information and codification: a philosophical approach. In: J. Ruesch & G. Bateson, *Communication, the social matrix of psychiatry*. Norton, New York.

Bateson, G. (1958), Naven (2nd ed.) Stanford University Press, Stanford, CA.
Bateson, G. (1972), Steps to an ecology of mind. Ballantine Books, New York.
Bateson, G., D.D. Jackson, J. Haley & J. Weakland (1956), Towards a theory of schizo-
    phrenia. Behavioral Science, 1(4), 251-264.
Beakel, N.G. & A. Mehrabian (1969), Inconsistent communications and psychopathology.
    J. of Abn. Psychol., 74(1), 126-130.
Bellack, A.S. & M. Hersen (eds.) (1979), Research and practice in social skills training.
    Plenum Press, New York.
Belliveau, F. & L. Richters (1970), Understanding human sexual inadequacy. Bantam
    Books, Boston.
Belz, S.E. (1969), Five years of altered marital contracts. In: G. Neuback (ed.), Extra
    marital relations. Prentice-Hall, Englewood Cliffs, NJ.
Bem, D.J. (1972), Self-perception theory. In: L. Berkowitz (ed.), Advances in experimental
    psychology, Vol. 6. Wiley, New York.
Bensing, J. & M. Dekker (1973), Goal Attainment Scaling II: Een methode tot evaluatie
    van psychotherapieën. Maandblad Geestelijke Volksgezondheid, 28(7), 342-356.
Berger, A. (1965), A test of the double bind hypothesis of schizophrenia. Family Process,
    4, 198-205.
Bodin, A.M. (1969), Videotape applications in family therapy training. Journal of Nervous
    and Mental Disease, 48, 251-261.
Bossard, J.H.S. & E.S. Boll (1950), Ritual in family living. University of Pennsylvania
    Press, Philadelphia.
Brinkman, W. (1974), Over de opleiding van gedragstherapeuten. Gestencild rapport.
    Afdeling Groepspsychologie. Universiteit van Amsterdam.
Bugental, D.E., L.R. Lowe, J.W. Kaswan & C. April (1971), Verbal nonverbal conflict in
    parental messages to normal and disturbed children. Journ. Abn. Psychol., 77(1), 6-
    10.
Bugental, D.E., L.R. Lowe, & J.W. Kaswan (1972), Videotaped family interaction: differ-
    ence reflecting presence and type of child disturbance. Journ. Abn. Psychol., 79,
    285-290.
Burger, A.W. (1976), Systematische desensitisatie in vitro. Tijdschrift voor Psychothera-
    pie, 2(6), 253-277.
Camp, H. (1973), Structural family therapy: an outsider's perspective, Family Process,
    12(3), 269-277.
Caplow, T. (1968), Two against one: coalitions in triads. Prentice-Hall, Englewood Cliffs.
Carter, E.A. & M. McGoldrick (1980), The family life cycle: a framework for family
    therapy. Gardner Press, New York.
Casey, G.A. (1973), Behavior rehearsal; principles and procedures. Psychotherapy: theory,
    research and practice, 10(4), 331-333.
Chin, R. (1964), The utility of system models and developmental models for practitioners.
    In: W.G. Bennis, K. Benne & R. Chin (eds.), The planning of change. Holt, Rinehart
    & Winston, New York.
Cleghorn, J.M. & S. Levin (1973), Training family therapists by setting learning objectives.
    Amer. Journ. of Orthopsychiatry, 43(3), 439-446.
Clijsen, M., L. de Groot & L. Hoos (1975), Een gestruktureerde vorm van psychotherapie
    in groepen. Tijdschrift voor Psychotherapie, 1(1), 26-35.
Conville, R.L. (1974), Linguistic nonimmediacy and communicators anxiety. Pychol.
    Reports, 35, 1107-1114.
Costello, C.G. (ed.) (1970), Symptoms of psychopathology. Wiley, New York.
Craighead, W.E., A.E. Kazdin & M.J. Mahoney (1976). Behavior modification; principles,
    issues and applications. Houghton Mifflin, Boston.
Davison, D.G. & S. Valins (1969), Maintenance of self-attributed and drug-attributed
    behavior change. J. Pers. & Soc. Psychol., 11, 321-327. Also in: M.R. Goldfried & M.
    Merbaum (1973), Behavior change through self-control. Holt & Co., New York.

De Bruyn, G. (1973). *Klaarkomen is ook niet alles.* Rapport Ned. Instituut voor Sociaal Sexologisch Onderzoek, Zeist.

Deci, E.L. (1975), *Intrinsic motivation.* Plenum Press, New York.

De Klerk, A. (1973), Lees dit niet . . . of een kleine verhandeling over paradoxen en tegenstrijdigheden. *Tijdschrift Maatschappijvraagstukken en Welzijnswerk,* 27(8), 193-197. Also in: A. van der Pas (ed.), *Gezinsfenomenen.* Samsom, Alphen a/d Rijn.

De Moor, W. & J.W.G. Orlemans (1972), *Inleiding tot de gedragstherapie.* Van Loghum Slaterus, Deventer.

Donnenwerth, G.V. & U.G. Foa (1974), Effects of resource class on retaliation to injustice in interpersonal exchange. *Journ. Pers. & Soc. Psychol.,* 29(6), 785-793.

Duvall, E.M. (1962), *Family development.* Lippincott, New York.

D'Zurilla, T.J. & M.R. Goldfried (1971), Problem solving and behavior modification. *Journ. Abn. Psychol.,* 78(1), 107-126.

Eisler, R.M. & M. Hersen (1973), Behavioral techniques in family oriented crisis intervention. *Archives of General Psychiatry,* 28(1), 111-116.

Ellis, A. & R.A. Harper (1975), *A new guide to rational living.* Prentice-Hall, Englewood Cliffs, NJ.

Epstein, N.B. (1972), Personal communication.

Epstein, N.B. & D.S. Bishop (1981), Problem-centered systems therapy of the family. In: A.S. Gurman & D.P. Kniskern (eds.), *Handbook of family therapy.* Brunner/Mazel, New York.

Epstein, N.B. & S. Levin (1973), Training for family therapy within a faculty of medicine. *Canadian Psychiat. Assoc. Journ.,* 18, 203-208.

Epstein, N.B., J.J. Sigal & V. Rakoff (1968), *Family categories schema.* Intern report, Dept. of Pychiatry, Jewish General Hospital, Montreal.

Epstein, N.B. & W.A. Westley (1969), *The silent minority.* Jossey-Bass, San Francisco.

Erickson, M.H. (1971), Indirect hypnotic therapy of a bedwetting couple. In: J. Haley (ed.), *Changing families.* Grune & Stratton, New York.

Faber, A. (1972), *Observeren van gezinsinteractie.* Intern rapport, Vakgroep Groepspsychologie, Universiteit van Amsterdam.

Farina, A. & K. Ring (1965), The influence of perceived mental illness on interpersonal relations. *Journ. of Abn. Psychol.,* 70, 47-51.

Ferreira, A.J. (1967), Psychosis and family myth. *Amer. Journ. of Psychotherapy,* 21(2), 186-197.

Festinger, L. (1957), *A theory of cognitive dissonance.* Row Peterson, Evanston, IL.

Framo, J.L. (1976), Family of origin as a therapeutic resource for adults in marital and family therapy. *Family Process,* 15(2), 192-210.

Frankl, V.E. (1960), Paradoxical intention. *American J. Psychiatry,* 14, 520-535.

Gardner, R.A. (1970), *The boys and girls books about divorce.* Jason Aronson, New York. (Quotes are from the Bantam edition, 1972.)

Garfield Barbach, L. (1975), *The fulfillment of female sexuality.* Anchor Book, New York.

Goldstein, A.P., L.B. Sechrest & K. Heller (1966), *Psychotherapy and the psychology of behavior change.* Wiley, New York.

Greenwald, J.A. (1975), The ground rules in Gestalt therapy. In: F.D. Stephenson (ed.), *Gestalt therapy primer.* Charles Thomas, Springfield, IL.

Gurman, A.S. & D.P. Kniskern (1981), *Handbook of family therapy.* Brunner/Mazel, New York.

Haley, J. (1963), *Strategies of psychotherapy.* Grune & Stratton, New York.

Haley, J. (1964), Research on family patterns: an instrument measurement. *Family Process,* 3, 41-65.

Haley, J. (1967a), Toward a theory of pathological systems. In: G.H. Zuk & I. Boszormenyi Nagy (eds.), *Family therapy and disturbed families.* Science and Behavior Books, Palo Alto, Calif.

Haley, J. (ed.) (1967b), *Advanced techniques of hypnosis and therapy: selected papers of Milton H. Erickson, M.D.* Grune & Stratton, New York.

Haley, J. (1970), Family therapy. *Internat. Journ. of Psychiatry,* 9, 233-248.

Haley, J. (1971a), A review of the family therapy field. In: J. Haley (ed.) *Changing families.* Grune & Stratton, New York.

Haley, J. (1971b), *Changing families: a family therapy reader.* Grune & Stratton, New York.

Haley, J. (1973), *Uncommon therapy; The psychiatric techniques of Milton H. Erickson M.D.* Norton, New York.

Haley, J. (1976), *Problem-solving therapy.* Jossey-Bass, San Francisco.

Haley, J., (1980), *Leaving home: the therapy of disturbed young people.* McGraw-Hill, New York.

Haley, J. & L. Hoffman (1967), *Techniques of family therapy.* Basic Books, New York.

Harper, J.M., A.E. Scorceby & W.D. Boyce (1977), The logical levels of complementary, symmetrical and parallel interaction classes in family dyads. *Family Process,* 16(2), 199-210.

Herbst, P.G. (1952), The measurement of family relationships. *Human Relations,* 5, 2-35.

Hersen, M., R.M. Eisler & P.M. Miller (1973), Development of assertive responses: clinical measurement and research considerations. *Behav. Research and Therapy,* 11(4), 505-521.

Hill, R. & R.H. Rodgers (1964), The developmental approach. In: H. Christenson (ed.), *Handbook of marriage and the family.* Rand McNally & Company, Chicago.

Hoefnagels, G.P. (1975), *(Niet)trouwen en (niet)scheiden.* Kooyker, Rotterdam.

Hoffman, L. (1971), Deviation-amplifying processes in natural groups.
   In: J. Haley (ed.), *Changing families.* Grune & Stratton, New York.

Hoffman, L. (1975), "Enmeshment" and the too-richly cross-jointed system. *Family Process* 14(4), 457-468.

Hoffman, L. (1981), *Foundations of family therapy: a conceptual framework.* Basic Books, New York.

Hoogduin, K. (1977a), De behandeling van anorgasmie. *Tijdschrift voor Directieve Therapie,* 5(1), 23-31.

Hoogduin, K. (1977b), De behandeling van clienten met hyperventilatie-aanvallen. In: K. van der Velden (ed.), *Directieve Therapie I.* Van Loghum Slaterus, Deventer.

Hoogduin, K. & R. Van Dijck (1976), De proefscheiding. *Tijdschrift voor Directieve Therapie,* 4(1), 5-10.

Ivey, A.E. & J.R. Moreland (1974), *Microcounseling: innovations in interviewing training.* Thomas, Springfield, IL.

Jackson, D.D. (1965), The study of the family. *Family Process,* 4, 1-20.

Jackson, D.D. (ed.) (1968), Communication, family and marriage. *Human Communication,* vol. I. Science and Behavior Books, Palo Alto.

Jacobson, N.S. & G. Margolin (1979), *Marital therapy: strategies based on social learning and behavior exchange principles.* Brunner/Mazel, New York.

Kanfer, F.H. & G. Saslow (1965), Behavioral diagnosis. *Archives of General Psychiatry,* 12, 529-538.

Kanouse, D.E., L. Hansen & W.J. Reid (1972), *Negativity in evaluations.* General Learning Press. Morristown, New York.

Kaplan, H.S. (1974), *The new sex therapy: active treatment of sexual dysfunctions.* Brunner/Mazel, New York.

Kazdin, A.E. (1974), Reactive self-monitoring: the effects of response, desirability, goal setting and feedback. *J. Consult. Clin. Psychol.* 42(5), 704-716.

Kazdin, A.E. (1976), Effects of covert modeling, multiple models and model reinforcement on assertive behavior. *Behavior Therapy,* 7, 211-222.

Keijser, J.A.M.P. (1975), *Handleiding bij scheiding.* Kluwer, Deventer.

Kelley, H.H. (1950), The warm-cold variable in first impressions of persons. *Journ. of Person.,* 18, 431-439.

Kempler, W. (1970), Experiential psychotherapy with families. In: J. Fagan & I.L. Shepherd (eds.), Gestalt therapy now. Science and Behavior Books, Palo Alto.

Kempler, W. (1973a), Het experientiële gezinsgesprek. Tijdschr. voor Maatschappijvraagstukken en Welzijnswerk, 27(20), 494-499.

Kempler, W. (1973b), Personal communication.

Kempler, W. (1974), Principles of gestalt family therapy. A.S. Joh. Nordahl Trykkery, Oslo.

Kempler, W. (1981), Experiential psychotherapy within families. New York: Brunner/Mazel.

Kiev, A. (1964), Magic, faith and healing. Free Press, New York.

Kilgo, R.D. (1975), Counseling couples in groups: rationale and methodology. Fam. Coordinator, 24(3), 337-342.

Kiresuk, T.J. & R.E. Sherman (1968), Goal attainment scaling: a general method for evaluating comprehensive community mental health programs. Community Mental Health Journal, 4(6), 443-453.

Knox, D. (1972), A behavioral approach to marriage happiness counseling. Research Press Comp., Champaign, IL.

Krech, D., R.S. Crutchfield & E.I. Ballachey (1962), Individual in society. McGraw-Hill, New York.

Laird, J.D. (1974), The self-attribution of emotion. J. Pers. & Soc. Psychol., 29(4), 475-481.

Lang, P.J. (1966), The transfer of treatment. Journ. of Consulting Psychol., 30, 375-378.

Lange, A. (1972), Opdrachten in gezins- en huwelijkstherapieën. Tijdschr. Maatschappijvraagstukken en Welzijnswerk, 26(15), 387-394. Also in: A. van der Pas (e.a.), Gezinsfenomenen. Samsom, Alphen a/d Rijn, 1973.

Lange, A. (1973), De double bind, empirisch bezien. Tijdschr. Maatschappijvraagstukken en Welzijnswerk, 27(8), 198-208. Also in: A van der Pas (e.a.), Gezinsfenomenen. Samsom, Alphen a/d Rijn, 1973.

Lange, A. (1976), Judo, oftewel het niet trekken aan clienten. Tijdschrift voor Psychotherapie, 2(5), 179-194. Also in: K. van der Velden (ed.), Directieve therapie I. Van Loghum Slaterus, Deventer, 1977.

Lange, A. (1977a), Allemaal misverstanden; communicatiepatronen in relaties. Intermediair, 13(51), 13-19.

Lange, A. (1977b), De zware last en enkele beschouwingen over zelfperceptietheorie. In: K. van der Velden (ed.), Directieve therapie I. Van Loghum Slaterus, Deventer.

Lange, A. (1977c), Directieve therapie en het verleden. In: K. van der Velden (ed.), Directieve therapie I. Van Loghum Slaterus, Deventer.

Lange, A. (1977d), Het gebruik van symbolen en het toepassen van de zelfperceptietheorie. In: K. van der Velden (ed.), Directieve therepie I., Van Loghum Slaterus, Deventer.

Lange, A. (1977e), Proefscheiding, gevolgd door een contract. Tijdschrift voor Directieve Therapie, 4(4), 45-49.

Lange, A. (1980), Timing. In: K. van der Velden (ed.), Directieve therapie 2. Van Loghum Slaterus, Deventer.

Lange, A. (1981), Het motiveren van clienten in directieve (gezins-)therapie. Dth. Kwartaalschrift voor Directieve Therapie en Hypnose, 1(1), 57-74.

Lange, A. & O. van der Hart (1973), De bestaande groep als gezin. Tijdschrift Maatschappijvraagstukken en Welzijnswerk, 27(3), 53-63.

Lange, A. & T. Brinckmann (1976), Effekten van een kursus relatietherapie op attitude, inzicht en eigen probleemoplossend gedrag der deelnemers. Gedrag, 4(3), 144-159.

Lange, A. & W. Zeegers (1978), Structured training for behavioral family therapy: methods and evaluation. Behavior Analysis and Modification, 2(3), 211-225.

Langer, E.J. & R.P. Abelson (1974), A patient by any other name . . .: clinical group difference in labeling bias. Journ. Consult. & Clin. Psychol., 42(1), 4-9.

Laquour, H.P., H.A. LaBurt & E. Morong (1971), Multiple family therapy: further developments. In: J. Haley (ed.), Changing families. Grune & Stratton, New York.

Lazarus, A. (1966), Behavior rehearsal versus nondirective therapy versus advice in effecting behavior change. *Behav. Research and Therapy,* 4(3), 209-212.

Lederer, W.J. & D.D. Jackson (1968), *The mirages of marriage.* Norton, New York.

Lefcourt, H.M. (1976), *Locus of control: current trends in theory and research.* Hilsdale, New York.

Leichter, S.R. & G.I. Schulman (1974), Multi-family group therapy. *Family Process,* 13(1), 95-110.

Lepper, M.R., D. Greene & R.E. Nisbett (1973), Undermining children's intrinsic interest with extrinsic reward: a test of the "overjustification" hypothesis. *J. Pers. & Soc. Psychol.,* 28(1), 129-137.

Lepper, M.R. & D. Greene (1975), Turning play into work: effects of adults surveillance and extrinsic rewards on children's intrinsic motivation. *Journal of Personality and Social Psychology,* 31(3), 479-486.

Levitsky, A. & F.S. Perls (1970), The rules and games of Gestalt Therapy. In: J. Fagan & I.L. Shepherd (eds.), *Gestalt therapy now.* Science and Behavior Books, Palo Alto.

Lewis, H.R. & H.S. Streitfeld (1971), *Growth games.* Harcourt, Brace, Jovanovich, New York.

Liberman, R.P. (1970), Behavioral approaches to family and couple therapy. *American Journal of Orthopsychiatry,* 40, 106-118.

Liberman, R.P. (1972), *A guide to behavioral analysis and therapy.* Pergamon Press, New York.

Liberman, R.P., L.W. King, W.J. de Risi & M. McCann (1975), *Personal effectiveness: guiding people to assert themselves and improve their social skills.* Research Press, Champaign, IL.

Lippitt, R., N. Polanski, F. Redl & S. Rosen (1958), The dynamics of power: A field study of social influence in groups of children. In: E.E. Maccoby et al. (eds.), *Readings in social psychology* (3rd ed.). Holt, Rinehart & Winston, New York.

Loeff, R.G. (1966), Differential discrimination of conflicting emotional messages by normal, delinquent, and schizophrenic adolescents. Doctoral Dissertation, Indiana University, Ann Arbor, University Microfilms, No. 66-1470.

LoPiccolo, J. & W.C. Lobitz (1972), The role of masturbation in the treatment of orgasmic dysfunctions. *Archives Sexual Behavior,* 2, 163-171.

Mandel, H.P., F. Weizmann, B. Millan, J. Greenhow & D. Speirs (1975), Reaching emotionally disturbed children: "Judo" principles in remedial teaching. *Amer. Journ. of Orthopsychiatry,* 45(5), 867-874.

Masters, W. & V. Johnson (1970), *Human sexual inadequacy.* Little, Brown & Co., Boston.

McFall R.M. & A.R. Marston (1970), An experimental investigation of behavioral rehearsal in assertive training. *Journ. Abn. Psych.,* 76, 295-303.

Mehrabian, A. (1966), Immediacy, an indicator of attitudes in linguistic communication. *J. Personality.,* 34, 26-34.

Mehrabian, A. (1967), Attitudes inferred from non-immediacy of verbal communications. *J. Verbal Learning and Verbal Behavior,* 6, 294-295.

Mehrabian, A. & M. Wiener (1967), Decoding of inconsistent communications. *Journal of Personality and Social Psychology,* 6, 109-114.

Meichenbaum, D. (1974), *Cognitive behavior modification.* Gen. Learning Press, Morristown, NY.

Merton, R.K. (1957), *Social theory and social structure.* Free Press, New York.

Minuchin, S. (1970), The use of an ecological framework in the treatment of a child. In: E.J. Anthony & C. Koupernik (eds.), *The child and his family.* Wiley, New York.

Minuchin, S. (1973), Personal communication. Family therapy training for the Dutch Association for Group Psychotherapy, Utrecht.

Minuchin, S. (1974), *Families and family therapy.* Harvard University Press, Cambridge.

Minuchin, S. & H. Ch. Fishman (1981), *Family therapy techniques.* Harvard University Press, Cambridge, MA.

Mishler, E.G. & N.W. Waxler (1968), *Family processes and schizophrenia*. Science House, New York.

Montalvo, B. (1973), Aspects of live supervision. *Family Process*, 12(4), 343-359.

Montalvo, B. & J. Haley (1973), In defense of child therapy. *Family Process*, 12(3), 227-244.

Moreno, J.I. & D.A. Kipper (1971), Group psychodrama and community centered counseling. In: G.M. Gazda (ed.), *Basic approaches to group psychotherapy and group counseling*. Charles Thomas, Springfield, IL.

Napier, A. (1976), Beginning struggles with families. *J. of Marriage and Family Counseling*, 2(1), 3-11.

Naranjo, A. (1970), Present-centeredness: techniques, prescription and ideal. In: J. Fagan & I.L. Shepherd (eds.), *Gestalt therapy now*. Science and Behavior Books, Palo Alto.

Nelson, R.O., D.P. Lipinsky & J.L. Black (1976), The relative reactivity of external observations and self-monitoring. *Behav. Ther.*, 7, 314-321.

Nevejan, M. (ed.) (1973), *Gezins- en echtparenbehandeling in Nederland*. Van Loghum Slaterus, Deventer.

Nordquist, V.W. & R.G. Wahler (1973), Naturalistic treatment of an autistic child. *Journ. of Applied Behav. Analysis*, 6(1), 79-87.

Norton, A.J. & P.C. Glick (1976), Marital instability: past, present and future. *J. Soc. Issues*, 32, 5-20.

Nunnally, J.C. (1961), *Popular conceptions of mental health*. Holt, Rinehart & Winston, New York.

Olson, D.H. (1972), Empirically unbinding the double bind: review of research and conceptual reformulations. *Family Process*, 11(1), 69-94.

Osborn, A.F. (1963), *Applied imagination: principles and procedures of creative problem solving*. Scribner's, New York.

Papp, P. (1977), The family that had all the answers. In: P. Papp (ed.), *Family therapy: full length case studies*. Gardner Press, New York.

Papp, P. (1980), The Greek Chorus and other techniques of family therapy. *Family Process*, 19(1), 45-58.

Passons, W.R. (1975), *Gestalt approaches to counseling*. Holt, Rinehart, & Winston, New York.

Patterson, G.R. (1971), *Families: applications of social learning in family life*. Research Press, Champaign, IL.

Patterson, G.R. & M.E. Gullion (1968), *Living with children*. Research Press, Champaign, IL.

Peck, B.B. (1974), *A family therapy notebook*. Libra Publishers, Roslyn Heights, New York.

Perls, F.S. (1969), *Gestalt therapy verbatim*. Real People Press, Lafayette, Calif.

Perls, F.S. (1970), Four lectures. In: J. Fagan & I.L. Shepherd (eds.). *Gestalt therapy now*. Science and Behavior Books, Palo Alto.

Perls, F.S. (1973), *The Gestalt approach & eye witness to therapy*. Science and Behavior Books, Palo Alto.

Poelstra, P. & A. Lange (1975), Evaluatie van een kursus gezinstherapie. *Tijdschrift voor Psychotherapie*, 1(3), 102-116.

Prochaska, J.O. & R. Marzilli (1973), Modification of the Masters and Johnson approach to sexual problems. *Psychotherapy: Theory, Research and Practice*, 10(4), 294-296.

Raapis Dingman, H. (1975), Over de doden niets dan goeds; verslag van een rouwtherapie. *Tijdschrift voor Psychotherapie*, 1(1), 11-20.

Ramsay, R.W. (1977), Behavioral approaches to bereavement. *Behav. Res. & Therapy*, 15, 131-135.

Rappaport, A.F. & J. Harrell (1972), A behavioral exchange model for marital counseling. *Family Coordinator*, April 1972, 203-212.

Ringuette, E.L. & T. Kennedy (1966), An experimental study of the double bind hypothesis. *Journ. Abnorm. Psychol.*, 71, 136-141.

Rodgers, R.H. (1973), *Family interaction and transaction: the developmental approach.* Prentice Hall, Englewood Cliffs, N.J.

Rose, S.D. (1972), *Treating children in groups.* Jossey-Bass, San Francisco.

Rose, S.D. (1977), *Group therapy: a behavioral approach.* Prentice-Hall, Englewood Cliffs, NJ.

Rubinstein, D. (1971), A developmental approach to family therapy. Excerpta Medica International Congress Series No. 274: Psychiatry (Part 1), 24-32, Excerpta Medica. Amsterdam.

Rubinstein, T.H. (1977), Personal communication.

Rubinstein, T.H. & O. Van der Hart (1977), Judo: de rechte weg, het steile pad. *Tijdschrift voor Directieve Therapie,* 5(1), 6-22.

Sager, C.J. (1972), Staff development for a therapeutic community. In: C.J. Sager & H. Singer Kaplan (eds.), *Progress in group and family therapy,* pp. 774-791. Brunner/Mazel, New York.

Schachter, S. (1971), *Emotion, obesity and crime.* Academic Press. New York.

Scheflen, A.E. (1971), Living space in an urban ghetto. *Family Process,* 10(4), 429-450.

Scheflen, A. & A. Ferber (1972), Critique of a sacred cow. In: A Ferber, M. Mendelsohn & A. Napier (eds.), *The book of family therapy,* Jason Aronson, New York.

Schulz, W. (1967), *Joy, expanding human awareness.* Penguin, Harmondsworth, Middlesex.

Selvini Palazzoli, M. (1974), *Self-starvation: from the intrapsychic to the transpersonal approach to anorexia nervosa.* Human Context Books, Chaucer, London.

Selvini Palazzoli, M., L. Boscolo, G.F. Cecchin & G. Prata (1974), The treatment of children through brief treatment of their parents. *Family Process,* 3(4), 429-442.

Selvini Palazzoli, M., L. Boscolo, G.F. Cecchin & G. Prata (1978), *Paradox and counterparadox.* Jason Aronson, New York.

Selvini Palazzoli, M., L. Boscolo, G.F. Cecchin & G. Prata (1980), Hypothesizing —circularity—neutrality: three guidelines for the conductor of the session. *Family Process,* 19(1), 3-12.

Sherman, M.H. (1968), Siding with the resistance versus interpretation: role implications. In: M.C. Nelson et al. (eds.), *Roles and paradigms in psychotherapy.* Grune & Stratton, New York.

Simmel, G. (1950), *The sociology of Georg Simmel* (Kurt H. Wolff, trans., ed., and introd.). Free Press of Glencoe, New York.

Sluzki, C.E. & D.C. Ransom (1976), *Double bind: the foundation of the communicational approach to the family.* Grune & Stratton, New York.

Smith, M.J. (1975), *When I say no I feel guilty.* The Dial Press, New York.

Sojit, C.M. (1971), The double bind hypothesis and the parents of schizophrenics. *Family Process,* 10, 53-74.

Solomon, M.A. (1973), A developmental conceptual premise for family therapy. *Family Process,* 12(2), 179-186.

Spiegel, J.P. (1969), Environmental corrections as a system process. In: W. Gray, F.J. Duhl & N.D. Rizzo (eds.), *General systems theory and psychiatry.* Little, Brown, Co., Boston.

Stelmachers, Z.T., S.H. Lund & C.J. Meade (1972), Hennepin County Crisis Center: Evaluation of its effectiveness. *Evaluation,* 1.

Stevens, J.P. (1971), *Awareness.* Real People Press, Lafayette, CA.

Storms, M.D. & R.E. Nisbett (1970), Insomnia and the attribution process. *Journ. Pers. & Soc. Psychol.,* 16(2), 319-328.

Stuart, R.B. (1969), Token reinforcement in marital treatment. In: R. Rubin & C.M. Franks (eds.), *Advances in behavior therapy.* Academic Press, New York.

Stuart, R.B. (1972a), *Marital pre-counseling inventory.* Research Press, Champaign, IL.

Stuart, R.B. (1972b), *Marital pre-counseling inventory: counselors guide.* Research Press, Champaign, IL.

Stuart, R.B. (1973), Behavioral remedies for marital ills: a guide to the use of operant-interpersonal techniques. In: T. Thompson & W.S. Dockens (eds.), *International symposium on behavior modification*. Appleton-Century-Crofts, New York.

Stuart, R.B. (1980), *Helping couples change: a social learning approach to marital therapy*. Guilford Press, New York.

Sturm, I.E. (1965), The behavioristic aspect of psychodrama. *Psychotherapy*, 18, 50-64.

Thibaut, J.W. & H.H. Kelley (1959), *The social psychology of groups*. Wiley, New York.

Tilmans-Ostyn, E. & J. Tijsma (1973), Enkele ervaringen van een co-therapeutisch team in gezinstherapie. In: M. Nevejan (ed.), *Gezins-en echtparenbehandeling in Nederland*. Van Loghum Slaterus, Deventer.

Toomim, M.K. (1972), Structured separation with counseling: a therapeutic approach for couples in conflict. *Family Process*, 11(3), 299-310.

Truax, C.B. & R.R. Carkhuff (1967), *Toward effective counseling and psychotherapy: training and practice*. Aldine, Chicago.

Underwood, B.J. & R.W. Schultz (1960), *Meaningfulness and verbal learning*. Lippincott, New York.

Valins, S. & R.E. Nisbett (1972), Attribution processes in the development and treatment of emotional disorders. In: E.E. Jones et al. (eds.), *Attribution, perceiving the causes of behavior*. General Learning Press, Morristown, NY.

Van den Berg, J.F. & M. van Loon (1976), *Effekt onderzoek van een groepsparentherapie*. Doct. Skriptie Vakgroep Groepspsychologie. Universiteit van Amsterdam.

Vandereycken, W. (1977), Anorexia nervosa. I. Leertheoretische beschouwingen. *Tijdschrift voor Pychotherapie*, 3(4), 151-165.

Van der Hart, O. (1973), Double binds, relaties en ervaringen. *Tijdschrift Maatschappijvraagstukken en Welzijnswerk*, 27(8), 181-192. Also in: A van der Pas (ed.), *Gezinsfenomenen*. Samsom, Alphen a/d Rijn.

Van der Hart, O. (1976), De ecologische behandeling van een schoonmaakdwang, *Tijdschrift voor Directieve Therapie*, 4(2), 5-29.

Van der Hart, O. (1977), *De last is te zwaar*. In: K. van der Velden (ed.), *Directieve therapie* 1. Van Loghum Slaterus, Deventer.

Van der Hart, O. (1983), *Rituals in pychotherapy*. Irvington Publishers, New York.

Van der Hart, O. & P.B. Defares (1973), Gezinstherapie. In: *Handboek Hulpverlenen en Veranderen*, vol. II. Van Loghum Slaterus, Deventer.

Van der Hart, O. & P.B. Defares (1978), Gezinstherapie 1978. In: *Handboek Hulpverlenen en Veranderen* (rev. ed.). Van Loghum Slaterus, Deventer.

Van der Hart, O. & J. Ebbers (1981), Rites of separation in strategic psychotherapy. *Psychotherapy: Theory, Research and Practice*, 18(2), 188-194.

Van der Hart, O. & T.H. Rubinstein (1972), Groepstraining en systeembenadering. In: K. Nijkerk & Ph. van Praag (eds.), *Groepswerk*. Samsom, Alphen a/d Rijn.

Van der Hart, O. & T.H. Rubinstein (1977), *Strategische en tactische aspecten van therapie*. In: K. van der Velden (ed.), *Directieve therapie*. Van Loghum Slaterus, Deventer.

Van der Hart, O. & R. Van Dijck (1977), Rouwtherapie door middel van afscheidsbrieven. *Tijdschrift voor Directieve Therapie*, 4(4), 24-35.

Van der Pas, A. (1969), Zoek de zieke mythe. *Tijdschrift voor Maatschappelijk Werk*, 12, 265-273. Also in: A van der Pas (ed.), *Gezinsfenomenen*. Samsom, Alphen a/d Rijn.

Van der Pas, A. (1973), Over co- en solotherapie met gezinnen. In: A. van der Pas (ed.), *Gezinsfenomenen*. Samsom, Alphen a/d Rijn.

Van der Pas, A. (1974), Vier grote gezinstherapeuten (III): Carl Whitaker, *Tijdschrift Maatschappijvraagstukken en Welzijnswerk*, 28(15), 215-290.

Van der Veer, J. (1974a), *Evaluatie met behulp van de Contract Fulfillment Analysis van een driedaagse gezinstherapietraining*. Unpublished Manuscript, Amsterdam.

Van der Veer, J. (1974b), Goal Attainment Scaling IV: doelenkontrakt als evaluatiemethode. *Maandblad Geestelijke Volksgezondheid*, 29(10), 469-480.

Van der Velden, K. (1976), Strenge religieuze opvattingen en directieve therapie: ervaringen met Jehova's getuigen. *Tijdschrift voor Directieve Therapie*, 3(8), 35-40.

Van der Velden, K. (1978), Een ritueel voor verwende kinderen. *Tijdschrift voor Directieve Therapie*, 5(3), 11-13.
Van der Velden, K., O. van der Hart & R. Van Dijck (1980), Positief etiketteren. In: K. van der Velden (ed.), *Directieve therapie 2*. Van Loghum Slaterus, Deventer.
Van der Velden, K., & R. Van Dijck (1977), Motiveringstechnieken. In: K. van der Velden (ed.), *Directieve therapie 1*. Van Loghum Slaterus, Deventer.
Van de Ven, P. (1973), *Gezinstherapie als agogische aktie*. H.Nelissen, Bloemendaal.
Van Dijck, R. (1977), Vormen van directieve therapie bij echtparen en gezinnen. In: K. van der Velden (ed.), *Directieve therapie 1*. Van Loghum Slaterus, Deventer.
Van Dijck, R. & K. Hoogduin (1977), Ruziemakende paren. In: K. van der Velden (ed.), *Directieve therapie 1*. Van Loghum Slaterus, Deventer.
Van Dijck, R. & K. van der Velden (1977), Valkuilen voor directieve therapeuten. In: K. van der Velden (ed.), *Directieve therapie 1*. Van Loghum Slaterus, Deventer.
Van Dijck, R., A. Lange & K. van der Velden (1980), Mislukte directieve behandelingen. In: K. van der Velden (ed.), *Directieve therapie 2*. Van Loghum Slaterus, Deventer.
Van Gennep, A. (1909), *Les rites de passage*. Libraire Critique, Emil Mourry, Paris. English edition: *The rites of passage*. Routledge & Kegan Paul, London, 1960.
Van Ree, F. (1977), *Inleiding tot interaktioneel psychiatrische diagnostiek: van Kraepelin tot Watzlawick*. Van Gorcum, Assen.
Vogel, E. & N.W. Bell (1960), The emotionally disturbed child as the family scapegoat. In: N.W. Bell & E. Vogel (eds.), *A modern introduction to the family*. The Free Press of Glencoe, New York.
Wagner, H. & K. Pease (1976), The verbal communication of inconsistency between attitudes held and attitudes expressed. *J. Pers. Soc. Psychol.*, 33(1), 1-15.
Wallerstein, J.S. & J.B. Kelly (1977), Divorce counseling: a community service for families in the midst of divorce. *Amer. J. Orthopsychiatry*, 47(1), 4-22.
Watzlawick, P., J. Beavin & D.D. Jackson (1967), *Pragmatics of human communication*. W.W. Norton & Co., New York.
Watzlawick, P., J. Beavin & R. Fisch (1974), *Change: principles of problem formation and problem resolution*. W.W. Norton & Co., New York.
Waxler, N. & E.G. Mishler (1970), Experimental studies of families. In: L. Berkowitz (ed.), *Advances in experimental social psychology*, vol. 5. Academic Press, New York.
Weiss, R.A. (1975), *Marital separation*. Basic Books, New York.
Wertheim, E.S. (1973), Family unit therapy and the science of typology of family systems. *Family Process*, 12(4), 361-376.
Whitaker, C.A. & D.V. Keith (1981), Symbolic-experiential family therapy. In: A.S. Gurman & D.P. Kniskern (eds.), *Handbook of family therapy*. Brunner/Mazel, New York.
Woodward, C.A., J. Santa-Barbara, S. Levin & N.B. Epstein (1978), Aspects of consumer satisfaction with brief family therapy. *Family Process*, 17(4), 399-407.
Zeegers, W. (1977a), *De efecten van overjustification*. Doctoraal scriptie Vakgroep Groepspsychologie. Universiteit van Amsterdam.
Zeegers, W. (1977b), *De vervaardiging van video demonstratiebanden t.b. v. onderwijs in gezins- en relatietherapie*. Rapport Vakgroep Groepspsychologie. Universiteit van Amsterdam.
Zelditch, M. (1955), Note on the analysis of equilibrium systems. In: T. Parsons & R.F. Bales (eds.), *Socialization and interaction process*. Free Press of Glencoe, New York.
Zuk, G.H. (1966), The go-between process in family therapy. *Family Process*, 5, 162-178.
Zuk, G.H. (1972), *Family therapy: a triadic based approach*. Behavioral Publications, New York.

NAME INDEX

287

SUBJECT INDEX